All That's Unseen

All That's Unseen

An Appalachian Memoir

EMILEE HACKNEY

PENGUIN PRESS NEW YORK 2026

PENGUIN PRESS
An imprint of Penguin Random House LLC
1745 Broadway, New York, NY 10019
penguinrandomhouse.com

Designed by Christina Nguyen

Library of Congress Cataloging-in-Publication Data

Names: Hackney, Emilee, author
Title: All that's unseen: an Appalachian memoir / Emilee Hackney.
Description: New York: Penguin Press, 2026. |
Identifiers: LCCN 2025054995 (print) | LCCN 2025054996 (ebook) |
ISBN 9780593831403 hardcover | ISBN 9780593831410 ebook
Subjects: LCSH: Hackney, Emilee | Hackney, Emilee—Family |
Hackney, Emilee—Religion | Coal mines and mining—Virginia, Southwest | Pentecostalism—Virginia, Southwest | Self-actualization (Psychology) |
Virginia, Southwest—Social life and customs | LCGFT: Autobiographies
Classification: LCC F232.T2 H23 2026 (print) | LCC F232.T2 (ebook)
LC record available at https://lccn.loc.gov/2025054995
LC ebook record available at https://lccn.loc.gov/2025054996

Printed in the United States of America
2nd Printing

The authorized representative in the EU for product safety and compliance is Penguin Random House Ireland, Morrison Chambers, 32 Nassau Street, Dublin D02 YH68, Ireland, https://eu-contact.penguin.ie.

To Jeremy,

wherever you are

After I had cut off my hands
and grown new ones

something my former hands had longed for
came and asked to be rocked.

After my plucked out eyes
had withered, and new ones grown

something my former eyes had wept for
came asking to be pitied.

—**Denise Levertov, "Intrusion"**

Author's Note

To maintain privacy, the names and identifying characteristics of most nonpublic figures, as well as the names of some institutions, have been changed.

All That's Unseen

Prologue

The church is in the shadow of a mountain, bordered by forest, a trailer park, and a creek that floods the parking lot every time it rains. The walls are stone. The few windows are narrow and darkly tinted. The American, Virginia, and Christian flags fly on the front lawn. Beneath the flagpoles is a large white sign: DELIVERANCE CHRISTIAN CHURCH, bold black letters except for the *t* in "Christian," which is a red cross in forward slant.

Inside, a large room with a high ceiling. In my first memory of Deliverance, I am five years old, and my mother is standing beside me, eyes closed, lips moving in silent prayer. The rest of the congregation is shouting, moaning, singing, chanting. *Yes, Lord. Yes, Father. Jesus. Jesus. Jesus. Jesus.* There are other sounds, guttural and repetitive: a holy language I won't understand even when I learn to speak it myself years later. The worship rises above the swaying bodies, above the waving arms and shaking heads and weeping faces, in a collective cry to God.

The lights grow dim. The music swells. People move out of their seats toward the front of the church. Some stand, arms high and open, at the altar beneath the pastor's pulpit. Some kneel and bow until their foreheads touch the floor. A few lie on their stomachs, still and silent as death.

In my memory, everyone is faceless, a congregation of amorphous figures behaving in ways I have never seen and do not at all understand. But something about the unashamed, unrestrained worship seems natural, even necessary, for the rapturous atmosphere. There *does* seem to be some kind of presence. Something sacred.

Whatever it is, I begin to sense it myself. It swallows me up in a slow wave of warmth. The whole of the room—the people, the music, the cries of praise—blurs into a great, urgent energy that settles heavily on my shoulders.

The pressure grows. My legs go soft.

My mother's eyes remain closed. I wonder vaguely what she will think if she happens to look down. I sense, inexplicably, that her thoughts do not matter, that nothing matters except conceding to the absolute whim of the mighty something that fills the room. My knees touch the floor, and I am Moses at the burning bush, hiding my face from the holy presence. It is a mysterious and all-consuming force: powerful enough to drive me to the ground, and heavy enough to hold me there.

Part
ONE

1.

In one of my earliest memories, I'm shrinking. I'm in the back seat of my parents' car, face pressed against the window, straining to see the peaks of the mountains outside. The road we're driving on snakes through a deep, narrow cut between two ridges. The farther we go, the steeper the mountains grow, and the smaller I feel. I am dwarfed by their magnitude and majesty.

Even as a toddler, I'm awed by the mountains. They are confining and comforting, ancient and noble. They radiate a soft old wisdom, as if they were born at the very dawn of the world. I feel as if I were born from *them*, as if my bones were formed from their dirt. In a way, they were: I'm an eighth-generation Appalachian, attached to the land by something more sacred, more mysterious, than mere blood and history. There is magic in that mystery, and in the darkness of the valley that sits between the sunny ridges. I bounce in my car seat, thrilled by the swoop in my stomach as we round the hairpin curves. My parents glance back at me, amused: A dying little coal town, deeply isolated even by Appalachian standards, is my favorite place on earth.

Not that I knew of many other places. There was Tazewell County, where I was born and raised, and there was Buchanan County to the west, where my parents—and grandparents, and their grandparents, and their grandparents—were born and raised. That little corner of southwest Virginia was my entire world, my family's entire world, too. Two and a half centuries ago, a German mercenary deserted the British army, fled the war, and settled in the mountains of what would eventually become known as Buchanan County. What drew him there, or made him stay, is unknown: The land was so rugged and rocky that it was never settled even by Native Americans. Since him, every one of my ancestors has lived and died within a few miles of his original homestead, in the shadowed hills and hollers that never see the sun.

I grew up feeling the weight of this legacy. It seemed congenital, so perfect was my family's loyalty to the land. I would not think about leaving—it would not occur to me that I *could*—for many years.

My mother's parents—Nanny and Poppaw, I called them—grew up in Grundy, Buchanan County's only town to speak of, and spent the early years of their marriage in Lexington, Kentucky. The city was small, but not to two kids from the coalfields. Poppaw dug ditches for a water company. Nanny raised my mother. Poppaw racked up promotions—"literally worked his way from the ground up," Nanny would say—until the little family moved from a trailer park to a real brick house in the suburbs and Poppaw had an office on the top floor of a building overlooking the city.

But no matter how far you go, you can never leave the mountains. Or rather, they'll never leave you. Poppaw got antsy living among all those people. He grew to hate the noisy streets and busy office and looking out his kitchen window to see the next-door neighbor looking back. He moved his family back to Grundy, traded his suits and ties for coveralls, and went back to digging. This time, for coal.

Each time she told the story about why they came back, Nanny's face shifted in a way I grew to expect. She spoke of my grandfather's hard work with bright, proud eyes, recalling the smallest details of her respectable suburban life as if she feared forgetting. Sometimes she'd illustrate the story by pulling out Poppaw's desktop nameplate, one of his few possessions she kept after he died. Her smile sagged when she spoke of his wild ache for home. She lamented the move, yet resigned herself to it long before it happened.

"The mountains are in our blood," she'd say. Every time, the same words. "I knew we wouldn't stay gone for long."

As the crow flies, there were thirty miles between my parents' house in Tazewell County and my grandparents' house in Buchanan County. The driving distance was double that. It took an hour and a half to go sixty miles, longer if you got stuck behind a coal truck, which happened more often than not.

My mother hated the drive. "It's like going down into a hole," she'd say, white-knuckling her seat belt through the scariest curves. The road descended from Tazewell's gentle hilltops to narrow canyons, winding deeper into Buchanan County until you finally reached the little town of Grundy. It sat in the shadows, cradled by mountains that held back the light. The buildings were dulled with age and coal dust. The ones nearest the river were slated for demolition, their walls soft and swollen with mold.

The Grundy of my grandparents' childhood would have been unrecognizable to me. Main Street was once as nice as any city's shopping district: You could find designer clothes, luxury furniture, and the latest record by any band you could think of. On weekends, the sidewalks were so crowded that you could barely squeeze through. Now the shops were empty, decaying. Nobody had a reason to walk down the sidewalk unless they were headed to the courthouse. In the time it took my grandparents to grow old, the coal industry waned sharply, and the town lost almost half its population. The aftermath of this exodus was the Grundy *I* knew, palpably unsettled by abandonment, shocked to silence by the awareness of what remained.

Still, Grundy enchanted me. Maybe it was my blood connection to its history. Maybe it was the oddity of its existence, the mythic lore of its rise and fall.

When people talked about the Appalachian coalfields—*my* Appalachia—I hung on to every word. Their voices were reverent, the fact of the mountains transcended to legend. They spoke about coal as if it were sacred, and it was: Grundy was a single-industry town, built by mining companies and the men who flocked to work for them a century before I was born. King Coal, as it was often called, was the reason Grundy existed, and the reason it continued to exist. Yet coal had doomed Grundy before the town was conceived.

Mining was a cruel and fragile industry. Even in its post–World War heyday, the coal market was unpredictable, a constant, rapid cycle of boom and bust. Mines would open; mines would close. Miners would walk into work not knowing if they still had a job. When Poppaw moved back to Grundy in the mid-1970s, he started mining in the fallout that followed a record production year. He'd keep a job for a few months, maybe a year with luck, then get laid off without notice or furloughed indefinitely. That was how it went for the rest of his life. I have a few early memories of him in his coveralls, black from head to toe in a film of greasy coal dust, but I mostly remember him stuck at his house for days and weeks at a time, pacing from the patio to the front porch to the patio again.

"Antsy," Nanny would say.

There's a bronze statue of a coal miner in front of the Buchanan County Courthouse. If you're passing through Grundy, you'll see him at a distance of about fifty yards, standing on a base of dark stone. He appears strong and proud, with broad shoulders and a wide stance. He holds a pickax with steady, confident hands.

If you look closer, there's a different story. The miner's neck is strained. His mouth sags. His hard, flat eyes gaze so high above the mountaintops that his pupils almost disappear into his skull.

As a child, I was unsettled by those eyes. Looking at them stirred something within me, a feeling I couldn't yet put into words. I sensed they were tuned to another world, somewhere far beyond the mountains. Years later, after I had made my way out of Appalachia, the mystery of the miner would remain. No matter how far I went, and no matter how many times I returned home, it haunted me always, the longing in his weary, heaven-bound gaze.

2.

The memory is my grandmother's, but it's as vivid to me as if it were my own.

She's young. Her father is drunk again. The woods are safer than her house, and she's wandering up the mountain alone. Something in the underbrush catches her eye: a big black rat snake, thicker than her arm. It's coiled, ready to strike. But it's not looking at her.

There's a bird standing mere feet from the snake. It's perfectly, unnaturally still, staring into the snake's onyx eyes. Nanny approaches slowly. Neither animal blinks as she bends down, picks up some rocks. She throws one at the bird to shock it out of its trance, but it doesn't flinch. She throws another, then another.

It's no use. The snake lunges forward and swallows the bird whole.

Nanny told all her stories over and over, but I listened to this one with special interest, terrified and captivated by every detail: her pity for the doomed and helpless bird; the electric chill in her spine when she saw something neither human nor animal in the snake's eyes.

"It was pure evil," she'd say with a shiver. "It was *of the devil*."

I didn't know what that meant, but I understood that something with the power to lure a bird to its death deserved my fear, too. I jumped at every rustle in the grass and did a double take at every branch in the yard. I peered into woodpiles, rock piles, holes, and shadows to see if wicked black eyes peered back.

Years later, I would learn that rat snakes don't eat live animals. They kill by constriction instead, squeezing their prey to a slow, suffocating death. Nanny swore to the truth of her memory with such conviction that I wondered if it really *was* true—if, in a miraculous defiance of nature, the snake *had* eaten the bird.

Of course, in the shadow of those mountains, you could believe in the possibility of anything. Nanny and Poppaw lived twenty-five minutes past the town of Grundy in a thin, deep vein of a holler called Home Creek, which seemed to be the very horizon between reality and imagination. It was the kind of place that attracted mischief: All the road signs were peppered with bullet holes, and mailboxes were always getting beaten off their posts. Occasionally you'd see tires burning in the road. Dad liked to tell me tales about red-eyed monsters roaming those woods, werewolves and wolf-bears and big, ugly man-beasts covered in fur. Sometimes I thought I could hear their whoops and howls, especially when coal trains passed through the tunnel down the mountain. Strange, feral harmonies wove through the grinding screech of metal on metal, falling out of tune as they echoed along the ridge.

Nanny had lots of stories. She told us about the tunnel, haunted by all the men who'd died digging it. Their bodies were buried in the walls, she said, stuffed into holes and bricked over.

She told us about the mine, a big pit in the mountain, just uphill in the woods behind my grandparents' double-wide. Inside, Nanny said, keeping me from getting too close to see, was a rickety old elevator that looked like a cage. Of course men had died down there, too, deep in the belly of the earth.

Then there were stories about Nanny's family. One was about her brother getting his head stuck in a bucket. One was about her grandfather who lived in a one-room house with his chickens. There was one about her uncle who got hit by a coal train—"they had to bury him piece by piece"—and one about her mother, who died young from a terrible cancer. There were stories about Nanny's childhood: how she and her five siblings grew up in clothes made from flour sacks, and without indoor plumbing. How luxury was a piece of fruit on Christmas morning.

Then there were stories about her father. He was a miner. An alcoholic. She said his eyes were black as a snake's, and that the devil had been in him, too.

Once, they got into a fight. A real, genuine, fists-flying brawl, Nanny and her father, her own flesh and blood, who was mad over who knows what: She just happened to be the closest object onto which he could discharge his fury. They wrestled around the front yard until he grabbed a piece of scrap lumber and split it over Nanny's skull.

When she got out of the hospital, Nanny knew she had to get out of Grundy. She dreamed of cities far from the mountains. She dreamed of going to college and becoming a nurse. She dreamed of having a family—a happy family—of her own, and married my grandfather. He was also from Grundy, but had been in the army and had seen some of the world.

Poppaw was red-haired and green-eyed and had freckled cheeks as round and firm as apples, but I remember him best by his hands. They were the hands of a miner, permanently black with coal dust in the deep, dry wrinkles of his knuckles. An inch of his right middle finger had been sliced off in the mines—so cleanly, he claimed, that he'd gone back to work as soon as the doctor tied his stitches.

The rest of my memories of Poppaw are less of *him* and more signposts of his presence. There was his soft cigarette smell and the twangy drone of his favorite bluegrass radio station. There were the muddy paw prints of his German shepherd mutt, Hank Williams, on the patio. Poppaw was so quiet that I have only one distinct memory of his voice. I was four or five, and I'd turned the bathroom faucet on too hot. The yellow water came out in a scalding blast, scorching my tiny fingers.

Poppaw heard me crying. He shuffled into the bathroom—he had the gait of a miner, too, all hobbled and hunched—and took my raw, wet hands in his dry, calloused ones.

"I'm gonna say some magic words," he said, "so you won't hurt no more."

Then he leaned down, eyes closed, and whispered into my fingers. The words were unintelligible, but whatever spell he cast worked. When he let go, the pain was gone.

My mother knew a different man. In most of her childhood memories, Poppaw is drunk. He's ranting about the "upper echelon" who live in luxury without ever lifting a finger. Or he's wondering how a man can work himself to the bone and still end up so poor. Or he's barricading himself in the spare bedroom, threatening to drink until he dies, until Nanny sends Mom, who's small enough to climb through the window, to unblock the bedroom door.

It's hard for me to imagine Poppaw, who quit drinking around the time I was born, this way. It's hard for me to imagine Nanny, with her baby-soft voice and placid smile, storming out of the house with a suitcase, barking at Mom to get in the car, and speeding down the mountain. She'd make it down the holler, or even into town. Eventually, she'd pull over and turn around. Nanny didn't have any money—Poppaw didn't want her working outside the home—and didn't have anywhere to go.

Still. She always packed the suitcase.

The stories Mom tells of her childhood are starkly reminiscent of Nanny's. They're threaded with terror, of tiptoeing around fathers who couldn't control their drinking or their rage. I sometimes wonder about the roots of that rage, if it was a manifestation of frustration at their miner's lives: the low wages, backbreaking work, and perpetual job insecurity. I wonder if Poppaw ever regretted leaving his office job. If living in the mountains was worth what he gave up to live there.

If there was anything truly strange about the mountains, it was that: You were never quite happy in them, and you were never quite happy beyond them.

End to end, Home Creek was about eight and a half miles. Nanny and Poppaw lived on the eastern end. The western end bumped up against the little community of Big Rock, a scattered collection of houses and mines, about a mile from the Virginia-Kentucky line. My other grandparents, whom I called Mamaw and Poppy, lived here—not on Home Creek itself, but in a holler that branched off it. It was a holler within a holler. A sub-holler.

Since both sets of my grandparents lived so close to each other, a visit to one usually meant a visit to the other. Mamaw and Poppy lived in a house about the size of a double-wide. Behind it, tucked so tightly against the mountain you couldn't open the back door all the way, was a smaller building—two outbuildings, actually, one brick and one vinyl, jammed together, with the dividing wall removed. Poppy had outfitted this Frankenstein building with a kitchen and a living room set to make it a second "house" of sorts. Even though it was only half the size of the main house, its open floor plan gave the illusion of space. Which, with a family as large as Dad's, was always in short supply.

Mom says she cried the first time she visited. Dad's family was so loud and rowdy that they startled her to tears. Mamaw, who was the loudest of them all, had been yelling over so many kids for so many years that she was oblivious to her own volume. Sometimes when she was especially loud, Dad would wince. "Mom, you're yelling."

She'd roll her eyes and shoot him a look. "I AIN'T *YELLING*," she'd yell back.

Dad was on a different frequency from the rest of his family. He was quieter. More inside himself. He was tough in a backwoodsy, I'll-prove-you-wrong kind of way, which came from growing up small and wiry, the youngest of five kids, and poorer than he'd ever admit. He rarely talked about his childhood—at least, not as it really happened. He claimed that he'd grown up seeing fanged deer in the woods, rabbits with eagle talons, and coyotes the size of trucks. He said that once he fell off a fifty-foot cliff and survived two days in the wilderness despite being chased by a house-sized bear, which he wrestled into submission and killed with his bare kid hands.

"After that, there wasn't nowhere I didn't take my gun," Dad would say. The way he told it, some kind of mutant mountain creature had lurked behind every tree, around every bend in the holler. My favorite story was about a werewolf with glow-in-the-dark eyes.

"He was a big ole thing. Twice as big as me." Dad wasn't very tall, but to me he was huge, especially when he told his stories. "Well, one night that son of a gun got to chasing me. I ran fast as I could up the holler, but he was right behind me. Breathing on my neck, *shoooo-wee*. Slobbering down my shirt."

I could almost smell it, the rancid wolf breath.

"Now I ran till there wasn't nowhere else to go, so I turned around and popped him." Dad would mime firing his gun. "But the bullets bounced right off."

Here I'd scrunch into myself.

"So I started running up the mountain. Got all the way to the top and turned back around. And he was getting closer and closer. Right on my heels. Nose in my hair. I thought I was done for. But then . . ." Dad would pause, a master of suspense.

"What? What?" I'd beg, even though I already knew what happened next.

"I remembered the silver bullet in my pocket."

Dad would let the miracle sink in. "I loaded her up and whipped around, and popped that bad boy for *good*."

It thrilled me to believe the mountains were so wild. My favorite thing was to be in them, deep in them, where rotting stumps took the shape of black bears, and scampering squirrels sounded big as coyotes. Poppy had a mud-crusted four-wheeler that my younger brother, Erik, and I loved riding. It wasn't hard to persuade Dad to take us, especially if my aunts, uncles, and cousins were visiting and the house was a riot. We'd pile onto the four-wheeler—Dad in front, me in the back, and Erik, the smallest, sandwiched between us—and go flying down the road, no helmets and no fear. Eventually Dad would cut into the woods. He'd creep over logs. Weave between trees. Sometimes he'd hit the brakes and claim in his most convincing, awestruck voice to have caught a glimpse of Bigfoot just ahead. I'd strain my eyes, searching every dark spot in the underbrush. I was fearsomely reverent of the mountains, of all that lurked unseen.

There was one adventure that was just the two of us, Dad and me, that sticks in my mind. It starts with us backing out of the driveway, my arms wrapped around Dad's belly. Poppy was watching from his porch chair. "Have a good time," he said, smiling. The gap in his front teeth was almost as wide as his cigarette.

From there, a blur of wind and speed. Dad punched the gas. We zoomed up the one-lane road until the pavement turned to dirt. There the curves got tighter, and the forest closed in. Nobody lived that far up the holler.

After a while, Dad veered onto an old mining road. It was barely visible under the brushy growth of the forest floor. He geared down, easing over fallen limbs, threading between adolescent tulip poplars and sugar maples. As we snaked up the mountain, the vegetation began to thin. The road grew bare, as if it had just been bulldozed.

It was a strange thing to behold. A moment earlier we'd been forging our way through the thickest part of the woods; now we were driving into a pit of scalped earth. A huge chunk of the mountainside had been blasted away, leaving behind high cliffs of stratified rock. Near the bottom of the rock face was the coal seam, a thin, shiny band of black.

The mine had been abandoned for years, Dad told me over his shoulder, but the land around it was ravaged beyond repair. A box turtle, nearly invisible in the yellow dirt, was the only sign of life. It crawled behind a rock as we passed. The rest of the forest kept its distance, as though it feared the mine and the wasted pit it had become.

Dad eased closer to the rock wall. There was a round, boulder-filled hole at the bottom, barely high enough for a man even as short as Dad to walk through upright. He told me that Poppy had mined in there years ago. That the deeper you went, the smaller the hole got.

"Just imagine it," Dad said to me. "Working a mile under a mountain, in a tunnel two feet high."

The next thing I remember, we were tearing back toward the trees, yellow dirt spraying behind us like smoke. We raced down the holler. When we got back to the house, Poppy was still on the porch.

"Y'all have fun?" he asked through his cigarette.

He stood up slowly, stiffly, to help me off the four-wheeler. First he leaned so far forward I thought he'd topple over. Next he strained to straighten his knees and back. All those years underground, and his body had curled in on itself, hardened like a fossil. When he offered me his hand, I rested my fingers on his as lightly as I could. He suddenly seemed too delicate to touch.

I never knew Mamaw and Poppy very well. I was one of eleven grandchildren and great-grandchildren, and they accidentally called me by my cousins' names more often than they called me by my own.

In my memory, they're opposites. Mamaw was slim and fidgety, always on her feet, either stirring a pot on the stove, washing dishes at the sink, or running between the two, in a perpetual hurry even when there was nothing to hurry for. Poppy, on the other hand, was large and laid-back. He had a big belly, big smile, and a crackling, phlegmy smoker's laugh. He was missing segments of several fingers: Once, as a young man, he'd lit a firecracker and held on too long.

Most of what I know of Mamaw and Poppy was told to me by other family members. A few years ago, I learned that their wedding picture is not of a wedding at all: It's a composite of Mamaw's eleventh-grade yearbook photo superimposed beside Poppy's army portrait. She's sixteen. He's nineteen. They're high school dropouts straight out of the holler, bright-eyed with youth and having never seen the world outside the mountains. Poppy was stationed in Germany soon after the wedding. He and Mamaw crossed an ocean they'd never seen before.

All through elementary school, I'd tell anyone who would listen that once upon a time my grandparents had lived in Germany. *Germany!* It was too exotic to even visualize. Most of my classmates, like me, had never seen much beyond southwest Virginia. They were impressed by the fact, and it made me feel special. Cosmopolitan.

In truth, I didn't know anything about my grandparents' lives in Germany—what it was like for them, or even which city they lived in. It was a brief stay. As soon as Poppy was discharged, he and Mamaw moved back to the very piece of land Poppy had grown up on. He built a little house and went to work in the mines. Mamaw stayed home, raised her babies. Dad, her fifth and final, was born when she was twenty-three.

I wouldn't realize until I was older how both sets of my grandparents led such similar lives. From growing up poor in big mining families, to fleeing Buchanan County young and coming right back again. From the military to the mines, to the back-in-the-holler houses set deep in the shadows of wild mountains. My grandfathers, in my eyes, were almost the same *person*, down to their mangled hands and the stilted way they walked.

My parents ended up together because they wanted something different. Neither wanted to stick around Buchanan County, living the rest of their lives under the iron thumb of King Coal. Neither wanted to live the lives of everyone around them. They met on the bus in high school, then dated through college. Their wedding was in Mom's Baptist church. Her preacher refused to perform the ceremony: Mom was baptized; Dad was not. It was an "unequal yoking," the preacher said.

Undeterred, they found a different preacher.

Growing up, I sensed the purposeful distance between where

my family lived and where my grandparents lived. I knew my parents loved the holler of their youth. I sensed the complexity to that love, too. I felt it in the acceleration of the four-wheeler when Dad took me and Erik riding, speeding as far from his childhood home as fast as he could. I saw it in the way Mom scanned her parents' wood-paneled living room with impatient eyes, arms folded and knees bouncing, in the minutes before she stood up and announced it was time to go.

I was too young to understand the chasm my parents had carved between past and present, but I *felt* it. I felt, too, that it didn't take much for the walls to shift, begin to converge. For my parents to remember that everything they'd left behind was not so far away.

3.

I was breathing into the cold glass of our living room window. I'd been watching outside for the better part of an hour, since Dad had called and said he was on his way home. It was a two-hour drive from Charleston, Mom reminded me every week, but I ran to the window as soon as she picked up the phone, trying to will Dad's truck into the driveway.

He'd been gone since Sunday night. He'd left after dinner with his travel bag of socks and undershirts and headed up the highway toward another week of tests, drills, and high-speed-chase simulations. State trooper training was serious business. Tonight—Friday—he'd come home half awake, sticky with sweat he hadn't had time to shower off, all lean and hard with new muscle, and spend the weekend with me, Erik, and Mom, before driving back up to the police academy Sunday night.

Since fall, around the time I started first grade, our family had marked time by Dad's coming and going. Each day was a countdown until the end of the week; each week was a countdown until the end of the month. Each month was a countdown until Dad graduated into his new job in the spring.

It was hard for me to picture Dad as a cop. Before, he'd come home at night smelling like new tires. He'd jerk his tie loose and yank at the collar of his too-big button-down, frustrated from all the schmoozing and hawking and haggling it took to sell cars. *You gotta do whatever it takes*, his bosses would scold. They essentially told Dad to lie through his teeth, say whatever potential buyers needed to hear to sign the paperwork. Dad either couldn't or wouldn't, even though no sales meant no commission, which meant Dad was working for minimum wage. Which, in the early 2000s, was a little over five dollars an hour.

Not that Tazewell was the best place to be a car salesman. It was half an hour from the nearest interstate. There were better, bigger dealerships that were a lot easier to get to unless you actually *lived* in Tazewell. The town itself was small, self-contained. I saw the same people at the grocery store, school, and church. Very rarely a new face.

My parents had ended up here just before I was born. Before that, they'd lived in Virginia Beach. They'd moved there the week they got married, fled as far as possible from where they'd grown up while staying in the same state. I can imagine the thrill of planning that move: mapping out the seven-hour drive, plotting all the cities they'd hit along the way; scoping out apartments with an ocean view.

How strange and wonderful it must have been, after a lifetime in rural Appalachia, to live somewhere so flat and expansive, with sand instead of trees, and condos instead of mountains. Restaurants you could walk to, and more than one grocery store. I used to ask Mom about the ocean. Trying to picture its breadth and power stretched my imagination to capacity. In many of the photos from that time, Mom's lying on the beach with a book and tanning oil, perfectly at ease.

Dad, meanwhile, grimaces up at the camera from beneath umbrellas and wide-brimmed hats. He didn't *dislike* the beach, necessarily, but he never fell in love with it the way Mom did. There was so much traffic. So many people. His new friends were always jabbing at his strong Appalachian accent, how he pronounced the words "bear" like "bar" and "pen" like "pin." Dad knew how to laugh at himself, but I can't help but think the teasing got to him a little.

Mom could have stayed on the coast forever. Dad, I think, would have put up with it for her. But they got to talking about kids, and they realized how lonely it would be to start a family so far from their own families, from the mountains of their DNA.

So they moved back to the coalfields. Not all the way back to Buchanan County, though. Tazewell County was a compromise. The northwestern half—the part that bordered Buchanan—was rugged and coaly, while the southeastern half relaxed into gentler mountains and wide, hilly valleys. My parents settled in one of those valleys. They bought a house in a nameless community of rectangular lots that were parceled out in a row, like teeth, on what had once been farmland. Just north, looking toward West Virginia, were some of the finest coal seams in the country.

On paper, Tazewell was exactly what my parents wanted: something *close* to Buchanan County and *like* Buchanan County without *being* Buchanan County. Tazewell's schools were a little better. Its poverty rate was a little lower. Its economy wasn't entirely dependent on the coal market, so there were more jobs outside the mines.

But few that paid like them.

Dad never wanted to mine. He saw what it did to the body, how it turned you old before your time. I think he feared becoming like Poppy, so stiff and pained that he was mostly confined to a chair, or like his brother Greg, whose back was broken by falling rock and who walked with a stilted limp for the rest of his life.

So he'd gone to college instead. No one else in his family had or ever would. And even though he was never more than an average student at best, he'd scraped through with a criminal justice degree, which seemed practical enough.

Still, even with a degree, good jobs were hard to come by. For most of his adult life, Dad ended up taking whatever work he could get. Which, until he got hired into the West Virginia State Police, meant selling—or trying to sell—cars.

My breath had formed a damp circle of frost on the window. It was a cold, brittle night, the kind that hinted at snow. Mom had promised we'd decorate the Christmas tree that weekend. Usually it was up by now, a week into December, but this year it was still crammed into its big, bulky box in the attic because Mom wasn't strong enough to wrestle it down alone. While I kept watch on the driveway, she banged around the tiny hallway that doubled as a laundry room. She heaved a small mountain of clothes into the washer. Stray socks rained to the floor. She swayed with exhaustion as she bent to pick them up.

During the week, Mom's day started at five. She taught kindergarten at the elementary school where I was in first grade. Every morning was a rush to beat the bell, especially since she had to drop Erik off at a preschool several miles out of the way. Every evening was a rush, too. She'd pick Erik up, drive home, start dinner, and chip away at the Sisyphean chore of keeping the house in an acceptably clean and organized state. Serve dinner. Wash dishes. Bath time. Finally she'd wrangle me and Erik into our beds, somehow still awake, and read to us from the books we'd picked out from the library that week, before collapsing into her own bed, hitting the pillow with her eyes shut.

Years later, Mom would tell me she'd wanted more kids. I balked at this. It seemed like a miracle she'd managed me and my brother. She clarified: If she'd had more money and time—if Dad's income would have allowed her to stay home—she would have wanted another kid or two.

But I can't imagine a life different from the one I had, with Erik and my parents in our cozy little house. It was modular, built concentrically around the staircase, so you were never far from anyone at any time, even if you were in opposite corners on opposite floors. The house always smelled warm, like maple candles and carpet. On Sundays it smelled like Mom's vegetable soup. The recipe was from an old Baptist cookbook with splatters all over the tattered cover. It called for cabbage, peas, carrots, potatoes, corn, stewed tomatoes, and a can of Spam for flavor.

Back in the summer, Dad had grown most of the soup ingredients in his garden. It was at the flat top of the hill that was our backyard, which butted up against the bigger hill of our neighbor's cattle farm. The garden was huge—twice the footprint of our house—and Dad worked it mostly alone, with occasional help from his brother Danny, who lived next door. I remember sweat streaming off Dad's face as he heaved the tiller through the soil. His wet shirt sticking to his shoulders and back.

Every year at harvest time, Nanny and Mamaw would come with twenty-gallon tubs. They'd comb the garden until nothing ripe remained, then pressure-cook it all into sealed glass jars. What resulted was enough for us and the whole extended family to stock their pantries, with plenty of leftovers. Those Dad gave away. Of course all our neighbors grew gardens, too, but Appalachian politeness dictated you couldn't accept a gift without giving one back, so when Dad went handing out vegetables, he'd come home with more than he'd started out with—Food Lion bags stuffed to splitting with squash, zucchini, peppers, lettuce, and enough tomatoes to line the entire length of our deck railing, where they'd come to full ripeness in the summer sun.

I loved the freedom of summer. I spent most days outside with Erik and the neighbor kids running from yard to yard. When we were a little older, one of our neighbors would let us ride his four-wheeler as long as we promised to not go too fast. We had no need for keeping time then, but could have by the coal trains. They ran like a clock, crossing the mountain every hour.

The texture of those days is gentle in my memory, like the slow roll of the sun over the ridge, or the sweet-earth smell of our neighbor cutting hay. Even rainy days—and there were a lot of them in the mountains—had a certain warmth. I'd pass the hours reading from my library books and, when I finished those, books from my own small collection. These were books like *Charlotte's Web* and *Little House in the Big Woods* that Mom had bought directly from Scholastic with her steep teacher's discount because she thought I ought to own them, not just borrow and return. When I tired of those, I dove into Mom's *Good Housekeeping* and *Southern Living* magazines. And when I tired of those, I'd write my own magazines and books. I made them out of folded notebook paper and illustrated them with colored pencils.

Mom tried to get Erik into reading, but he didn't take to it like me. He was a lot like Dad that way. I only remember Dad reading one book ever. It was called *Heaven Is for Real,* about a toddler who claimed he'd left his body during surgery, went to heaven, and met Jesus. Mom, on the other hand, kept her nightstand stacked with beach novels, crime novels, coffee-table art books, and her giant Max Lucado study Bible, which had a picture of a foot and washbowl on the cover. She made sure I always had a steady supply of books, too, and read to me every night. This was one of my favorite things. Mom took on a different voice for each character, and slowed down to build tension, and got louder when something exciting happened, so I'd stay with every word, waiting for whatever the next sentence would bring, even when I didn't care much for the stories themselves.

A Wrinkle in Time was one of those. It was Mom's pick. We read it when I was five or six, long before I was able to understand the vaguely evil "Black Thing" or the abstract way in which the characters traveled through time and space. Mom's enthusiasm made up for my lack of understanding, though. She loved that book, and all things outer space.

Most hours of the day, Mom kept her kitchen radio quietly tuned to the news. She liked background noise, the absence of silence. It was only when a story about rocket launches or solar flares or meteors hurtling close to Earth came on that she jumped for the volume dial.

"We're all made of star dust," she liked to say.

Those could be fighting words, depending on Dad's mood. He fundamentally disagreed with the big bang theory. His stance was staunchly creationist, which was that all of humanity originated by God's hand, not by some giant explosion.

By this token, he was skeptical of all theories that had to do with the universe, especially the idea that it was infinite.

"It can't just go on forever," he reasoned. "It's gotta end somewhere."

"No it doesn't." Mom was always ready to play defense. "Because if it ends, that means it's contained. So what's containing it? And where does *that* end?"

Dad, a little flustered, would double down. "Space has got limits. It's *got* to."

"Does not," Mom would sneak in.

Dad: "Maybe it's contained within itself somehow. Or within heaven."

Mom: "Then wouldn't that mean heaven's infinite? Or is it contained in something, too?"

Then Dad—who, once he formed an opinion, stuck to it—would roll his eyes and grumble in a half-joking-half-not way about Mom's left-wing-liberal radio. Mom would reply that NPR was barely left of center, actually, and the argument would die there, unresolved, until it inevitably flared back up a few weeks or months later. Mom and Dad disagreed on a lot, but rarely argued. The concept of infinity, for some reason, was the one exception.

4.

I don't remember the shock of cold. I don't remember the hand on my forehead, big as my whole face, or the breathless going-under. All I remember is climbing out, wrapping myself in a towel handed to me by the pastor's wife, and the weird wet mush of carpet under my bare feet.

There's one picture of my baptism. Just one, tucked into a scrapbook with photos of Dad's state police graduation, Erik's first day of kindergarten, and the blue ribbon I won in the second-grade spelling bee. The baptism photo is a little shaky. I imagine Mom was trying to focus the camera while shushing Erik, who was barely patient enough to sit through a normal church service. You can see the water up to my chest. My hands are clasped and my eyes are closed. Pastor Ron towers behind me, a giant arm raised in prayer.

I liked Pastor Ron even though he was different from most people I knew. It mainly had to do with his accent, or lack of one, how his words stood upright instead of tumbling over themselves like mine. He was from Oklahoma. He'd spent his whole life and pastoring career there until a fateful visit to southwest Virginia in the late 1990s. All he saw was hopelessness and despair, he said, unlike anything he'd seen before. A lightning bolt to the heart, and he uprooted his wife and kids to Tazewell County. He got funding to build a church. Deliverance opened when I was five.

Pastor Ron was a thunderboom of a man. He was one of the biggest, tallest people I'd ever seen and had a voice that matched. He'd been a linebacker in college and could have gone pro, he often said, if God hadn't called him to the ministry. Most Sundays, Erik and I opted out of his sermon and went to Children's Church instead. It was held out back, separate from the main church building, in a single-wide trailer. There were metal folding chairs and *VeggieTales* coloring sheets. The children's pastor was a blonde-haired mom with a voice so soft and girlish that she seemed more like a kid than a teacher.

But I must have stayed for the sermon the day Pastor Ron passed out the baptism sign-up sheet. I wrote my name down—probably in my loopy beginner's cursive, the way I wrote everything when I was eight—although I don't recall what went into making the decision. I didn't understand the meaning or purpose of baptism any more than I understood the Bible verses I memorized for Children's Church every week. Maybe I decided to do it because I'd heard enough times that it was something I was supposed to do. Maybe I decided to do it simply because the option was there. Maybe I didn't think much about it at all.

Where we lived, you didn't see many new churches popping up. The ones that did were usually in dying shopping plazas or rundown buildings bought for cheap. The brand-new Deliverance was *nice*. It had a shimmer of decadence that most mountain churches lacked: a high-ceilinged foyer with a coffee bar, upholstered chairs for pews, and a sleek black synthesizer instead of a piano. There were big purple tapestries on the sanctuary walls with the many names of God embroidered in silky gold letters: Jehovah Rapha, Jehovah Shalom, Jehovah Nissi, Jehovah Jireh. Despite all the grandeur, Pastor Ron rebelled against the usual formalities of church. He showed up most Sundays in T-shirts and jeans. The congregation, which was mostly young families and college-age kids, followed suit.

Deliverance was a Pentecostal church, although I wouldn't know this until I was in middle school. While browsing Deliverance's website for reasons I don't remember, I saw a small line of text at the bottom of the home page. It said Deliverance was associated with the International Pentecostal Holiness Church.

This confused me. Deliverance, as far as I'd ever understood, was nondenominational. I couldn't recall a single time Pastor Ron had labeled our church otherwise. For some reason, the very truth of us was something of a secret.

Years later, I'd realize why. The word "Pentecostal," if you knew anything about it, had a certain connotation, brought to mind certain images: people speaking in tongues, writhing on the floor, and screaming to Jesus with red sweat-streaked faces. Such rapturous intensity did not appeal to general audiences.

But "nondenominational," that said something else. It said welcoming. Progressive. Different.

To some, that might have sounded a little hippie-dippie, if not downright sacrilegious. It made Mom curious. She'd grown up in a Baptist church with stained-glass windows, wooden pews, and a cotton-haired pianist who played hymns like dirges. There the men wore slacks and the women wore hose, and to deviate in any way meant spending the whole service with eyes on the back of your head.

As a teen, Mom had liked the predictable orderliness of the Baptist church, a refuge from her father's drinking and rage. But she went a little sour on it after the "unequal yoking" incident, and in the years after, her faith grew into something all its own, something big-minded and hungry. No church seemed to offer what she needed, so she stopped going entirely.

Until Deliverance.

It must have been so strange to her at first. The contemporary Christian rock preferred by Deliverance's worship team. Pastor Ron's casual style. His passionate, unscripted preaching, delivered thunderously, as if he were trying to broadcast his voice up to heaven.

The most unusual thing about Deliverance was that there were no expectations for what your faith looked like—how you prayed, how you worshipped. You could run up and down the aisles screaming your praises to Jesus, and nobody would bat an eye. If anything, people would be energized by the spectacle. Some might start screaming and running themselves.

Unexpectedly, Mom loved it. It was religion undone, fresh and expansive. Mom went to church every Sunday with me and Erik in tow. Though she never expressed her faith as loudly and openly as the rest of the congregation—that was the one buttoned-up Baptist sensibility she couldn't shake—she appreciated that others were free to do so.

Deliverance was my first experience with church. To me, all the emotion, noise, and movement, as intense as it was, seemed *right* for the atmosphere. Curated, even. When the room went dark and the drummer rolled his cymbals in low, gentle reverberations, cries would rise across the sanctuary, and the congregation would flood the altar and fall to their knees in heaving sobs. When the worship team danced and shouted and the stage lights flashed across the ceiling in bright, dizzying patterns, the congregation would jump and shout and wave their arms in the air, spasming in spiritual ecstasy.

I didn't know if everyone behaved that way by choice, or if they were so overwhelmed by God that they *couldn't* behave any other way. Once I watched a sweating woman shriek and flail as a circle of congregants held her down. Pastor Ron got on his knees and put his hand to the woman's forehead.

"Be gone in the name of JESUS!" he shouted into the woman's face. It seemed to me as though he were speaking *past* her, to someone, or some*thing*, no one could see.

After a few minutes, the woman fell limp and silent. Someone covered her sprawled body with a blanket.

"Is she dead?" I whispered to Mom.

"No," Mom whispered back. "God's just working inside her."

I had only a vague understanding of what that meant. I remembered being five years old, the warm heaviness on my shoulders, and my knees bending under its irresistible weight. The force that had acted on me then, I understood, was the same force acting on the woman, and everyone else who lost control of their bodies in church.

I didn't understand what it accomplished, though, God working inside you. I didn't know why or how it even happened. Why or how it had happened to *me* the very first time I'd gone to that church. In the three years since, God had never returned to me in that way. Not once. Not even in a whisper.

When I looked at the rest of the congregation, I wondered how others seemed to feel him every week.

Dad didn't come with us to church. He was raised Pentecostal and got his fill of it—stopped going as a teenager as soon as he was old enough to have the say-so. It wasn't that he didn't believe; he would always call himself a Christian. He just preferred to keep his faith personal, and quiet.

Most Sundays, I asked to stay home with Dad. "Why do we have to go to church if he doesn't?" I'd whine to Mom.

"Dad's a grown-up," she'd say. "When you're a grown-up, you can choose not to go."

That was rarely enough to placate me. "Why do we have to go every week?"

Mom always gave the same answer. "Because church is *good* for you."

Even though Dad only went to Deliverance when Erik and I were in Christmas or Easter plays, he seemed to agree with Mom: that church was good, and its teachings were valuable, and it was important Erik and I learned them. He shut down my whining the second it began, making it clear that church wasn't optional. I didn't—and still don't—know what he thought church gave us that he didn't need.

There were a lot of things that went unsaid because they were hard to explain. The big one that winter was Dad's job. He'd been working long hours in Princeton, West Virginia, forty minutes north of our house. It was a rough place. Dad told stories about robberies, shootings, and drugs. It wasn't just meth and crack and heroin, but pills now, too. He pulled over a lot of erratic drivers who were high on who-knows-what, and half of them would have kids in the back seat. It bothered Dad a lot, people playing recklessly with their children's lives.

I knew this not because he *said* it bothered him but by how extra quiet he got after telling those stories. Dad's feelings were revealed mostly in the space between his words. To understand him, you had to learn to read his silence.

One night, I woke from a bad dream. I hollered for Dad, who came and tucked himself into my bed, then told me a story to soothe me back to sleep. Somewhere along the way he nodded off, too. When his alarm went off, Mom shuffled into my room.

"Tom," she whispered in the dark. "Time for work."

Dad rolled over beside me. He was quiet for a moment.

"I can't do it no more," he whispered back in a strange voice.

Mom didn't say anything for a few seconds. When she finally replied, her voice was different, too.

"You *have* to," she said.

Dad didn't move. I pretended to sleep and held my breath. The ceiling could have fallen in, and it wouldn't have been any more terrifying than this, Dad as tender as an open wound.

My parents had always been careful not to discuss money around me and Erik, but I wasn't oblivious to the precarious nature of our lower-middle-class stability and how it all hinged on how much money my parents brought home. Once I knew Dad hated his job—even though he eventually got out of bed and went anyway—there was something newly threatening in his silence, all the things he didn't say. Was he thinking about quitting? What would happen to our family if he did?

This uncertainty was soon overshadowed by another. Poppaw was sick. He'd spent weeks in the hospital, until one day he was suddenly home again, confined to a hospice bed that took up most of his and Nanny's bedroom. Everyone but the nurse, who visited twice a day in Looney Tunes scrubs, tiptoed around the word "cancer."

I came to dread our visits. Poppaw shriveled and yellowed. His breathing alternated between shallow gasps and big, sucking gulps. The sight and sound of him terrified me. The doorway of the bedroom was as close as I would go.

Once, Mom urged me to go inside. "Just say hello," she said. "Tell him you're here."

I inched forward. Up close, Poppaw's pallid face seemed barely human. He stared at the ceiling, eyes glazed with morphine, in what looked to me like terror.

I started crying and ran from the room.

From then on, I stuck to the den at the opposite end of the house. I strayed only to go to the bathroom or sneak away to the basement where no one ever came looking for me, until one night when I sensed a sudden heaviness. I crept back to Poppaw's room and peeked inside. Nanny and Mom and several relatives were gathered, their heads bowed and cheeks wet.

In a shattered voice, Nanny begged God to receive Poppaw into heaven.

"Have mercy, Lord," she whispered. "Have mercy. Have mercy."

When Poppaw died an hour later, I didn't cry right away. It seemed as if he'd already been gone for weeks, and the reality of his absence was less shocking than the fact that Nanny's prayer, in my mind, had worked. I didn't realize that Poppaw had been in his last moments and would have passed soon anyway. My understanding was that the prayer, more so than the cancer, had precipitated his death.

Though I'd heard in church that God answered prayers, I'd never actually seen a prayer answered—at least, not so obviously or immediately. The miracle, as I saw it, of God answering Nanny's prayer lodged itself in my brain, seeded a new awareness of his power and omnipresence. It was both comforting and alarming to realize God's *realness*. To know there was an actual someone on the receiving end of my bedtime prayers.

The full gravity of being at God's mercy was still years beyond my comprehension, but the pinprick of knowledge was enough to open me up just a little. Terrifying, this God who controlled the fate of each human life. Who was everywhere, always, with the weight of eternity behind his crushing presence.

5.

The months after Poppaw died were cold and slow. They passed heavily, with bitter mornings and pale, snowy skies. Mom was on the phone with Nanny a lot, making sure she'd gotten out of bed, had something to eat. Dad was quieter than ever. Something seemed to be hanging over our house.

The cloud burst in late winter, just before I turned nine. One evening I was reading in my room when the house went still. I crept downstairs to spy on my parents. They were in the kitchen, thumbing through stacks of bills.

"I don't know what we're going to do," Mom finally said. Her voice warbled with panic.

"We'll be fine, Debbie," Dad said, although he sounded uncertain himself.

"No we won't." Mom slapped the bills down on the counter. "No we won't."

Dad, who was usually better at escalating conflict than resolving it, tried to calm her down.

Nothing he said helped. I don't remember who started yelling first, or what was said. My parents' faces contorted with stress and fear, and the slice of each other's angry words. Mom started shouting above Dad.

"We're going to have to sell the house!" she shouted.

At that, I revealed myself uncertainly.

"Are we moving?" I asked.

"No," Dad barked.

Mom glared at him with burning eyes. Then she turned, walked down the hall to the bathroom, and shut the door. She didn't come out for a long time.

It was rare to see Mom lose her temper. She usually approached problems with a cool matter-of-factness that didn't allow for the frivolity of emotion. I'd heard her yell only a handful of times. I'd seen her cry only twice: once, briefly, at Poppaw's hospice bedside, and then a few weeks later at church, once the sanctuary lights were dimmed for worship. Tears had started rolling down her cheeks, a flood of them, one after another. They'd dripped off her chin and landed in tiny splashes on her ironed blouse.

Just after the New Year, Dad had quit his police job. I didn't know at first. I'd only realized something was different after several nights of him leaving for work around the time Erik and I went to bed and getting home around the time we woke up for school. When I asked, he told me he was now an overnight security guard at a junkyard in Grundy, an hour's drive away.

This job was meant to be temporary, and conducive to the college classes he'd signed up for. His new career plan was to teach middle or high school history. His textbooks, which were rubbed soft on the corners by their previous owners, had names like *Introduction to Curriculum Planning* and *Principles of Classroom Instruction*. He read them in the junkyard office between patrolling scrap heaps.

Since Dad was making less money *and* paying for college classes,

Mom had started tutoring after school for extra cash. She'd also enrolled in a program to get her master's degree, paid for by the Tazewell County school system, which would come with a thousand-dollar salary increase when she graduated.

The thing was, my parents needed money *now.* A couple weeks after their argument, they announced we were going for a drive. Erik and I climbed into the car. Dad drove to the end of the road, Mom silent beside him, then turned and headed back the way we came. This time we bypassed our driveway. Two cars I didn't recognize were parked out front. A Realtor and a pair of interested buyers were talking on the porch.

Every Sunday from then on, when Mom's eyes were shut in concentrated prayer, I'd search her wrinkled brow and quivering mouth, intrigued by both the showing of her emotion and her restraint in showing it. Everyone around us cried openly. Mom never allowed herself to. On the occasions she let her tears flow, she kept them quiet, controlled.

As winter turned to spring, my parents' barely contained worry seemed to lighten a little. I forgot about the house being for sale until I realized Mom and Dad hadn't taken me and Erik on a car ride in a while.

"Are we still moving?" I asked one day.

They looked at each other, then answered at the same time. "No."

It was around then that I noticed my birthday money was missing. In the back of my top dresser drawer, I kept a red zipper pencil pouch as a makeshift piggy bank. One day I pulled it out. Forty dollars—the sum of the cash my aunts, uncles, and grandparents had given to me in birthday cards—was not there.

I dug out the remaining fives and ones, the rest of my life savings, and counted again. I was definitely forty dollars short. I knew I hadn't spent it.

This had happened before, my money disappearing. Usually just a few dollars at a time—small amounts I figured I'd lost somewhere, left in a pocket or dropped at school. Or maybe I'd miscounted: Math was my worst subject, after all. Or maybe my count was off because I sometimes lent Dad money for gas.

"Just five bucks," he'd say. "Promise I'll pay you back."

And he always did. It didn't occur to me that he might have taken my birthday money without asking, or without promising to repay.

But then Erik noticed *his* cash missing. He had a real piggy bank, the kind with a rubber stopper in its belly. One evening he popped it open. I heard the soft shatter of coins draining out on his bedroom rug, then the dull scratch of him scraping at the pig's empty innards.

A moment of realization, and he started wailing.

"Someone *stole* my *money*."

By the time I peeked into his room, Erik's eyes had turned as red as his shirt. Through his tears, he tried to explain: All the cash he'd saved in the five and a half years of his life was gone.

It was such an unbelievable thing that my mind went first to other explanations. Maybe Erik and I had *both* misplaced our money. Or maybe I'd miscounted, and Erik had spent his and forgotten.

Suddenly he turned to me in rage.

"What'd you do with it?" he yelled.

"I didn't take your money," I said.

"Yes you did!"

"No I didn't!"

"Hey!" Dad hollered up at us from downstairs. "What's all the commotion?"

Erik burst into a fresh round of tears and bawled, "Emilee broke into my piggy bank!"

For too long, Dad said nothing.

My memory skips a beat here. The next thing I remember, my parents were upstairs, trying to explain themselves in that embarrassed, half-desperate way when you know that no amount of explaining will suffice. I don't remember their words, exactly, only that Dad swore he'd intended to pay us back. He said sorry, and that he and Mom wouldn't borrow any more money without asking first.

"Borrow," that was the word they used. Not "steal."

I was confused by it all. I couldn't wrap my head around my parents stealing. *Thou shalt not steal*: the eighth of the Ten Commandments. I knew this because I'd memorized them for Children's Church. My prize for perfect recitation was a tombstone-shaped magnet printed with the commandments, which I'd given to Mom. She'd stuck it on the bumper of her car.

Another layer to my confusion was that my parents didn't *borrow* things. Dad's philosophy was "Don't owe nobody nothing," which meant that if you couldn't afford to pay for something up front, you went without. (Exceptions were made for the house, and the car my parents bought when I was five.) He carried only cash and refused to even own a credit card. Mom, who had a debit card, was only slightly less extreme. So for my parents to "borrow"—or steal, or whatever you wanted to call it, because no word seemed quite right to me—well, that was sheer desperation.

Years later, Mom told me how close she and Dad had come to losing our house. They'd cobbled together mortgage payments from my money, Erik's money, Mom's after-school tutoring, Dad's seven-day workweeks, and the change that accumulated in car cup holders. Erik and I unknowingly helped fund groceries, gas, and our own doctors' visits and medicine when we got sick, too.

Somehow, Mom said, they always came up with just enough money in the nick of time. My parents would get bills they knew they wouldn't be able to pay, but then cash-filled cards from our relatives would arrive in the mail for me and Erik—not just on birthdays and Christmas, but on holidays that didn't warrant gifts at all, like Valentine's Day and Halloween. Or one of my aunts, uncles, or grandparents would come visit, then fold a couple bucks into my and Erik's hands on their way out the door. "For good grades," they'd say. Even without seeing our report cards.

I'm certain this was more than serendipity. It seemed as if my extended family was most generous to me and Erik when our parents' budget was tightest. Lending and borrowing was a delicate dance of courtesy and discretion—it would have been something of an insult for my relatives to directly offer my parents help, or to even vocalize the presumption they needed it, and my parents, who were fiercely anti-charity, wouldn't have accepted—so to avoid it altogether, my relatives slipped money to me and Erik instead.

Not that *they* had a lot of extra cash to spare. But that was their way of showing love—giving. Or, more accurately, sacrifice. Taking care of everyone else before themselves. Going without so others wouldn't.

Easter came in mid-April, when Home Creek was in full bloom. Dad's family always celebrated in a big way, with an egg hunt for the kids and a dinner that put all other dinners to shame. Mamaw started cooking before dawn. She used every eye on her stove and both racks in her oven. When one dish was done, she'd put it to the side, wash whatever pot or pan she'd cooked it in, and start on another. By the time all the family flooded in around noon, every inch of the countertops and tables was covered in food, so much that you had to eat holding your plate. There was nowhere to set it down.

The little house felt like a million degrees, with about as many people. Mamaw dished me up a volcano of mashed potatoes and a slab of country ham. Beside it she heaped some greasy green beans from Dad's garden, a couple deviled eggs, and a fat, fluffy dinner roll. I perched on the couch armrest beside my uncle Danny, who was tearing into the pineapple casserole I'd opted out of. "That plate's 'bout as big as you, girly," he teased. Every forkful tasted a little like the cigarettes Poppy puffed on between bites.

We ate ourselves to bursting. After, the grown-ups lounged around in a heavy, happy daze, while my cousins and Erik and I grew eager for the egg hunt. We whined until our parents finally heaved themselves up and went to hide plastic eggs outside. Mamaw pulled the curtains to keep us from peeking.

When it was time, we shot out of the house, baskets in hand, searching wildly for slivers of color along the sidewalk, in the grass. I found my first egg in the cinder blocks that served as the stoop of the main house. I found another in a strawberry pot, and another in the ditch that drained into the rust-colored creek. They all jangled, somewhat disappointingly, with dimes and quarters. Our parents and grandparents had filled most eggs with spare change. A rare few were stuffed with dollar bills, to make things more exciting.

After a few minutes, my cousin Dylan hollered from the edge of the yard. He'd found the "golden egg," the prize egg, hidden in the unmowed grass of the bank. Inside it was a twenty-dollar bill.

Burning with jealousy, the rest of us kids flocked to see. The bill was crinkled and soft, like cotton. As if someone had been holding on to it a while. I didn't know who'd contributed it, but I knew twenty dollars was no small amount for anyone.

The discovery of the golden egg always ended the magic of the egg hunt. I followed my cousins to the patio, where we counted our loot. We ended up with a few dollars each, mostly in change. When I put mine in my pocket, I felt as if it were *really* mine. A month had passed since my parents had admitted to taking money from me and Erik, and in that time they hadn't taken or asked to borrow a single penny.

Which didn't mean they hadn't needed it. A couple weeks earlier, I'd brought home an order form for the school yearbook. The form and its payment envelope lay on the counter untouched for days until they finally disappeared. I was disappointed, but never said so. I knew the twenty-five-dollar yearbook was a luxury none of us could afford.

Back in the house, Mamaw was almost done cleaning up dinner. She'd heaped leftovers onto plates and wrapped them in aluminum foil, then stacked them on the dining table by the door.

"Lordy mercy, somebody better take some a this food!" she yelled. As my aunts and uncles stood to go, Mamaw passed plates around. "Take some more, honey," she urged. "Take a little more."

Everyone protested at once. *You gotta keep some. Just a little. You're not gonna have none left for yourselves.* Poppy insisted they didn't want any of it, and Mamaw hushed and shushed everyone in her loud, stubborn way until every last plate was gone.

Loaded down, my parents started making their way to the door. Mamaw hollered for me as I followed them out. "Hold up, sissy," she said. "Come back here a second."

I turned around. Mamaw pulled me into her and gave a loving squeeze. Then she pointed to the ceramic flour jar by the oven. "Go see what's under there."

I did.

It was a fifty-dollar bill.

I snatched it up and stuffed it into my pocket, then beamed my thanks up at Mamaw. Her eyes weren't on me, though. She was looking across the room to my parents, to make sure they'd seen.

6.

It was a blue-sky day but cold, especially for early April. Each spring, Tazewell Elementary sent its fourth graders on a tour of Virginia Tech, the nearest university, an hour and a half's drive east. My friends and I sat at the back of the bus. These were the best seats, the most coveted seats, even though you could feel every bump in the road and the windows rattled violently in their metal frames, because they were farthest from the teachers up front.

Not that we were trying to escape their watchful eyes. My friends were all like me—quiet and bookish. We were in our school's "gifted" program, meaning we got pulled out of our classes once a week to do schoolwork intended for higher grade levels, meaning we were a little too nerdy to fit in with anyone but each other. But that morning we shrieked and laughed along with everyone else, high on the excitement of field trip day.

My impression of Virginia Tech was that it was the college you went to if you were really smart. A couple of Tazewell High's top graduates went each year. Others went to Bluefield College, a tiny Baptist school on the northern end of Tazewell County, or Southwest Virginia Community College on the western end. I imagined

Virginia Tech would look similar to these smaller colleges, with their steep hillsides and old brick buildings.

As it turned out, Virginia Tech's campus was sprawling and almost flat. The nearby mountains were hidden behind tall buildings and trees. There were lots of sidewalks, and lots of people on those sidewalks, and neatly pruned rows of bushes and budding flowers. I pressed my face to the bus window, imagining this was what a city must look like.

Outside the bookstore, student tour guides with crisp, upright accents welcomed us to campus. They led us first across a wide lawn. We passed a stately stone hall that loomed like a castle. We toured a geology museum, then peeked into an empty classroom—a "lecture hall," the guides called it—that was so oddly hushed it seemed as if all the sound had been vacuumed out. Last we went to the football stadium. Our guides led us to the top of the bleachers, where we got an almost-bird's-eye view of the field.

But what sticks most vividly in my memory about that day is how everyone on that campus was so *different* from me, my classmates, and my teachers. I couldn't say exactly what that difference was, though I sensed it ran deeper than their non-Appalachian accents—something I occasionally saw in strangers at the grocery store that immediately made me know they weren't from southwest Virginia. Maybe it was in the set of their mouths, or the way of their walk. Maybe it was only that I'd never seen their faces before. Virginia Tech was just eighty miles from Tazewell, but it was so opposite from what I knew that it seemed to belong to another planet.

Ten days later on the evening news:

Limestone buildings I recognized. Big green lawns I'd walked across. Zoomed-in shots of caution tape and police carrying limp, bloodied bodies from buildings. People embracing, crying. Through the night, the death toll ticked up and up and up.

In the morning, teachers cried in the hallways. Almost everyone wore orange and maroon, Virginia Tech's colors, and black. My classmates wore shirts they'd bought from the campus bookstore. The whole school was quiet with shock, especially fourth grade, knowing that less than two weeks earlier we'd walked the grounds of what was now the worst mass shooting in American history.

Over the next few days, black wreaths and ribbons popped up in storefronts all over town, and churches organized prayer services and vigils. Everyone had ties to Virginia Tech; either you'd gone to school there or knew someone who had, or you were a football or basketball fan. If nothing else, you were connected by sheer proximity. It was *our* school, one of the very few things that put southwest Virginia on the map. The tragedy was personal.

Suddenly Virginia Tech didn't feel so far away.

There was a lot of crying in church on Sunday. Pastor Ron wept. The worship part of service turned into an unstructured hour of prayer where some cried with their arms in the air, reaching up to God, while others sobbed into the carpet around the altar. The feeling in the room was hollow, of helplessness. Prayer, it seemed, was the only control we had over our lives.

Pastor Ron had a different take. He rose from the altar and wiped his eyes. His shoulders were slumped, as if the heaviness of the week were a physical weight.

"There is so much *evil* in this world," he said. He took a long breath. "We have to be vigilant. Proactive."

That morning's sermon wasn't a sermon at all. It was a request, a plea, for the gun owners of our congregation to start coming to church armed. "God forbid a gunman ever walk through that door,"

Pastor Ron said, pointing to the back of the sanctuary. "But if he does . . . we *cannot* be defenseless."

It wasn't unusual to see at least one or two men wearing handguns on their hips, but the next week half the congregation had holsters clipped to their belts. When we stood for worship, I eyeballed the sanctuary. There were dozens of stocky black grips ready at a second's notice.

This made me feel safe—or safer, at least, in a world that suddenly wasn't. I'd never given much thought to the pistol in Dad's sock drawer, or the shotguns in Mamaw and Poppy's living room gun case, or the rifles under the bench seat of my uncle's truck, except when he and Dad went hunting in the fall. Now I was glad they were there. Obviously, terrible things could happen anywhere, anytime.

Spring slipped into a warm, then hot, summer. The black ribbons and wreaths faded in the sun. To take them down even months after the fact was too soon.

Mountain people didn't let go of their dead easily. There were a dozen or so roadside memorials for car crash victims along the crooked road between my house and Grundy, wooden crosses with flowers, stuffed animals, and family photos in plastic baggies to keep the rain out. Most had been there the entire span of my memory, but I noticed them acutely that summer. I paid attention to the names. Calculated the ages.

One sweltering afternoon on Home Creek—the kind where you sweated sitting still, praying for rain clouds to snap and break the heat—Nanny sat on the patio with my parents and announced she was going to sell.

"There's talk of Concoal buying up Home Creek," she said. Concoal was one of the biggest coal companies in Buchanan County. "They're wanting to dig up the mountain. Open a couple mines. There's talk of big money."

The patio looked into the backyard, which looked up into the woods. Now that Poppaw was gone, Nanny owned forty acres of wild, rugged mountain. Most of it was so steep you couldn't walk it upright.

"How much money?" Mom asked.

"A million dollars per lot, maybe," Nanny said.

She'd heard the rumor from Mildred Fletcher down the road, who'd heard it from her sister Edna, whose daughter's husband had heard it from Coy Estep, who was a supervisor at the Buchanan No. 1 mine and heard these things from corporate firsthand.

"Don't believe anything till you see it in writing," Mom said.

Rumors of potential buyouts were always circulating the hollers, moving as fast as you could pick up the phone. They never seemed to amount to anything, though—died like a gust of wind, as hard and fast as they began.

"Well," Nanny said, "this just came in the mail." She stepped inside and grabbed a piece of paper off the fridge.

It was an invitation from Concoal's lawyers, addressed to Nanny and a dozen other landowners on Home Creek. Come fall, there'd be an interest meeting for anyone who might want to sell.

Mom and Dad scanned the letter with skeptical eyes. "No harm in going, I guess," Mom said. "Just don't get your hopes up."

Most people, whether they admitted it or not, knew that coal was never going to recover from decades of decline, never going to make Buchanan County as prosperous as it had once been. Still, whispers of possibility, of turning tides, happened every time there was a slight uptick in the coal market, as there'd been the previous year. A lot of people had taken that to mean—or rather, *hoped* to mean—coal wasn't in a death spiral after all. Because you couldn't *not* hope. Coal was the past, the present, and, since there were no promising alternatives, the future. Hope was the only option.

If she sold, Nanny said, she'd want to move to Tazewell County to be closer to me, Erik, and my parents. She'd want to be somewhere she wouldn't have to drive twenty-five minutes to the nearest grocery store or doctor's office. Somewhere power outages didn't last a week, and where coal trucks wouldn't wake her up at six in the morning.

At the same time, Nanny feared leaving Home Creek. She'd grown into it even though she hadn't wanted to move there in the first place all those years ago. "I don't know how I could ever leave," she'd say. Yet leaving was all she talked about.

I didn't understand how Nanny could feel two very different ways about the same thing. In my mind, she was so much a part of Home Creek, and Home Creek so much a part of her, that the two couldn't be separated. It was unnatural. A cleaving. Like if you'd suddenly decided to salvage the old tools from the mine up the hill, after they'd spent decades sinking into the earth.

Mom was certain Nanny wasn't going anywhere, though, not on Concoal's dime.

"They're never going to open more mines up here," she said. "Not now. Not with how things might go."

I didn't know what that meant until summer turned to fall. The 2008 presidential election was still a year away, but talk of it was suddenly everywhere, all the time. There was near-constant coverage on Fox News, Dad's favorite TV channel, and NPR, Mom's favorite radio station. It dominated most of the conversations I overheard in Food Lion, the parking lot after church, and every other place grown-ups had the time to stand around worrying themselves about how Democrats were going to "kill coal."

As fall gave way to winter and winter gave way to the presidential primaries and caucuses, buzzy phrases like "carbon tax" and "renewable energy" passed like vapor through my ten-year-old consciousness. I only remember contemplating "clean coal" because it made no sense to me. Coal was just about the dirtiest thing I could imagine. Poppaw had always showered with Dawn dish detergent after work to get all the dust off. And even then it remained in his cuticles, and the waterlines of his eyes.

In spring, there was a fresh bloom of anxiety as Obama emerged as the favored Democratic candidate. Hillary Clinton, his opponent, dropped out of the race in June, to Mom's disappointment. She'd really wanted a woman president.

Dad, on the other hand, had said all along that Slick Willie's wife was the last person we needed in office—besides Nobama, of course. A lot of people seemed to share this sentiment. The feeling in the air was that an Obama presidency wouldn't just be bad; it would be ruinous.

My friend Hunter, who went to a church like mine, said it meant the end of the world. He said Obama was the Antichrist. This didn't seem entirely implausible: I'd also heard that the Antichrist would be smart and charming, and that he'd rise to power shortly before Jesus's Second Coming.

I must have not been too convinced, though, because for Halloween that year I decided to dress up as one of Obama's campaign slogans. I hot-glued plastic coins to a large piece of felt, cut a hole in the center, and draped it over myself like a poncho. I wore it to a school costume contest the week before the election.

Just before the contest, one of the judges, a teacher, gave me a strange looking-over.

"I'm *Change*," I explained.

She gave me the wrong kind of laugh then, sharp instead of amused. "You're representing the wrong party."

I don't remember what I said to that, if anything. I turned away, my cheeks hot, and fell in with the crowd of kids who weren't participating in the contest. Obviously I'd already lost.

7.

That fall, on a day the valley dazzled with red and gold, Dad got a call.

He took the kitchen receiver to the hallway, stretching the spiral cord around the wall. It was a quick conversation. He returned with a smile so big all his teeth showed.

"I got the job!" he announced.

It was an administrative position at Knox Creek Mine. Dad would keep the books, order equipment and supplies, and answer the phone when miners called from deep inside the mountain. Knox Creek was on the other end of the county, closer to Home Creek than our house. The drive was a slow, curvy thirty-five miles, and the shifts were ten hours a day, five and sometimes six days a week. But the money was good. Too good to turn down. By far the best money Dad had ever made.

For the past year or so, Dad had been substitute teaching. He'd finished his college classes and earned all his credits, then failed his licensing test twice.

I could hardly believe this. Dad was one of the smartest people I knew. It was nothing for him to fix broken things by scrappy and unconventional means, or spot imperceptible animal trails in the woods, or spin fantastical stories from thin air, but these weren't things you could test for on paper, or needed to prove to be a history teacher. After he failed the test the second time, he sold his textbooks on eBay and started applying for other jobs.

I don't know why Dad applied for the Knox Creek job—the pay, I suppose—or how he got it. It was office work, which he'd never done, and at a *mine*, where he'd never wanted to work—although this was different since he'd be aboveground, except for annual safety trainings where he had to actually go down into the mountain. The job must have sounded tolerable enough. For the first time ever, he seemed excited to go to work.

I didn't understand what the new job meant for our family until two weeks after Dad started, when he took his first paycheck to the bank. The next morning, a Saturday, he woke me, Erik, and Mom up early.

"Get dressed," he told us. "We're going shopping."

To me, shopping meant going to Food Lion for groceries. That wasn't what Dad was talking about.

He drove south for an hour and a half, toward Tennessee. In Bristol, he pulled in to a plaza with half a dozen stores and parked in front of one called TJ Maxx. I had never heard of TJ Maxx. It turned out to be a theme park of a store, packed with way more people than I ever saw at Food Lion, with bright lights and cramped aisles and shelves and racks overflowing with *stuff*. Next door, Books-A-Million was just as overwhelming. It was twice the size of the Tazewell County Library. I'd never seen so many books in one place.

But Target was the grandest store of all, and my favorite—mainly because of the Starbucks in the corner, which looked and smelled luxurious, and because the girls' clothing section was so big and nice. When a pair of leggings caught my eye, Dad threw them in the cart without looking at the price tag.

We left the plaza with armfuls of shopping bags. I felt strange, as if we'd stolen it all, as if it couldn't all belong to us. In the car, we jammed our loot onto the floorboard, piled it on our laps. I held the bag with my new leggings. It seemed they might evaporate if I didn't keep them under my eyes and hands.

Dad didn't tell us where we were headed next. He wanted it to be a surprise. I saw him grinning in the rearview mirror as we turned in to the Olive Garden parking lot. This was new to me, too: We almost never ate out. When we did, it was at McDonald's, Wendy's, or, on special occasions, a buffet called Ryan's where kids ate free. I had no memory of ever going to a sit-down restaurant with a menu.

Inside, Erik and I twisted around in our seats, taking in the dim dining room. Behind our booth, a waitress in head-to-toe black grated cheese onto a salad. We stared shamelessly until Mom told us to turn around and read the menu.

Ziti al forno. Eggplant parmigiana. Mouthwatering descriptions of foods I'd never heard of. I was intimidated by their unfamiliarity, and the occasion seemed too momentous to risk trying something that I might not like. I settled on a bowl of minestrone, which sounded a little like the vegetable soup Mom made for Sunday dinner. "Mine-stroan," I pronounced it to the waitress.

For weeks after the shopping trip, my parents didn't spend a dime more than they had to. Dad cashed his checks into neat stacks of bills and tucked them away in the back of his sock drawer. He and

Mom didn't seem to know what to do with the new leftover income. Slowly, though, they started pulling cash out for small projects—ripping up old carpet, replacing bathroom faucets. Then they started giving me and Erik a small allowance each week to pay back the cash they'd taken.

Their penance annoyed me. The shopping trip had been nice, of course, but an allowance was too much. I couldn't explain why, couldn't put my feelings into words. There was embarrassment at my parents' obvious guilt. There was fear that Dad would lose his job and need the money back—mines were always shutting down, after all—and preemptive anger that I might build up my savings just to lose them again. Then there was my own guilt for having needs and wants that cost money.

Erik, on the other hand, took his readily, and without thanks. He did it with a face that said, *That's right. You owe me.* He'd tuck the cash in his piggy bank and pull out the notebook where he meticulously tracked every addition and subtraction to safeguard against my parents' sticky fingers. Erik wasn't the type to forget. That annoyed me, too. I understood his grudge, but I wished he'd just let it go. Like I was trying to.

He and I were opposite in just about every way two people could be. He had blue eyes, strawberry-blond hair, and Mom's golden skin. I was pale like Dad, with fine chestnut waves and murky green eyes. Erik was stubborn; I was pliable and eager to please. He was a hothead, quick to throw a tantrum, whereas anger shut me down, turned me in on myself. At school, he could barely sit still through a test. My report cards boasted long lines of A's.

It's a mystery how we came to be so remarkably different, and the fact of it meant we were always knocking heads, getting under each other's skin. In the winter, Dad started taking us shopping again. Erik always ended up asking for something expensive—a pair of basketball shoes, a new video game. My parents rarely said no.

I hated that Erik had no shame in asking for expensive things, that he took advantage of my parents' guilt for everything they hadn't been able to give us in the past. Their eagerness to buy made me feel that *I* needed to regulate their spending—which I did, in a way, by almost never asking them to buy things for me. I worried the luxury of Dad's paycheck wouldn't last.

Because they seemed to quietly fear this, too. Dad counted the cash in his wallet after every purchase, even small ones, and both he and Mom were timid about buying for themselves. Every shopping trip went the same way. Mom would put something small, like a decorative pillow, in the cart, push it all over the store, then set it back on the shelf before approaching the register, saying we had enough pillows at home and didn't really need another. Or Dad would try on a pair of boots, stare at them long and hard in the mirror, then put them back in the box to "think on them." Finally, he'd decide that his old boots weren't *that* worn and could probably last another winter.

My parents' feelings about money were complicated beyond my understanding. It was a perpetual dilemma, I think, whether they should enjoy the extra money while they had it or prepare for the day they didn't. Both required sacrifice. Spending now meant less security in the future. Saving now meant continuing to live the way they always had, tightly and carefully. As it turned out, deciding what to do with the money was almost as stressful as not having it.

In January, I watched Obama's inauguration on TV. He was sworn in with his hand on the Bible, which proved to me he wasn't the

Antichrist. It would have been like garlic to a vampire. Hunter said the Bible must have been a fake.

I remember hearing the word "recession" a lot around this time, in tones that ranged from resignation to worry to full-throttle panic. I understood it to mean that businesses were closing and people were losing their jobs. I worried a lot about Dad's. It was almost supernatural luck, and sheer irony, that our family was finally doing all right while so many families around us struggled.

One chilly Friday night, I went to my friend Brooklyn's house for a sleepover. At dinner, I told her parents I'd be waking up early.

"Dad's picking me up in the morning," I said. "We're going shopping."

Across the table, Brooklyn's father raised his eyebrows. "Christmas was just last month."

"We're just going to look at clothes and things," I replied.

"That's nice," he said flatly, like he didn't think it was nice at all. "Brooklyn only gets new clothes at the start of the school year."

I wanted to say that Mom and Dad rarely even bought anything for me, that my favorite part of "shopping" was actually eating at Olive Garden. Instead, I stayed silent. Brooklyn's mother was a receptionist, her father was disabled, and her older brother worked full-time hours at Food Lion to help his parents out even though he was still in high school. They never went to restaurants.

The next day, and for many shopping trips after, I feigned disinterest and dislike. I kept my eyes on the floor so Mom or Dad wouldn't see me looking at something and insist on buying it. Still, when they saw something I might want, they'd toss it into the shopping cart when I wasn't looking. When *they* weren't looking, I'd pull it out and tuck it away on a shelf. When they *did* manage to get things past me and through checkout, I'd feel a dreadful sort of guilt. I didn't want anyone at school to see me with nice new stuff. The shame of being poor was nothing like the shame of being rich.

And at Olive Garden, I always ordered the minestrone—not just because I liked it, but because it was one of the cheapest things on the menu.

8.

I could hear my aunt in the receiver. She might as well have been on speakerphone, as loud as she was. Her voice was so garbled with rage I could pick out only a few words and phrases.

"Laid him there . . . left to die!" she shouted. "Lord God! . . . piss poor . . ."

Dad held the receiver way out from his ear. He looked pained, every muscle and vein taut, as if whatever he was holding in were straining against the surface.

Poppy was sick. It was a sudden sickness—something with his heart, someone said. He'd been rushed to the hospital in Grundy, where he'd only gotten sicker. "Septic" was the word my aunt used. My family blamed the doctors and nurses—"neglect," that was another word. Those details went unexplained to me, too. Now Mamaw was having Poppy transferred to a better hospital in Kingsport, two and a half hours away.

It was too late, though. Poppy died not long after arriving. Grundy Funeral Home brought his body back to Buchanan County, where he was interred in a mausoleum in the aptly named Mountain Valley Memorial Park. It was a steep mountainside cemetery on the west end of Home Creek. It overlooked the ridges and hollers Poppy had set his eyes on almost every day of his life.

The hours after the funeral were strange and liminal. Mamaw's hot, cramped house seemed to pulse with the question of "What now?" My family picked from the heaps of food friends and neighbors had dropped off in sympathy, listening to my aunt stew about how terrible the Grundy hospital was, how poorly they'd cared for Poppy, until she ran out of steam and her anger evaporated into a resigned grief. Then she took on the face everyone else wore, the one you got when you exhausted yourself by caring too much about something you couldn't help and couldn't change. *It's over and done with*, said Mamaw's vacant eyes. *What's the point in being mad?* said the flat line of Dad's mouth.

Soon, the conversation turned the way it always did when my family spent enough time together. Grown-ups loved talking about the dead—the recently deceased and the long, long gone, and the many ways they'd left the world. Like the woman down the holler who'd overdosed in her bathtub. And the cousin so-many-times-removed who'd been eaten up by cancer because he was too scared to go to the doctor. And the girl in town who'd been murdered by her brother-in-law, who swore until the day he died he didn't do it, until DNA evidence proved otherwise, decades after he'd been pried from the electric chair.

I suppose there was something morbidly comforting about this kind of talk—that by discussing death with such grisly bluntness, you got a sense of control or peace or *something* over the cruelty and randomness of life. As if you could defeat the Grim Reaper by staring straight into his greedy eyes.

By now I'd sat through enough church services that certain phrases and concepts had rooted themselves in my mind. The one that came to me that evening was "conquering death." It was the idea that if you believed in Jesus, you'd live after dying just as you had on earth, except in a billowy, golden heaven where you'd never be sick or sad or feel pain. It was a perfect place. A hopeful place. Even more so in times like this, I understood, watching my family's tired eyes, when the weight of earthly living was so heavy.

I was in middle school now, at the weird in-between age of too old for Children's Church and too young to follow Pastor Ron's sermons. Still, most Sundays I opted for the sermons.

The specifics of them are largely gone from my memory, if they ever took at all. What sticks is the *feeling* of them. The prickle on my arms when Pastor Ron preached about the narrow gates of heaven and the broad road to hell. The pit in my chest when he pleaded for us to get right with God, because Jesus would soon return to earth in the Rapture. Later I'd call these feelings "conviction," but I didn't have that word yet. It was just fear to me then, vague and cold.

The concept of salvation—and with that, the afterlife—was beginning to form in my mind, and it was impenetrable, more complicated and far less gentle than the watered-down version I'd learned from the baby-voiced children's pastor. According to her, getting saved was as easy as declaring you loved Jesus. But as far as I understood Pastor Ron, getting saved had less to do with loving Jesus than with sparing yourself from an eternity of suffering. And it involved a lot more than a simple declaration.

Like "living righteously." That was the big thing. Not lying, not stealing, not cussing, and, according to Pastor Ron, being careful about what movies, books, and music you "let into your spirit." Pop culture was riddled with satanic influences, he said. Especially horror movies and Halloween. (Every year, Deliverance held a trick-or-treating alternative called "Hallow-him," where grown-ups in biblical costumes handed out candy in the church parking lot.) Hunter's parents went to a different church that believed similarly, and wouldn't let Hunter read Harry Potter or watch the vampire movie *Twilight.*

My parents let me read and watch whatever I wanted as long as it wasn't R-rated. Which I didn't get. How could "living righteously" mean different things to different people? There was a boy at my church who wasn't allowed to watch *SpongeBob* or *Scooby-Doo.* There was a boy in my grade who wasn't allowed to say the Pledge of Allegiance. There was a girl on my school bus, Sarah, who wasn't allowed to cut her hair or wear pants. Once I asked her how she rode a bike in her long denim skirts.

"I don't," she said.

At the time I didn't know that Sarah was Pentecostal, like me, but of a more fundamentalist brand. *Apostolic.* In her church, men dressed normally, if not a little stiffly, in nice jeans and button-downs; women stood out in their long skirts and long hair. Sarah's mother was one of the only women I knew who didn't wear makeup. This was her interpretation of righteousness, I understood, though I didn't get *why.* Makeup seemed pretty harmless to me. Mom, Nanny, and all my aunts and teachers, even the old ones, wore it. Pastor Ron's wife even sold Mary Kay.

It didn't make sense how two people of the same faith could believe such different things. Still, I accepted the mystery of it because, like most aspects of religion, the complicated logic of it was beyond my comprehension. Most Sunday mornings I retreated into my own mind, as far as possible from Pastor Ron's thunder, trying to unscramble the strange puzzle of it all.

The summer before eighth grade, I started hearing words like "aggressive" and "advanced" and "terminal" in whispers, as if not talking about it at full volume made it not true.

For a while I thought Mamaw would be okay. It wasn't until Christmas, months after her diagnosis, I noticed a change. Suddenly she was ghostly frail, and her yell-talking was turned down to a near whisper. Still, at dinner, she insisted on pulling the roasted turkey out of the oven herself. She swatted away my aunts' offers to help. Everyone held their breath as she heaved the giant bird onto the stove. After, she tried to disguise her labored breathing, and didn't lift anything heavier than a fork for the rest of the night.

She died a month later, in early February.

By then, I'd become unhappily familiar with the Grundy Funeral Home—its dusty carpet smell and ancient love seats, and half-papered, half-paneled walls. The chapel's cross-shaped sconces and red-purple color scheme resembled Deliverance's sanctuary. When I walked in, I felt as if I were in church.

And I was, more or less. To this day, I've never been to an Appalachian funeral where there wasn't a preacher and a sermon.

The preacher of Mamaw's church officiated her funeral. He stood on a platform behind her glossy casket and spoke about salvation. Mamaw, he said, was looking down on us now from heaven.

"Ohhhhh, Lord," the man said. He was an old-timey mountain preacher, the kind who wailed his words instead of saying them. His voice was too loud for the microphone.

"'For who can find a virtuous woman?'" he quoted from his Bible. "Yesssss, oh, Lord. Ann was steadfast in yoooou all the waaaaay to the end."

Sometimes the preacher addressed God. Sometimes he addressed the mourners. The longer he went, the louder he got, and the less he talked about Mamaw. His voice pitched and dipped. Some words were shouts; some were whispers. Some were staccato and some were miles long. Behind him, a pianist played slow, mournful hymns. Sobs erupted across the chapel.

I couldn't tell if the preacher and music encouraged the emotion, or if the music and emotion were encouraging him. Eventually he started hollering and didn't stop. "DEATH comes to us ALL!" he said. "One day it'll be YOOOOOU lying there"—he pointed to the open casket, where Mamaw wore a mask of makeup—"and YOU will be answering to the LOOOOORD of LORDS and KIIIIING of KINGS!"

In the pew in front of me, my cousins were bent over in tears, pressing soaked tissues into their faces. One of my aunts jumped out of her seat. "Mommy!" she screamed. "Mommy!" She ran to the front of the chapel and flung herself across the open casket.

I turned my head, overwhelmed by her grief on top of my own. Beside me, Dad sat rigid, dry-eyed and tense.

It always scared me a little, seeing him like that. I wondered what he was thinking. Dad never talked about the church Mamaw and Poppy had raised him and his siblings in. I figured—although I couldn't be sure and was too afraid to ask—that it had something to do with this: the untamed displays of emotion, and the preachers who goaded you into feeling it.

Almost everyone I knew would have claimed they were Christian to at least some degree. To some, like Dad, that looked like practicing in the most private of ways; to others, that meant going to church every time the doors were open. I didn't know that not every preacher was like Mamaw's or mine. I didn't know that charismatic Christianity was so polarizing. Several years later, I'd hear a friend of a friend call Pentecostalism "a cult." She was a Christian herself—Methodist—and the word shocked me, as did the way she said it, with a condemning bite in her voice that I wouldn't understand for several *more* years. At that moment, though, sitting in the pew of the funeral home chapel, I was blind to that future knowing, except for the shadow I saw in Dad's eyes.

The preaching went on for an hour, maybe longer. All my attention went to tuning it out and keeping my eyes from Mamaw's body. At the end of the funeral, when everyone lined up to say their final goodbyes, I tried to slip away in the opposite direction.

"It's okay," Mom said, urging me toward the casket. "A body's just a shell."

That was what scared me: the lack of animation; the air of sudden abandonment. I couldn't wrap my head around the opposite of existence, or what another existence looked like, even if it was one of golden streets and angel trumpets. It was hard to imagine something so pleasant when the fact of death was so frightening.

This is what heaven looked like in my head, when I tried to picture it. There were massive glistening gates. Blue sky above me, clouds at my feet. And then there was God, a light as blinding as the sun, with an angry, booming voice that rattled my bones and the air around me. He'd read off a list of every wrong I had committed, things like fighting with Erik and lying to my parents about the secret Myspace account I'd created. And then he'd judge me for my faith. Was I baptized? How many times had I skipped church or my bedtime prayers? Did I love Jesus with all my heart?

I still didn't understand how it worked exactly, the whole getting-into-heaven ordeal. All I knew was that the alternative was unacceptable.

After the funeral, my family drove caravan-style to my great-uncle's house on Slate Creek. Inside, every inch of the refrigerator, kitchen counters, and even the coffee table was crammed with foil-covered casseroles, cakes, dips, trays, and finger foods—edible condolences from Mamaw's neighbors and church friends. At first, the house was somber. Everyone was still puffy-eyed and reeling from the sermon. We picked at our food in near silence, most of us standing since there weren't enough chairs, until someone cracked a quiet, halfhearted joke. Someone else chuckled lightly. Another person added to the joke. Another chuckled a little louder.

And then, all at once, an avalanche of laughter and levity bowled over the house. Almost everyone ended up on the floor, either on their backs or slumped against the couches and paneled walls, clutching their trembling bellies.

Dad, who had for hours been as stiff and impassive as a slab of granite, was almost doubled over near the dining room radiator. He laughed so hard that no sound came out, quaking silently as a flood of tears streamed from his closed, crinkled eyes. This image of Dad is one of the most vivid in my memory. I had never seen him so unrestrained.

I didn't laugh. I didn't even smile. In the space of Mamaw's funeral, I'd crossed into some new awareness about mortality. The visceral finality of it branded me like an iron, hot and astoundingly clear. This was what I suddenly knew: Death was coming. Death was always coming. Death was absolute and irrevocable. One second you were alive and the next you were extinguished, either rejoicing in heaven or burning in hell. The holy terror of this pulsed to the very ends of my nerves. So did the terrible, trembling uncertainty of where I'd go after.

9.

It was late afternoon, after the final bell. I was walking from the high school to the elementary school down the street where Mom taught kindergarten. As I started down the sidewalk, a long-haired senior hollered at me from the passenger window of a red Ford Ranger.

"Heeeeey, baby!"

I waved as he passed. He waved back, smiling, and wolf-whistled as the truck sped away.

It almost stopped my heart.

The senior had been hollering at me every day since the start of the school year a few weeks earlier. At first I'd hated it: I was a wallflower of a freshman, drowning in the fourteen-year-old self-consciousness that told me everyone else thought I was seriously uncool, and I thought I was being made fun of. After a week or so I'd stopped caring, gotten bold. I began looking forward to the catcalls, hearing myself called things like "cutie" and "sexy." I started waving back, putting up whichever hand wasn't carrying my Hello Kitty lunch box.

The senior's name, I found out, was Sam. He was cute and charming and seemed to be friends with everyone. I always looked for him between classes—he was one of the tallest guys in school—and headed in his direction, trying to get close enough so he would notice me. I was lucky to get even a nod of acknowledgment before he looked away. Still, every day after the bell, he hollered at me out of his friend's truck. And that was enough.

Sometime after Mamaw died, my understanding of salvation began to crystallize. I started getting small bursts of clarity, slowly piecing together how Jesus's sacrificial death atoned for my sins. I didn't *feel* all that sinful. But I'd learned that it didn't matter what I felt.

Salvation was difficult at times for me to wrap my head around. How were God, Jesus, and the Holy Spirit all the same being? Why did Jesus have to die for sinners? What counted as a sin? I heard the word "saved" all the time, but its meaning was just beyond my reach, a cloud of religious buzzwords and ideas that I couldn't organize into a single strand of comprehension.

"ALL have fallen short of the glory of God," Pastor Ron often quoted. He'd hold his Bible high in the air, a beacon of absolute authority. "And the soul who sins *shall* die."

Pastor Ron preached that humanity was in the end times, which is why salvation was such an urgent and necessary matter. Soon—maybe only months, or even minutes from the present moment—Jesus would return to the world unannounced, *like a thief in the night*, and whisk the saved away to heaven. The unsaved would be left behind in a desolate, flaming, postapocalyptic world, condemned to suffer all kinds of plagues and torments.

I didn't have what "saved" people had. At least, I couldn't do any of the things that the front-row believers at Deliverance could do:

prophesy, speak in tongues, or "fall out" in the Spirit, which meant collapsing to the floor, overwhelmed to unconsciousness by God. These were "gifts" God gave you when you were deeply in touch with him, receptive to his Word and will.

I wasn't sure why some people got gifts and others, like Mom, didn't. I figured it had something to do with your degree of devotion. That the more devoted you were, the more gifts God gave you. Apparently there were levels to being saved.

Which probably meant I was on the bottom tier. I didn't feel synced with God the way a lot of people in my church seemed to. In fact, I didn't feel him at all. What I felt was fear—a hard knot of worry, heavy in my stomach—at the thought of dying and going to hell, or the possibility of being left behind in the Rapture.

While I knew I should *want* to get saved, the effort sounded as if it outweighed the reward. Getting saved was supposed to be an all-or-nothing commitment. To do it right was to dedicate every word, thought, and action to God. It seemed like a lot of responsibility. A lot of work.

I considered it for months, rolled it over and over in my mind, until one day in December, when Sam approached me in the hallway for the first time.

"I want to take you on a date," he said.

For a moment I couldn't speak, so I stammered out the first thing that popped into my head. "I'll have to ask my parents."

I knew Mom and Dad would never let an eighteen-year-old senior pick me up for a date, and I was too young to drive. Still, I cringed at the words as soon as they left my mouth.

"That's okay. We'll figure something out," Sam said, winking as he walked away.

Suddenly salvation wasn't at the front of my mind anymore.

I called my friend Brooklyn that night to tell her the news. She squealed into the phone. "Think he'll ask you to prom?"

Ninth and tenth graders were allowed to go to prom only if invited by upperclassmen, so the invitation was highly coveted among underclassman girls. Getting to dress up and show off on the arm of an older guy bumped you up a few rungs on the high school food chain.

Which I wanted badly, being a "gifted" kid. I hadn't given much thought to the label before, but now, in high school, it suddenly defined me, and not in a good way. Some of my friends had tried to shed their gifted identities by joining a sport, or drifting to slightly cooler groups like the theater kids and Future Farmers of America, or by simply toning down their zeal in the classroom—letting the occasional B slip into an otherwise-perfect report card.

I didn't want to join another friend group, and I couldn't *not* make good grades. I'd never allowed myself to make anything below an A minus, not even in math. Purposely bombing my assignments would have been more difficult than acing them.

But it wasn't cool to care about your grades, especially when the guy you liked almost certainly didn't. I worried what Sam might think if he found out I was such a nerd. I desperately wanted to be worthy of him.

Sam and I started dating in December. At least, we called it dating: I saw him outside school only once, at a New Year's Eve prayer service in the basement of his grandmother's church. Mom and Dad let me go only because there would be other people around and they'd all be talking about Jesus. They maintained that I wasn't allowed to date until I was sixteen, and that Sam was too old for me, anyway.

Still, I was infatuated. I thought about Sam nonstop. *Sam. Sam. Sam.* I thought about his melty brown eyes and easy smile. I whispered his name to myself when no one was listening, satisfied by its brevity and the way it rested on my lips. Truthfully, I didn't really know that much about him—I knew he liked superhero movies, and he could kind of play the guitar, and he'd been raised by his grandparents because his dad had run off and his mom was in prison—but that didn't matter. I couldn't believe that I'd somehow caught the attention of such a cool, popular, outgoing senior.

For three months, Sam walked me to every class. He carried my books. He held my hand. He surprised me with candy, gum, and flowers. When his friend's truck broke down, Sam started riding the bus home. He lingered with me in the schoolyard, smothering me with kisses, until the bus driver flashed her lights and yelled out the door, "Are you getting on or not?"

For three months, I floated on a cloud.

Then, in mid-March, Sam came to my locker and said he had something to tell me. There was a girl on his bus, he said. A girl he had a crush on.

He didn't tell me she was twelve years old.

I found out from Brooklyn, who rode Sam's bus. She told me he'd started sitting beside a seventh grader who lived in Brooklyn's neighborhood.

It crushed me. Not so much the fact of the girl's age, but that Sam had broken up with me for her. I wondered what she had that I didn't. Of course the six-year age gap was weird—Sam had already been pushing the limit with me—but I don't remember being *disturbed* by it, as my parents were. The girl was only two grades below me, which didn't feel like a big difference.

If Sam ever acted on his crush beyond sharing her bus seat, Brooklyn never reported it, and I never heard otherwise. Because of this, I found it easy to forgive him when he texted me a few months later over summer break, swearing he was over the girl and that he regretted our breakup every day.

By the beginning of my sophomore year, he and I were together again.

"He's a predator!" Mom said when she found out. "He's *nineteen.* He had a crush on a *middle schooler.* You're young enough as it is."

"He was eighteen then," I quietly corrected. I regretted telling my parents why Sam had broken up with me. I was embarrassed by how bad it sounded.

"Big whoop," Mom replied. "You need to stop talking to him."

But I didn't.

I was fifteen now, still not old enough to drive. My parents wouldn't let Sam pick me up from my house. For a while, the only time I saw him was after school. He'd wait for me in the parking lot in a car he borrowed from his grandpa, then drive me the half mile to the elementary school so I wouldn't have to walk. Mom never knew.

Those brief interactions weren't enough. After a couple months of sneaking around, we decided we had to find a way to get my parents to like Sam.

Our solution was perfect: church.

I can't remember if it was my idea or his. Either way, church had allowed us to see each other once before. We schemed up a plan. Sam would visit Deliverance one Sunday morning. He'd dress up nice, make sure to cross paths with me and Erik and Mom, say hello, be extra friendly. Try to show that he was nice and respectable—that he wasn't whatever Mom thought of him. Then I'd invite him to sit with us. The week after, he'd show up to church again, smile, and slide into the pew beside me. He'd repeat week after week until Mom softened, leading her and Dad, I hoped, to let me spend time with Sam outside church.

One Sunday in October, we put our plan into action. Sam walked into Deliverance in a wrinkled dress shirt and slacks. He sat down across the aisle from me and Mom.

Her eyes widened. I feigned surprise.

"Well, hey there!" I waved to Sam.

He followed my lead. He smiled politely at me and Erik and then Mom, who refused to meet his eyes. I invited him over. As he sat down beside me, Mom, who was on my other side, stiffened. She offered Sam a polite but hard "hello," then ignored him for the rest of the service.

That middle schooler meant nothing to Sam, I'd explain to her later. *It was a lapse in judgment. He didn't know what he was feeling. He was confused.* These were the words Sam used to justify his crush to me. In turn, I used them to try to justify Sam's behavior to Mom. I could have thought of a million excuses to make her change her mind about him, although she never would.

After that Sunday, Sam stuck to the plan. He showed up every time Mom and I went to church. Soon he started sitting beside me without being invited.

Mom refused to warm to him, though. At home, Dad silently stewed. After a few weeks, they seemed to reluctantly accept that Sam and I weren't budging. "So you're a *thing* again," Mom would say scathingly.

October turned to November, and November to December. I inched closer to sixteen. Sam never missed church.

One day, I decided to push my luck.

It was a snowy Sunday morning. Mom had woken up late and was slow getting out of bed. "I think I'll just skip church today," she told me, turning off the Weather Channel and burrowing back under her comforter.

My heart leaped. I'd been waiting months for my chance.

"But I really want to go," I said. "You know I hate to miss."

Mom gave me a skeptical look. Before she could say anything, I rushed on. "Sam's coming from town. He could pick me up on the way."

If she let me go this once, I reasoned, she couldn't say no the next time. And after all, it was *church*. Innocent, innocent church. Would she really deny me the right to spend time in the house of the Lord?

Mom sighed. I begged. She told me to go ask Dad. He sighed and said nothing.

It wasn't a no. I texted Sam. He was in my driveway ten minutes later, and I was in his passenger's seat before he even had time to cut the engine. He grinned at me, and I grinned at him, and we spent the whole ride to church hand in hand, glowing with our victory.

Sometime around my sixteenth birthday, after my relationship with Sam had been firmly reestablished, I returned to the question of my salvation. It had been sitting on a shelf in my mind for more than a year and had started to nudge its way back to the front.

The more time I spent in church, the more frightening and more real Satan, hell, and the Rapture were becoming to me. They'd materialized from vague, abstract concepts to terrifyingly concrete visualizations. I'd begun having dreams of angry red thunderclouds and splitting skies, toppling skyscrapers, agonized screams. Cataclysmic earthquakes would shake the ground beneath my feet, and suddenly I would be tumbling breathlessly into a hot black pit. Before I splattered at the bottom, I'd wake to a racing heart and sweat-soaked sheets, certain I'd just received a warning, a sign.

The visceral terror of those dreams lingered with me into the day. At night I'd lie awake for hours, too scared to fall asleep. God was urging me toward salvation, I figured. I was going to have to make the commitment, or the terror would only get worse.

Sam, like me, had grown up with only lukewarm interest in God, had gone to church only because he was made to. But now he told me of his own apocalyptic dreams. He took notes on sermons, and prayed loudly and earnestly. Sometimes he threw his arms up in rapturous worship. His newfound belief seemed strong, sincere.

That finalized my decision. If Sam was going to take God seriously, then I was, too.

Dear Jesus, I accept you as my Lord and Savior. Forgive my sins. Come into my heart. I want to live my life for you.

This was my prayer of salvation. The words formed on my lips as I sounded them out in my head, sending them up to God.

For many Pentecostals, salvation comes like a lightning strike. It is an emotional reception of the Holy Spirit, a flash of divine enlightenment and assurance. Many Pentecostals remember the exact moment they are saved, and are able to recall the details with perfect clarity.

Nothing happened to me. I prayed the prayer again, then again, then dozens of times a day for weeks, waiting to feel different, changed.

I thought that salvation, when asked for sincerely, was instantaneous. I worried God didn't think I was sincere enough.

To prove my sincerity, I decided to get baptized a second time.

The baptism happened in May, on a spring day that felt like summer. The air conditioner inside the church was cranked up high, and I should have been shivering as I waded out of the ice-cold baptistery. When I stepped out, dripping all over the carpet, I was instead awash in a faintly warm satisfaction. The feeling was unexpected—I hadn't expected to feel anything at all—so I was cautious. Was this my confirmation? Was I saved?

A splash behind me interrupted my thoughts. A wave rolled over the lip of the baptistery as Sam stepped out. He had decided to get saved himself, and then we'd decided to get baptized together. This was doubly symbolic: Our individual baptisms signified our respective commitments to God; getting baptized together signified a commitment to each other in God.

In the weeks before, Pastor Ron had given a series of sermons on relationships. The secret to a successful relationship, he'd preached, was to ground it in biblical principles: God only blessed relationships that followed his rules. If Sam and I wanted our relationship to be blessed, we would have to pray for each other, and with each other. Encourage each other's spiritual journey. Devote ourselves first to God and then to our relationship. Be pure in body and mind. Let God work in our hearts daily, strengthening and convicting and changing us, so that we would continually grow in both faith and love.

I write these words and phrases as I heard them preached, and as I used them myself. They sound odd to me now—rehearsed, cloying, uncomfortably idealistic. To my sixteen-year-old self, that was their attraction. Here was the formula for a fairy-tale relationship. I hadn't forgotten about the twelve-year-old girl or Sam breaking up with me at my locker. I feared a similar incident happening again. Of losing Sam a second time.

Before getting saved, I had worried whether obeying God would be worth the reward. But the promise of divine blessing over me and Sam, of God protecting our relationship from sinful influences, was more than worth it. Salvation was a safeguard not only for my soul but for my relationship. And to sixteen-year-old me, the two were equally important.

10.

There's a sort of fervor that overcomes the newly saved. It's a glowing, buzzing, almost anxious feeling—a feeling that you have something special, that God cares for you intimately, personally. You're ablaze with a new sense of purpose: to show gratitude to your loving Father for saving you, a hopelessly lost soul dangling over the fiery pits of hell. How close you were to death and damnation. How graciously and mercifully you were redeemed.

Sam's transformation was immediate. All he wanted to talk about was Jesus. He carried his Bible everywhere, always ready to crack it open and share the Gospel. In church he'd raise his arms high in worship, jump and dance and sing and cry, totally overcome.

The feeling came to me more slowly. I didn't get the hype. So I was saved. Now what? What did it mean, exactly, to love Jesus?

I figured that the best way to learn was in church, listening to Pastor Ron and mimicking the congregation around me.

It wasn't as easy as it looked. One morning during worship, I tried raising my arm in praise. Slowly, after checking to make sure no one was watching, I lifted a hand off the back of the chair in front of me. After just a few inches I felt an inexplicable rush of embarrassment, and quickly dropped my hand.

I glanced around to make sure no one had seen. Beside me, Sam was occupied by his own worship, eyes closed. Mom wasn't there. She'd been coming to church less often since Sam had been coming more.

After service, I told Sam I didn't get the point of raising your arms. "It feels silly," I said as we climbed into his car. He always drove me to and from church now.

"It's a sign of surrender," he explained. "You're opening yourself up to the Holy Spirit. If you want to feel God, you have to stop resisting him."

Stop resisting. Stop resisting. That was what I told myself the next Sunday as Sam and I stood for worship. The music grew louder as the lights dimmed.

I closed my eyes, trying to block out the rest of the congregation, and lifted my hand.

Stop resisting. I didn't raise it far, only to shoulder height, as if I were scared to ask my teacher for permission to go to the bathroom. The music was getting faster. My face burned.

I held steady anyway. *Help me understand you, Lord,* I prayed. *Fill me with your Spirit.*

My closed eyes crinkled with focus. The music was at full volume now. I imagined other people were starting to sway and jump with the quick beat. I kept my arm up, trying not to think of it or anyone around me, only my prayers. I wanted to feel whatever it was that made others dance and cry and scream. I wanted to *understand.* I turned my mind to the memory of the holy presence I had never been able to explain, the one that had made me sink to my knees as a child, and concentrated on it with a force that made my forehead ache.

And then I was there.

I was *there.*

I was five years old and on the floor.

Except I wasn't. I was standing, but not conscious of my body, only the presence surrounding it. It was warm and heavy, just as I remembered, and its force wiped every thought from my mind. I could focus only on the sensation, its mystery and power.

What was it, this all-consuming presence? Assurance? Enlightenment? Love?

It didn't matter. It was the Holy Spirit, returned.

The feeling lasted only a few seconds. I became aware of my body again, the space I occupied. The dark room faded back into focus. My face tingled. I grabbed the back of the chair to steady myself. Sam leaned into my ear and asked if I was okay.

"I felt it!" I said, smiling, realizing what had just happened. "The Spirit!"

So *this* was what it was all about. I felt I'd just received a much-needed answer to a question I hadn't known to ask—as if I'd unlocked a new realm of existence, one where I was personally acknowledged by the creator of the whole universe. He saw me in my ignorance and came to meet it with infinite mercy. There was a seductive promise in his holy presence: one of care, guidance, and protection until the end of time and beyond.

I decided the feeling *was* love, and the weight of my salvation was realized.

In June, a wave of sticky heat rolled over the mountains. It was the kind that makes the air feel like a damp rag, where nothing cools you off, even riding with all the windows down.

Which we did, my parents and Erik and I, all sixty miles to

Home Creek. We didn't visit much anymore. Nanny was the only one of my grandparents left, and she preferred to come to Tazewell. Any chance to get out of the holler, she took.

Mom had been right about Concoal. At the first interest meeting years earlier, Concoal's lawyers had shown PowerPoints of projected mine sites, promising big buyouts were on the horizon. But then the lawyers went silent—wouldn't even return calls—and the contracts they'd promised never materialized. Months went by. One day, another letter came in the mail announcing another meeting. Nanny and her neighbors went to it, too, and listened to the same promises, and went home to more months of silence. Then another letter. Another meeting. And still no contracts.

No one could make sense of it, the cruel and absurd stringing-along. Nanny had given up on leaving Home Creek. Nobody was ever going to buy an old double-wide with moss on the roof and tap water that smelled like rotten eggs, in a middle-of-nowhere holler twenty-five minutes from a sleepy, struggling coal town, two hours from the nearest interstate.

That evening, my parents drove back to Tazewell. Erik and I stayed with Nanny. Almost every June, we spent a week with her so we could attend Vacation Bible School at her Baptist church. Bible School was run like a carnival, with bouncy houses, sno-cone machines, balloons, and prizes, no expense or effort spared. One year, for an East Asian theme, someone hung hundreds of paper cranes from the church ceilings. Another year, for a tropical island theme, someone decorated the sanctuary stage with a pair of inflatable plastic pineapples, which were so big they had to be deflated to fit through the door.

Nanny always volunteered in the kitchen. This year I decided to volunteer with her. We were tying our aprons when the church secretary hollered through the door.

"We've got two hundred out here!" she yelled. Behind her was a mass of screaming kids in neon Bible School shirts. "And more coming in!"

Nanny and the three other cooks—all women, all named Mary—flew into motion. They banged around the cabinets, dug out the biggest cook pots, and set them to boil. Then they dumped in what seemed like a thousand packs of hot dog wieners, while Nanny lined aluminum roasting pans with yellow buns. Someone relegated me to drink duty. I spent the rest of the evening pouring red Kool-Aid into plastic cups.

Near the end of the night, an old friend wandered through the drink line. Trey was my age, and had been coming to Bible School almost as long as I had.

We usually saw each other only once a year, but the previous fall we'd bumped into each other at a cross-country meet. I was new to running, and Trey was the fastest kid on his team. I'd asked if I could train with him the next time I was in Grundy. Earlier in the week we'd planned a five-mile route through town.

"Still up for that run tomorrow?" I asked him.

Trey smiled and took a Kool-Aid. "See you in the morning."

Once all the dishes were washed and the kitchen was swept, Nanny and Erik and I headed back to Home Creek. I kicked my shoes off at the door and went to call Sam from the landline.

He picked up on the second ring. "Where have you been?"

"Hello to you, too," I said. "I was at church."

"I texted you like ten times," he said.

"I was busy. Sorry."

Sam exhaled loudly and said nothing.

I asked Sam about his day, ignoring the annoyance in his voice, then talked about mine. I told Sam about Trey, that we were going running in the morning.

There was a pause. "Just you and him?"

"Well, yeah," I said.

On the other line, silence.

"You still there?" I asked.

"Yep," Sam replied. His voice was clipped.

"Is something wrong?"

Sam exhaled again. "I think that's a bad idea."

"What do you mean?" I asked. "We're just friends. We're just going to go for a run."

"That's what *you* think." Sam was more than annoyed now. "Guys can't be *just friends* with girls. They always want more. You don't know what he'll try when he's got you alone."

I started to say something about how we *wouldn't* be alone, that we were going running through the center of town, and that Trey wasn't like that, besides.

Sam cut me off. "I'm just trying to protect you," he said.

Now I was frustrated, too. "I don't need protecting. I can make my own decisions."

"Well, I pray you make the right one," he snapped, and hung up the phone.

I put the receiver back on the base with more force than necessary. Sam had always been suspicious of my male friends. He didn't like me talking to them, or even about them. He especially didn't like me spending time with them.

Which was ridiculous—wasn't it? I went to bed stewing over Sam's paranoia. He had never met Trey, didn't know anything about him.

Then again, Trey and I had never hung out alone. Maybe he *would* flirt or make a move. I couldn't be sure that he wouldn't. Sam had a man's brain. He knew what men thought about.

And that was the thing. I had come to believe that men had an inherent, God-given wisdom that women didn't have. I'd never heard Pastor Ron say so explicitly, but I'd heard plenty of sermons about how men were supposed to use their divine authority to lead and guide their wives and families. The Bible, on the other hand, was more direct: *The head of every man is Christ, and the head of every woman is man.* Since men were spiritually closest to God, women were supposed to defer to men. It was biblical.

And I wanted a biblical relationship.

This was the first time in my memory that I let Sam's will and reason supersede my own. I lay awake for an hour or two considering the matter, slowly becoming more and more convinced that I was wrong and Sam was right. I began to believe—and not just because I was supposed to, but because I really, truly felt it—that he *did* have my best interests at heart, that he *did* want to protect me. I believed that his godly wisdom alerted him to something about Trey that as a girl I couldn't detect.

Very early the next morning, before the sun broke up the fog, I walked to the end of Nanny's driveway. I could sometimes get weak reception if I stood under the open sky, away from the trees, and held my cell phone high and still in the air.

Something came up, I wrote to Trey. *I won't be able to make it. Sorry.*

His reply came through with a ding. *Want to try for tomorrow instead?*

I looked at the text for a moment, unsure of how to respond. What could I say? *My boyfriend has a bad feeling about you*? It sounded ridiculous even though it was true. I put my phone in my pocket and turned back toward the house, choosing to say nothing at all.

11.

Now that I was sixteen, I was free to go on dates with Sam. Actual movie, dinner, pick-me-up-in-the-car dates, not just going to and from church. That had always been my parents' rule—I could date when I turned sixteen—but I saw their regret every time Sam's car showed up in the driveway. Dad's face said, *I should have made her wait another year or five.* Mom's said, *This guy? Still?*

I stopped caring what they thought. I practically sprinted out the door.

Sam was embarrassed of his car, an old Mitsubishi Eclipse he borrowed from his grandpa. The front bumper was tied on with bungee cords, and the rearview mirror was always falling off. To me, that car was the greatest thing in the world. It meant the freedom to be alone with Sam, away from my parents' disapproving eyes.

Not that we had anywhere to go. Most of the time we were too broke for dinner or a movie, so we'd browse the aisles at Walmart or Lowe's instead, talking paint colors and light fixtures and what we wanted our future house to look like.

We were just joking around. Sort of. When I imagined my future, Sam was always there, at the center of everything I did.

He and I spent almost every day together that summer. Even when he had to work, Sam would pick me up and take me with him to the restaurant where he waited tables.

Once, another waiter made fun of how close we were. "When's the wedding?" he teased.

"Oh, I'm saving up." Sam flashed a smile and winked at me, then grabbed my left hand and caressed my ring finger with his thumb.

There was jest in Sam's voice, so I knew not to take him seriously. I wanted to, though. I couldn't tell him or anyone else that I fantasized about marrying him. I was only sixteen, impossibly young.

And impossibly in love.

I loved Sam's long hair and big smile. I loved how he was just as bold as I was shy. I loved that he was taller and older and spiritually wiser, that he worshipped passionately and studied his Bible and devoted himself totally to God. Every night he'd send me a short prayer or devotional. Throughout the day, even if we were together, he would send me scriptures. He cared so much about me and my faith, I thought. He knew so much that I didn't.

A few weeks after Vacation Bible School, I'd gotten a message from Trey.

You ghosted me, the text read. *And I don't know why.*

I hadn't talked to Trey since canceling our run together, and the thought of not responding again made me feel guilty.

It didn't have anything to do with you, I replied. *My boyfriend just doesn't like me hanging out with other guys. I'm sorry.*

There was a long pause before Trey's response. *That's not healthy. Good luck with that.*

The text rubbed me the wrong way, so I didn't reply. I showed the conversation to Sam.

"See!" Sam puffed with pride, the fact that he'd been right. "If Trey was a real friend, he'd respect our relationship boundaries."

His logic made sense. A *healthy* relationship was one in which I honored my boyfriend's wishes. If Trey was a real friend, he would understand.

To me, this was proof of Sam's wisdom, his spiritual gifts. I was still so new to my faith that I didn't have any spiritual gifts at all. At least, that was what Sam told me. "They'll come in time," he promised. "When you spiritually mature."

Until that happened, I would have to defer to him.

The necklace was silver. From the front, the pendant was a cross; from the side, it was an ichthus, a Jesus fish.

"Pretty," Mikayla said. She examined it between her fingers, then passed it across the lunch table to Sarah, who agreed. Sarah passed it back across the table to Chelsea, who sat beside me.

"Derek gave me something like this when we got married." Chelsea caressed my pendant for a moment before dropping it into my palm. I hooked the clasp behind my neck.

The necklace was from Sam. I showed it off to my new friends to prove I was one of them. Mikayla, Chelsea, and Sarah were some of the most religious girls at school, and I'd gravitated to their lunch table at the start of the school year. My old friends, who were mostly boys, sat on the other side of the cafeteria. I barely talked to them anymore.

"I've never seen you wear a necklace," Mikayla said to Chelsea.

"I don't like jewelry that much," Chelsea said. "Except for this." She flashed her wedding ring, a fake diamond on a sterling silver band. Chelsea was always showing it off, taking any opportunity to talk about her wedding—the Walmart dress, the courthouse ceremony, the honeymoon in a camping tent because she and her new husband couldn't afford a night at the motel in town. That was two years ago, right after she'd turned sixteen.

My new friends were all quiet, like me, and had a nice, churchy wholesomeness about them that I wanted for myself. Sarah, from my bus, had hair that was now long enough to sit on. Mikayla always carried a Bible around.

I'd started bringing my Bible to school, too. It was a monster of a thing, thick and heavy as my textbooks. I took it to every class to read in my free time. It occupied most of the space on my desk.

Early in the summer, I'd begun in Genesis: *In the beginning, God created the heavens and the earth.* Now, months later, I was still only in the eleventh book, 1 Kings, slogging through Solomon's temple and wisdom and wives. Reading cover to cover had been a larger undertaking than I'd expected. I read anyway, though, every day and every night, chapter by chapter, word by word.

When I tired of reading chronologically, I'd pray. *Speak to me through your Word, Father.* I'd run my thumb up and down the pages of my closed Bible until I felt God urging me to stop. Then I'd open the book to whichever page my thumbnail caught, aiming my eyes at the paragraph closest to my finger.

Most of the time, I could glean some meaning from the passage. The story of Job, for example, was a reminder to trust God's timing and wisdom; the parable of the mustard seed was a reminder to always keep my faith.

Sometimes I found meaning less in the whole of a passage and more in a single verse or phrase. It would jump out at me, announcing its importance with a tiny jolt, and I would know, inexplicably, that I'd stumbled upon something God wanted me to study and take to heart.

Bad company corrupts good character. My old friends had talked about sex, alcohol, parties, and marijuana—teenage curiosities I tried not to think about, because the mere thought of such things was sinful. Once, when a freshman shouted the word "penis" over the noise of the cafeteria, my whole lunch table turned red with scandal. Sarah escaped to the bathroom, practically faint from secondhand unholiness.

Beauty should not come from outward adornment. I'd mostly stopped wearing makeup except for yearbook photos and choir concerts, when I was in front of an audience. Even that I felt a little guilty about. Sam told me there was no point in wearing makeup unless I wanted to attract attention. If people were looking at my appearance, they weren't looking at my faith.

By this logic, I'd decided to dress more modestly. I got rid of my bikinis, shorts, and sleeveless and low-cut shirts. Knees, collarbones, shoulders, curves—the body was a minefield of sin.

I'd started growing my hair out, too. *If a woman has long hair, it is her glory.* My hair had never come past my shoulders, and Sam wanted me to stop cutting it anyway.

That was another thing: *Man was not created for woman, but woman for man.* I couldn't ignore the theme of female submission that spanned the Bible. Even though most of the verses concerned married couples and Sam and I were only dating, I understood the principle that men were designed by God to lead, protect, and provide for women, and that women were supposed to obey the wisdom and authority that God had given men.

Such a clear-cut dynamic appealed to me, though I wasn't sure it would work for me and Sam. He couldn't save up more than a couple hundred dollars at a time, and then he'd blow it on things he didn't need. The fish necklace was pretty, of course, but I wondered why he hadn't put a down payment on his own car. Or paid the deposit on an apartment so he could move out of his grandparents' house. Or taken a couple of night classes to finish his degree.

Sam had dropped out of community college in the spring, halfway through his second semester. College was a scam, he'd told me. A money racket. When I'd asked him what his plan for the future was, he answered with one word: "Jesus."

"I'm going to preach," he said. "I don't need college for that. All I need is the Word of God."

After some consideration, I decided I was okay with this. Preaching was an honorable profession. The Lord's work. As personable and devout as Sam was, he would surely excel.

And I couldn't criticize him for dropping out of college when I wasn't sure about going myself. My parents expected me to go—and probably my teachers and friends, too, since my grades were so good—but I was secretly terrified of college culture, or what I imagined college culture to be. I thought of movie scenes with shirtless frat boys and girls in tube tops chugging beer. I didn't even allow myself to watch those kinds of movies anymore. There was no way I could actually *witness* something like that.

Of course, there were Christian colleges. Mikayla and Sarah were both going to Liberty University to study music. Liberty was expensive, though, and hours from Tazewell besides. I didn't see the point in paying that much money to move somewhere I didn't want to live to earn a degree I didn't want to get.

Really, my skepticism boiled down to a fear of the unknown. It was impossible for me to picture a life other than the one I was living, away from Tazewell or my church or especially Sam. College, according to a campy flyer hanging outside the guidance counselor's office, was supposed to "expand your horizons." I saw it as a secular distraction with no spiritual benefits. If I wanted to truly expand my horizons, I would have to seek God, not the world. *He* was the great knowledge giver, the one who opened doors and provided opportunities. I wanted to grow in him, and him only.

And that, ironically, made my world grow smaller.

12.

My Bible was open on my bed. I'd been reading in Psalms when I was overwhelmed by a sudden heaviness. The Holy Spirit was in the room. It commanded me to stand and pray.

I didn't have words as much as a willingness to receive. *Speak to me, Father,* I thought, arms stretched toward the ceiling in supplication.

A whisper of urgency tugged at my heart, telling me to close and reopen my Bible. I moved quickly, letting the book fall open.

Matthew, the first book of the New Testament, chapter 19. My eyes landed on verse 5 near the top of the page. *So a man shall leave his father and mother and be united to his wife, and the two will become one flesh.*

For a moment nothing happened, and then I was being sucked out of myself, a thousand miles from my room and body. There was a desert. The sand was as black as coal, and the ground parched, shattered like broken glass.

Suddenly the jagged cracks glowed orange, then red. Magma was rising just beneath the surface of the earth. I waited for it to spill over. Instead, the broken pieces of ground began to converge. The cracks were filled and fused by the red-hot liquid. The magma cooled. The black earth was healed, solid and perfectly smooth.

When I returned to my body, I was on my knees beside the bed, breathless and overwhelmed. I pulled myself up and reached for my Bible, which was still open to Matthew. I read verse 5 again.

Warm and calm, awash in the Spirit, I knew with that powerful, inexplicable knowing what God was trying to tell me.

He wanted me to marry Sam.

I'd never had a vision before, at least not like that. Occasionally an image would come to my mind so strongly that it almost materialized in front of my eyes, a quick flash of a translucent still. I had never been carried away from my body, or seen something as clearly as if I'd been watching a movie screen.

The next day, I told Sam what I'd seen. He was silent for a moment. Then he said that he, too, had had a vision. In his, there was a chasm in the earth, a deep valley between two high cliffs. The ground rumbled, trembled, roared; the mountains converged, closing the divide, and came together with seamless precision.

Before this, I'd sometimes wondered if I mistook my desires for God's will—if my wanting to get married precipitated the evidence that seemed to say I should. But the metaphor of convergence in both Sam's vision and my own seemed like divine confirmation, an occurrence beyond the scope of human will or force. *And the two will become one flesh.* I could think of no other explanation for what we'd seen.

Sam said he couldn't either, then went quiet again. He seemed stunned—at the startling coincidence of our visions, I hoped, not because he didn't want to marry me. Then something shifted, and he warmed up. "We have to pray about this very hard," he said, smiling at me.

From then on, it seemed as if my eyes caught on verses about marriage every time I opened my Bible. I had more wedding dreams. More visions. More still small voices when I prayed. Sam reported the same.

In December, Sam started going to Deliverance's Wednesday night youth group. At twenty he was too old to be a member, so he volunteered under the youth pastor. I had never gone to a youth group service, but Sam persuaded me to give it a try.

The first night I went was around Christmas. The room was dark and the worship music was reverent. Right away, I felt the Holy Spirit in the air. I felt it wanting to speak to me. I moved out of my seat and toward the altar, where other teens were bowing on the floor, crying out to Jesus.

Sometimes I felt the urge to worship on my knees, but that night I felt that I should stand. I raised my arms, ready to receive.

A hand landed on my shoulder.

I became aware of Sam beside me, but the hand was not his. A boy around my age whose name I didn't know held Sam's shoulder along with mine.

"Father, Father, Father," he cried.

He was praying for me and Sam both, I realized. He said something about unity, something about love. After a while he stepped closer. Now he was speaking more to me and Sam than to God.

"They are no longer two, but one flesh," the boy said. His grip closed tighter on my shoulder. "God told me to tell you that."

I didn't decide to get on the floor, but suddenly I was there. The concrete was hard and icy on my knees. I wept without control, overcome by the impossibility of such divine coincidence—of receiving this verse a second time, and from a total stranger.

Sometimes God spoke in whispers; sometimes he spoke in shouts. He spoke most clearly, at least to me, in repetition, in coincidences that were too perfect and inexplicable to doubt or deny. There was no mistaking his will: Sam and I were destined to marry. I had never been so sure of anything.

Sam didn't have money for a ring, but from that night on we considered ourselves engaged. It wasn't an explicit decision so much as a mutual agreement that the decision had been made for us and we had a responsibility to act on it. We decided we'd get married in a year and a half, the day after I graduated from high school.

I didn't tell Mom or Dad our plans. There was no point. Their chief complaint was no longer that Sam was too old for me. Now it was that he had dropped out of college and was working a dead-end job. "Is he going to wait tables forever?" Mom would ask, a lilt of disapproval in her voice.

"No, he's going to preach," I'd reply.

We had that conversation a dozen times. Mom would ask what Sam was doing to become a pastor, and I would say that he was studying his Bible very hard. Mom would ask why he didn't go to seminary school, and I would say that you didn't need a college education to preach, only a calling from God. Mom would sigh and give me a whatever-you-say look, and I would walk off in a huff, angry that Sam was never good enough for her.

I didn't quite understand how one became a pastor. Sam didn't either, but he told me he was "working on it" and I believed him. I believed he would have no trouble finding a pastoring job, even without experience or qualifications, if it was truly God's will. And I believed it was. Devotion aside, Sam fit the evangelical pastor stereotype in my head: tall, extroverted, big-smiled, charming. He made fast friends with Pastor Will, Deliverance's youth pastor. That seemed like a step in the right direction.

I liked Pastor Will and his volunteers. They were all Sam's age or a little older, and were deeply in touch with God. They knew what Sam and I meant when we said that God had commanded us to marry.

"If it's his will, you have to obey," Whitney, a volunteer, told me after service one night. "God brings people together for a reason." She was married to Jared, who led worship.

Jared and Whitney were one of the most spiritual couples I knew. Jared sang and danced and spoke in tongues onstage, modeling to the teens what true worship and surrender looked like. Whitney floated around the room laying hands on whomever the Holy Spirit urged her to pray for, always bringing the person to healing tears. I imagined me and Sam doing the same. Surely that was why God had commanded us to marry so young: Our life's work was to bring as many lost souls to Christ as possible before the Rapture. Our marriage would serve a divine purpose. A purpose far bigger than ourselves.

Which was something few people understood. People like my parents, whose faith was only "lukewarm." This was a term used by the highly devout, like my youth group friends, to describe those who were less so—people who called themselves Christians, yet didn't submit their whole selves to God. People like that, they couldn't understand my visions. They couldn't understand my calling to support my husband's ministry, or to go forth and spread the Good News. They would only balk like Gentiles and argue that it made no sense, financially or otherwise, to become a teenage bride.

And that was how I justified not telling my parents about our plans. To not *honor thy father and mother* was a sin, but it was an even greater sin to obey human will over God's. I'd underlined a verse in Matthew, which had become my favorite book of the Bible, so many times that the pen marks dimpled the other side of the page. *Anyone who loves their father or mother more than me is not worthy of me.*

It seemed extreme, but that didn't matter. I was willing to sacrifice a relationship with my parents to obey God. Sometimes he asked you to do things that didn't make sense to the rest of the world.

13.

There was a snow day. I woke to the quiet whir of the heat pump outside as flakes drifted by my window, pale against the gray slate of sky. I stared up at the popcorn ceiling, then turned to face the wall where I'd hung some of Mom's old vinyl record covers.

As I laid my eyes on them, my chest tightened. The feeling was heavy, something between worry and guilt, but I couldn't name it. I knew only that the records had to come down right away.

Thriller was first. I took it out of its frame and put it face down on the bed, hiding Michael Jackson's seductive gaze. Same for Prince and *Purple Rain.* Next was the J. Geils Band's *Freeze Frame*, then the Rolling Stones' *Tattoo You.* Last was Van Halen's *1984.* It was my favorite, though by far the most blasphemous: On its cover was a winged cherub smoking a cigarette.

How had I not recognized the sinfulness before? The album covers were suggestive, and the songs alluded to sex and drugs and every manner of immorality.

Thank you, Lord, for opening my eyes to the impurities in my life. I put the albums into a box and pulled the nails out of my wall.

It was late in the winter. I'd been saved not quite a year. My faith was still fresh, driven by a sustained burning fervor to know and serve God. I rarely missed a Sunday morning service, and I never, ever missed Wednesday night youth group. The room was always filled with the Holy Spirit. Pastor Will radiated righteousness and godly wisdom.

I wanted that for myself—to glow with God's favor. The key, Pastor Will preached, was to be fully attuned to the Holy Spirit at all times. You had to listen for conviction, for a *still small voice* to chime like alarm bells in your head, warning you away from sin.

I grew more and more sensitive to that voice. In no time, I was obsessed with purging every possible sinful influence from my life. *Convict me of my sins, Lord. Convict me. Convict me.* I repeated the prayer so often that I usually didn't realize I was saying it; it simply popped up in my mind and played in a loop.

The albums were only the beginning. Next I took down a Pink Floyd poster behind my bed, then a *Twilight* movie poster on the opposite wall. Vampires were too close to witches, and witchcraft was a sin worthy of death.

That brought to mind my Harry Potter box set. It left a gaping hole in my bookshelf when I pulled it off. I scanned the shelf for other abominations and weeded out a paperback on astrology, a guide to dream interpretation, and a couple of educational books about puberty and sex.

"What are you doing in here?" Mom poked her head into my room and studied my blank walls, the heaping box on my floor.

"Just getting rid of some things I don't need." I didn't explain further, sure she wouldn't understand.

She pressed her lips together and gave me a hard look. I knew she knew that I'd gotten some strange idea in my head. "You're not selling all this, if that's what you mean." She crouched down to dig around the box. "These are good albums and books. I'm sure you'll want them someday."

"I doubt it," I said.

"Just put them under your bed," Mom said.

"I don't want them in my room."

"In your closet?"

"I *don't* want them in my room."

"Fine." Mom threw her hands up. "Put them in the attic."

I took the box downstairs and out to the garage. Before I even touched the ladder to the attic, I felt an urgent tightness in my chest, a whisper of conviction. It was a sin to keep any evil influence within the walls of my house. I picked up the box and took it to the backyard shed, stuffing it away in a cluttered corner where no one would ever see.

Tennis season started a few weeks after my birthday. The uniform—a tight, sleeveless top and pleated skirt—was impractical in the mid-March cold, so I layered a long-sleeve thermal under the top and swapped the skirt for a loose pair of yoga pants. When the weather started to warm, I tried on the top and skirt in the privacy of my bedroom. It was shockingly revealing, at least by my standards—even more than my cross-country uniform, which was sleeveless but baggy. There was no rule I *had* to wear the uniform—my friend Sarah, who was my doubles partner, wore homemade ankle-length skirts—so I opted for the pants and thermal for the rest of the semester, except on the hottest, most humid days in May, when I allowed myself the luxury of an oversized shirt.

In church I'd learned that there should be little division between my personal faith and my public life. If people didn't know I was saved, if I wasn't a walking testament to God's goodness and mercy, how could I influence anyone to seek salvation for themselves? Modesty was an outward symbol of inner devotion. I lived in fear of projecting the wrong image.

Not that I owned anything even slightly provocative. After purging my walls and shelves, I'd felt compelled to go through my closet. I touched every shirt, dress, and pair of pants, let my fingers linger on the fabric. If I felt a tug of conviction, the clothing went into a box.

At the time, I thought this hypersensitivity to the voice of the Holy Spirit was a spiritual gift: It was a blessing to be convicted so easily, to be warned away from any and every potential sin. What was actually developing, even though I didn't realize it until much later, was a nonstop, round-the-clock, every-waking-moment obsession with being perfectly holy, as blameless as Jesus himself. I was always watchful. Always on high alert. Anything could be a sin, and everything became one.

The fact of my sexuality was particularly troubling. I was perpetually aware of my body since its very existence invited sin. It was *my* responsibility to prevent temptation, to ward off men's lustful thoughts. It was *my* responsibility to keep them from wanting to sleep with me.

One day months earlier, when we were alone in Sam's car, I'd climbed over to the driver's seat and curled up in his lap. I kissed him. He kissed back. We kissed again and again and soon the kisses turned sloppy, and he untucked my shirt from my jeans and ran his fingers up my stomach, under the band of my bra. He grazed a nipple with his thumb.

The touch shocked me back to my senses. I leaped back over to the passenger's seat and burst into tears. My perfect purity was ruined.

And it was all my fault. Sam's touch had nothing to do with it. *I* was the one who crawled into his lap. *I* was the one who planted the first kiss. *I* was the one who had let his hand travel up my shirt, and *I* was the one with the breasts, the body, the power of enticement. Even that slight, split-second act had hinted at sex. Put it on my mind and, worse, on Sam's. I apologized to him over and over. Then, that night, I apologized to God.

Forgive me. Forgive me. Forgive me. I called myself a slut and a whore through my tears, hoping that if I berated myself, God would see the sincerity in my remorse. Until my wedding night, I was supposed to be as snow-white as a sheet of copy paper.

I didn't understand why that was, exactly, but I knew it was so. It was a sermon I'd heard a dozen times. "Go to bed with someone," Pastor Ron would warn, "and your soul is tied to them forever." These *soul ties*, he preached, were unbreakable. They were an enduring reminder of sin that caused everlasting damage to your relationship with God. A few moments of pleasure, a lifetime of fallout.

Such permanence frightened me. I couldn't imagine the shame of being supernaturally tethered to someone besides my husband, or committing a sin I could never come back from. Once I did it, there was no undoing.

From that night on, I quickly pulled away from Sam's hugs and kisses. I started avoiding everything that might involve sex or any other manner of immorality: books, music, movies, TV. I even stopped browsing the internet. As far as I was concerned, mass media and pop culture were nothing more than a corrupting cesspool of godlessness. The only entertainment *I* needed was the Bible. Every night I'd read it for an hour or two or three. Whatever the Spirit told me. It was a sin to read even a minute less than the assigned amount. I felt sickeningly guilty if I fell short.

And sometimes I felt guilty anyway for no apparent reason at all.

It would come from nowhere and everywhere. One minute I'd be fine; the next a crushing weight would fill my chest. What had I done to displease God? I'd anxiously rack my brain, trying to pinpoint the source of my sin. Had I told a white lie? Had I forgotten to say my nightly prayers? Had I let my eyes linger too long on the TV when I'd walked through the living room?

Usually the answer was no, so I began to assume that my sin was in whatever I was thinking or feeling at the moment. One day I was moping around after getting a B on an advanced biology test. Without warning, guilt descended upon me in a crushing wave. My chest grew so tight and heavy that for a moment I couldn't catch my breath.

Is it a sin to be sad? I texted Sam.

Sam replied with Bible verses. *Always be joyful. Never stop praying. Be thankful in all circumstances, for this is God's will for you who belong to Christ Jesus.*

So it was, then.

Scripture as I understood it was black and white. This one meant that *every* emotion other than joy was sinful. And, when I thought about it, the guilt only appeared when I was already feeling worried, angry, frustrated, or annoyed. Of course, feeling guilty because of a negative emotion caused *more* negative emotion, which then perpetuated even more guilt. The cycle was exhausting, and I started finding myself stuck in it more often than not. Sin and guilt stalked my every waking moment.

14.

Jared from youth group had a brother, Alan, who pastored his own church. The summer before my senior year, Sam and I decided to check it out.

Lighthouse Worship Center was mostly a family affair. Pastor Alan's parents, aunts, uncles, and cousins all went there, plus his wife Lindsey and their two kids. The three-room building was on the side of a hill. It was cramped, made to feel even smaller by the black ceiling, blacked-out windows, and crimson walls and carpet. It had the hushed air of some ancient holy place. I could sense the Holy Spirit as soon as I walked into the room.

Sam and I started going to Sunday morning and Thursday evening services. We liked that the congregation was so small and devout. Everyone spoke in tongues. Everyone danced and screamed in worship. No one batted an eye at my and Sam's engagement, because most of them had been married young, too. Pastor Alan's style of preaching was even more thunderous than Pastor Ron's: It was sin and Satan, hellfire and brimstone. He jumped and shouted and ran around, speaking in tongues almost as much as he spoke in English, and preached the Bible to its most literal meaning.

He also preached something different, something I'd never heard of: that there was power in my faith to influence tangible change. By declaring my authority as a child of God, I could speak all of my desires—as long as they aligned with biblical principles and God's will—into existence.

I wouldn't hear the phrase "prosperity gospel" until years later, but that was the core of Pastor Alan's teachings. "Mark 11:24!" he would shout, pacing wildly in front of the altar. "The Lord says, 'Whatever you ask for in prayer, believe that you have received it, and it will be yours.'" A chorus of "amens" would rise from the congregation, and Pastor Alan would lift an arm out toward them. "I DECLARE that the sick will be healed! I DECLARE that marriages will be repaired! I DECLARE that bills will be paid! I DECLARE IT DONE in the name of JESUS!" Beads of sweat would shine on his forehead. He'd open and close his raised fist over the crowd, as if squeezing God's favor out of the air.

I liked the idea that I had the power to bring about my own prosperity. My desires could materialize through mere declaration—how easy was that? A simple solution to complicated problems. *Sam will find a good preaching job. I will be a good wife. We will have enough money.* The phrases were half prayer, half mantra, and I repeated them over and over in my head, believing that the more I said them and the more strongly I believed, the more likely they were to come true.

"Faith healing" was another phrase I wouldn't hear until much later, but I practiced it without knowing its name. At the end of each sermon, Pastor Alan would call the congregation to the altar. "Who here needs a touch from God?" he'd ask. Someone would step forward for prayer. Pastor Alan would move in front of the person and drape a linen prayer shawl over their shoulders. Next he'd dip his thumb into a golden bottle of oil and draw a cross on their forehead.

"How would you like us to pray for you?" he'd ask. The person would state their need: to resolve a conflict with a family member, to make a decision about a career change, to heal from an illness. Pastor Alan would lay his hand on top of their head. The rest of us would enclose them in a circle, stretching out our own hands, and command that, by the power of faith and the blood of Jesus Christ, God would give the person everything they had asked for.

After a few minutes of praying and Pastor Alan's forceful declarations, the person would usually "fall out" on the floor. "It is FINISHED!" Pastor Alan would declare. The congregation would sing and shout their praises. I would, too. I didn't quite understand what was happening—falling out never happened to me—but it seemed like proof that God was answering prayers.

One Sunday morning, I decided to step forward for prayer myself. My shoulders and upper back had been aching constantly for months. (Both Mom and my doctor attributed the pain to anxiety. I blamed it on Satan.) Pastor Alan stepped in front of me, draping the shawl across my shoulders. It was delicately embroidered with Hebrew script. The tassels tickled my arms.

"How can we pray for you?" he asked, drawing an oily cross on my forehead.

"I've been having some back pain," I told him. He laid his hand on my head. A wall of bodies moved toward me, and then a dozen hands reached out, coming to rest across my back and shoulders.

"Lift your arms," Pastor Alan said. "Praise God like you're already healed."

Thank you, Father, I prayed, *for healing me.*

Pastor Alan's hand was heavy. The heel of his palm pressed into my forehead.

"Ohhhhh, Lord. Yesssss, Lord." He stepped in closer to me, eyes closed, and turned his face toward the ceiling. "I feel the Holy Spirit moving."

I didn't feel anything except the force of Pastor Alan's hand. Still,

I closed my eyes and tried to focus on the healing that was supposed to be flooding my body.

"Thank you, Father. Touch Emilee right now. Heal her pain in the name of Jesus."

Thank you, Father. In the name of Jesus. I echoed Pastor Alan's prayer, and so did everyone else. A chorus of voices rose around me. *Heal her . . . Thank you . . . Name of Jesus . . . Yes, Lord . . . Holy Spirit.*

"Jesus, Jesus, Jesus." He stepped in closer, mere inches from my face now. My impulse was to step back—I didn't get this close to any man except for Sam—but I didn't dare move, fearful of disrupting the work of God.

"There's a healing taking place right now!" Pastor Alan pushed harder on my head. His breath was hot in my face. "I declare this body free from Satan! I DECLARE this body FREE from pain!"

The congregation pressed harder, too. *Free from Satan! Free from pain!* My arms were getting tired and starting to sag. Pastor Alan's mother put a hand under one, boosting it higher.

I was being pushed in all directions: front, back, up. Pastor Alan was shouting now, his words growing less and less recognizable. I didn't know what he was saying, but I knew the words were holy.

I kept waiting to lose consciousness, to slip outside myself and onto the floor. As much as I wanted it, as much as I tried to will it, the feeling never came.

Finally Pastor Alan's tongues slowed.

Hand still on my head, but lighter now. Pastor Alan sighed as if his soul were exhausted. I opened my eyes a sliver and saw him looking down at me. "God has done a mighty work in you today," he said solemnly. "Now set your eyes on him and declare your healing."

I snapped my eyes shut again. "I am healed," I said.

"Louder." The hand clamped down again.

"I AM HEALED."

"Again."

"I AM HEALED!"

"Again."

"*I AM HEALED!*"

And at this, Pastor Alan dropped his hand.

"Now show us what the Lord has done," he said.

I hesitated. How was I supposed to prove my pain was gone?

Pastor Alan answered the question before I could ask. "Come on, now. Bend over. Twist around. Walk in your victory."

I stepped back from him a bit, bending and twisting at the waist. I felt silly: These were things I could do before the prayer. My back pain didn't make me immobile. It was just an uncomfortable ache.

And it still was, even now. Disappointment surged as the tension returned to my shoulders. If anything, they hurt worse than before.

"How do you feel?" Pastor Alan asked.

I hesitated again, then lied. "Perfect."

Hallelujah! Praise God! Rapturous praise filled the room. My chest constricted with the guilt of my lie and the fact that I hadn't been healed.

I couldn't admit that the prayer hadn't worked. Obviously there was something wrong on *my* end: I hadn't concentrated hard enough, or prayed hard enough, or truly believed that I was healed. I hadn't had enough faith.

My eyes burned with tears. I shut them to keep from crying. For everyone else, prayer always worked. *Always.* I'd never seen someone walk away from prayer without a healing, a revelation, or some sort of divine intervention.

Unless they were all lying, too.

"I'm not going to say marriage is easy, because it's not."

Lindsey rested an arm along the back of the pew. I was sitting one row behind, and she was turned toward me.

"The best advice I've got," she said, leaning closer and lowering her voice, "is to pick and choose your battles."

The marriage counseling from Pastor Alan and Lindsey had been Sam's idea, and I'd eagerly agreed to it. Lindsey knew what it was *really* like to be a young bride. She was twenty-two, five years older than me. I foresaw my life unfolding the same way hers had: She'd gotten married at eighteen to an older man, Pastor Alan. They'd started a church and then a family. Now they had a toddler and a newborn.

I didn't know much else about Lindsey. She spent most church services in Pastor Alan's office watching their kids, so I rarely even saw her. Occasionally she'd slip out when Pastor Alan called the congregation forward for prayer. She'd step forward silently, tears streaking her pale cheeks, and tremble with sobs underneath our hands, soaking tissue after tissue as we declared peace and healing in the name of Jesus. I never knew why we were praying for her. Pastor Alan never asked, I noticed, and Lindsey never said.

I felt drawn to Lindsey. She and I were a lot alike—soft-spoken, careful, anxious.

"If Alan asks me to do something I don't want to do, I'm still going to do it," Lindsey said. Though she wore a gentle smile, her eyes were tired. "I might not feel like vacuuming or taking out the trash. But Alan's my husband, and I'm his helpmate. That's how God intended it to be."

She tucked a loose blonde curl behind her ear and dropped her voice again, glancing toward Pastor Alan's closed office door. He and Sam were on the other side. "Like I said, it's not always easy."

It took hard work, she said, and lots of it. Sometimes it was impossible to agree, or get along, or even be in the same room together. She laughed off that last part, but with the same tired half smile that quietly betrayed the humor.

As she talked, a tiny bud of anxiety started in my chest. It wasn't the idea of submission that bothered me, but fear that submission alone wasn't enough to make a happy marriage. My assumption was that following the Bible's framework for marriage naturally resulted in a strong relationship. That was the crux of Pastor Ron's relationship sermons, and of every Christian marriage book and article I'd ever read: If you served God together, loved each other the way God intended, and adhered to the gender roles God had dictated in the Bible, marriage would be easy, uncomplicated.

I hadn't expected Lindsey to say otherwise.

I searched her face, trying to meet her eyes, but she mostly kept them to the floor. Was she just being brutally honest about the reality of marriage, or was she warning me against it?

I read between the lines. I could hear the exhaustion in her voice.

To some degree, I understood Lindsey's frustration. Even though I supported the concept of submission, practicing it was difficult. It was hard to allow someone authority over you, to let them make all the decisions and win all the arguments. Hard to hear someone tell you no and not say it back. After two and a half years, I'd realized that Sam and I got along best when I let him have his way. It was painful to swallow my pride, of course, but it was well worth keeping the peace.

Before talking to Lindsey, I thought that it would get easier to submit. I thought, with teenage naivete, that a godly marriage would magically smooth out the bumps in my relationship. Of course we'd face obstacles. But with God at the center of our relationship, Sam and I would always gravitate back to blissful harmony.

Right?

For months I'd been full steam ahead about getting married. Now Lindsey's words gave me pause. Suddenly, anxiously, I worried otherwise.

But worry was a sin and so was doubt. God's will for my life was to marry Sam. And I was not, under any circumstance, going to disobey.

15.

In late September, the fall of my senior year, I got a text while in class.

I got kicked out, Sam said. *Don't know where to go. Don't know when I'll be able to talk again.*

I wasn't used to him sounding so serious. I immediately sent back a string of texts—*What happened? Where are you? Are you okay?*—but got no response. I would hear from him only sporadically over the next couple of days.

Sam had been living with his grandparents, who had raised him, and had seemed to get along with them well. His explanation of what happened would change several times over the coming months. Each retelling was drastically different from the one before, and none seemed to warrant getting kicked out in the middle of a weekday with nowhere to go. His grandparents, he'd say, were disappointed that he didn't want to join the family construction business. Or they said he came home from work too late. Or they thought he didn't keep his room clean enough. Eventually Sam would say that leaving was his choice.

I didn't care if any of it was true or not (although I didn't, and would never, know what the truth really was). The reason Sam was kicked out mattered far less to me than the fact that he was suddenly homeless, and carless, and had almost nothing to his name. He was still waiting tables, but he'd told me that he'd built up his bank account, that he had enough money saved up for a small wedding, an apartment, and the engagement ring I'd been waiting almost a year for. I knew that wasn't true either, when he couldn't afford the deposit on the cheapest apartment in town.

After a few days of searching, Sam ended up in the spare bedroom of a single-wide trailer near his job. His housemates were a pair of brothers, some friends of a friend's. Their rent was three hundred dollars a month. Sam's portion was a hundred dollars. That he *could* afford.

I went to visit the day after he moved in. There were three other trailers in the park that all shared a driveway. Sam lived in the trailer at the back of the lot. It was faded yellow with dirty white skirting. The wooden steps wobbled beneath my feet.

I knocked on the door. Sam's face appeared in the diamond window.

He let me inside, then led me to his room. It was so small that the bare twin mattress took up most of the floor space. There was a tiny desk, a broken chair, and a dresser topped with a dusty TV set that looked older than me.

"It's better than nothing," Sam said, reading my face.

He turned to two garbage bags on the mattress. They were filled haphazardly with all of his belongings from his grandparents' house—books, blankets, shoes, clothes. He'd barely unpacked, as if he'd been waiting for my help. I got started right away.

Even though we'd barely spoken in days, we sorted in silence. Sam worked through one bag while I tackled the other.

Suddenly my chest was pulsing tightly with each heartbeat. I pulled out a T-shirt that was creased with a spiderweb of wrinkles, like a piece of paper that had been crumpled and then unfolded, and suddenly I felt myself crumpling. Hot tears spilled onto my cheeks. I inhaled sharply, and the ache in my throat spread to my stomach, my arms.

"What?" Sam asked. "What is it?"

The annoyance in his voice made me cry harder. "What are we going to do?" I asked.

Sam looked at me blankly. "About what?"

"About us. The wedding. Everything."

Sam stared. He still wasn't following.

I wiped my tears with my sleeve, but they kept coming. In eight months I would graduate from high school. In eight months we were supposed to get married. I wasn't ready. *We* weren't ready. I didn't have a job, and Sam's job only paid for three pieces of old furniture and a mattress. We had no money for an apartment or groceries or bills, let alone a ring or a wedding, and we had very little time to save.

When I tried to explain this to Sam through my tears, his annoyance hardened to anger, and he cut me off.

"God will provide everything we need," he said. "You just have to have faith."

It was a sin to doubt, but in my panic I couldn't help it. "How? Look around us."

"Yeah. Look around. God *provided* a roof over my head. God *provided* a place for me to sleep at night." Sam looked down at me. "And he'll *keep* providing, if you trust him."

I wiped my eyes again. "Maybe we should push the wedding back a little," I said. "It doesn't have to be in May. If we wait, we can save up—"

Sam looked so offended that I stopped talking.

"You *don't* trust God, do you?" he said.

His disapproval was cutting. I tried to retort, but he talked over me. "You think worldly problems like money are bigger than God?"

"No!" I exclaimed. Of *course* God would provide. Why couldn't we give him a little more time, though? What was wrong with that?

"You don't trust him," Sam said again.

"I do!"

"You don't."

Now I was crying out of shame. Maybe I *didn't* trust God, or at least not as much as I was supposed to. Not as much as Sam did. He seemed perfectly unconcerned about the future, confident that in a few short months we'd have everything we needed to be a self-supporting married couple.

Help me trust you, Father, I pleaded silently. *Forgive my doubt. Help me have faith.* I pulled another crumpled shirt out of the bag, praying hard as I folded it on the bare mattress.

Suddenly I was jolted out of my prayer by a low rumble. The floor vibrated beneath my feet.

"What is that?" I asked.

Sam refused to look at me. "Train's coming," he said.

I glanced out the rattling window and saw railroad tracks in the backyard. The whole house trembled as the great engine passed.

After I suggested postponing our wedding, Sam seemed to think I was getting cold feet. I promised I wasn't. I promised I still wanted to marry him—but not until we could support ourselves.

It was our only sustained argument, and the only time that I didn't immediately concede to Sam's will. Reason and reality were constantly warring against my faith. When I was trying to wash Sam's dishes and the water wouldn't heat up, or when he wore holes in his shoes and had to pay for a new pair with dollar bills and change, all I could think about was how irrational it would be to *choose* struggle. Who wanted to live like that?

I didn't.

Sam, on the other hand, didn't seem to mind. Living humbly made you more like Jesus, he said. That attitude infuriated me. Couldn't you be like Jesus without living paycheck to paycheck?

It made me even angrier that Sam wasn't looking for a better job. I'd nagged and nagged until he finally told me that he wasn't going to start looking until I stopped nagging. Even after I stopped, he didn't show any sign of looking, despite needing the money now more than ever.

All I could do, I figured, was pray. When I think back to that fall, I only remember church. Between Lighthouse and Deliverance, I went four to five times a week: Tuesday worship service, Wednesday youth group, Thursday night service, Sunday morning service at Lighthouse and sometimes Deliverance afterward. In my memory I'm always on my knees at the altar, asking and declaring for God to provide. Prayer was my only power. I pressed into it, threw my whole heart and head into it, until I emerged breathless and disoriented. Often I was too dizzy to stand. Once I walked out of service with my face numb. I got in my car, cheeks and forehead tingling, and drove out of the parking lot. Then my brain started tingling, too, as if it were falling asleep. My vision blurred. I pulled over and called Sam.

"You'll be fine," he said. "It's just God working inside you."

I wished that God would work outside me for once instead.

The day before New Year's Eve, the Deliverance youth group headed down to Pigeon Forge for its annual retreat.

Winter Ramp was something between a conference, a revival,

and a Christian rock concert. It was a three-day event. Each day was packed with hours-long sermons called sessions that began early in the morning and ended late at night, with speakers who commanded constant shouts of "hallelujah" and "praise Jesus" from the crowd of thousands. The music was either a slow, reflective ambience, reverberating guitar chords and rolling cymbals, that brought the room to its knees in tears and worship, or energetic rock with electric guitars, unintelligible lyrics, and bass that shook the walls, the kinds of songs that made people jump around and throw their hands up and scream their praises to God. Seeing the room fall under the spell of the Holy Spirit made it easier for me to, too. I lost myself in each session. I pushed my way into the mob of bodies, sobbing and shouting along.

The final day of Winter Ramp was a Saturday. The next-to-last session was at two o'clock. It was a powerful one that pulled me to the stage at the front of the room and then to my knees. There, I prayed and worshipped. I asked God for a breakthrough with Sam. I prayed and worshipped some more.

The session ended at four, but I felt a quiet urge to skip dinner and keep praying. For hours I'd been concentrating on God with all the force in my exhausted brain—the past three nights had been near sleepless, spent on a lumpy rollaway bed with three other teens—and I hoped if I kept focusing, if I pushed through my exhaustion and denied my hunger and thirst, God would reward my faithfulness. *See how much I love you*, the sacrifice said.

So I prayed as the room emptied.

I prayed through the silence.

I prayed as the worship leaders returned from their dinner and the crowd flooded in once again.

It was then that I finally stood. My back and legs felt as if they might shatter from stiffness. As I hobbled to rejoin my youth group, a spiky-haired preacher named Casey Doss jogged onto the stage.

"Does anybody in Pigeon Forge love Jesus tonight?" he yelled into his microphone.

Screams and arms rose across the room.

Casey launched into his sermon. It mirrored the other sermons that had been given over the course of the conference. I figured it was because we were a crowd of mostly teenagers, but every speaker at Winter Ramp had fervently preached against "sins of the flesh": homosexuality, pornography, fornication. The sermons always ended with a call to renounce our sins, to receive the strength and guidance of the Holy Spirit.

"You need the Holy Ghost to live pure, clean, and sanctified!" Casey shouted. "If you're NOT baptized in the Holy Ghost, you NEED to get baptized in the Holy Ghost!"

This was a concept I understood but had never experienced myself. A "Holy Spirit baptism" occurs when you are filled—"baptized"—by God's spirit. It is a gift bestowed only on the spiritually mature, on those who have an intimate connection with God. Like salvation, it is usually instantaneous, emotional, and loud. The initial and most obvious evidence of a Holy Spirit baptism is speaking in tongues.

What I *didn't* understand was the purpose of speaking in tongues. I had a vague notion that it was supposed to be a more powerful form of prayer, though I didn't understand that either. How could praying in nonsense words be more effective than praying in English?

"The fire of God is going to come out of you," Casey shouted, pacing the stage. "Something's going to come up out of your belly that bypasses your intellect, and you're going to begin to pray in a heavenly language!"

I'd always held a secret slight suspicion that tongues were often used for show, a put-on by people who wanted to appear more spiritual than they really were. Sometimes I'd peek around in church and see people speaking in tongues while looking around the room, digging through purses, or scrolling through phones, eyes open and distracted. Or worship singers would derail their songs with tongues, then step back from their microphones to speak to the guitarist or drummer in English, and resume tongues as they came back within earshot of the rest of the church. I found it hard to believe that people could command their tongues—essentially, the Holy Spirit—at will.

Another person appeared onstage now. Karen Wheaton, the founder of Winter Ramp, was a tiny woman, visible to me only on the giant screens that flanked the stage. A camera followed her face, a floating head of sorts, her black clothes and dark hair disappearing into the backdrop. The music softened suddenly. So did the crowd. Her presence hushed the whole room.

"The Spirit of the Lord is in this place so strong, I'm shaking all over," Karen said to the crowd. She paced the stage, too worked up to keep still. "People are going to be baptized," she shook her head, voice rising, "in the fire of God!"

A pause, and she smiled. "IT'S GLORIOUS!"

The room exploded in agreement.

"Tonight," she declared, her words coming louder now, "you will receive," she pulled her fist to her stomach, looking up and closing her eyes, "the Holy Ghost!"

And the room screamed its praises.

I found myself shouting along with everyone else, arms raised high, so exhausted I couldn't think. Tears soaked my face. I didn't know why I was crying or when I'd started.

Karen kept going, her words rolling faster. The music picked up, and the crowd vibrated with anticipation. "I feel faith in this room right now!" Her voice was on the edge of breaking. "So come right now, Spirit of God—"

We screamed, a sea of hands grasping toward the sky.

"And baptize us in the Holy Spirit!"

The music swelled toward crescendo.

"We receive you in the name of Jesus!"

The voices around me started to bleed from English into the unfamiliar.

"In Jesus's name, RECEIVE THE HOLY GHOST!"

Hundreds of people collapsed onto the lacquered concrete. The floor shook with the collective fall. Karen shouted in tongues into her microphone. All around me the crowd cried out to God in strange words, nonsense words. Each person's language was different: rapid-fire repetitions of vowels; long, steady consonants, *L*'s and *S*'s and *H*'s; guttural utterances that sounded distinctly Old Testament, ancient, holy.

But I was less aware of the strangeness of these sounds than the fact that I, too, was speaking in tongues.

16.

In early March, I landed a job interview at the Subway restaurant in town. A few hours before my interview, a blizzard moved in.

"Can't you reschedule?" Mom asked. Snow was falling in a white sheet. It was impossible to see where the yard ended and the road began.

"No!" I stuffed my arms into my coat. "I *need* this job."

Mom let out something between a groan and a sigh, then yanked her coat out of the closet. "Then I'll drive."

Since Sam had gotten kicked out of his house in September, I'd put in job applications at almost every business in Tazewell—Food Lion, Dollar General, McDonald's, Wendy's, Pizza Hut, and Sonic—with no luck. At least Subway had bothered to offer me an interview. There was no way I was rescheduling.

Mom idled in the parking lot as I shuffled across the slick sidewalk to the door. A bell chimed when I stepped inside, and a woman with scarlet hair peeked out of the prep room.

"I'll be damned!" The woman turned and hollered toward an invisible someone behind her. "Angie, she showed up!"

The interview was all of five minutes. Crystal, the red-haired manager, sat me down at a wobbly table. Angie, the owner, plopped down across from me, skimmed my application, and told me that pay was $7.25 an hour, with a twenty-five-cent raise after three months. "Can you start tomorrow?" she asked.

"Yes!" I said, practically bouncing in my seat. Minimum wage was better than no wage at all.

The next afternoon, I walked onto my first shift.

"Lord, honey, I'm so glad you could start today. We needed someone A-S-A-P." Crystal led me to the cash register and told me to clock in with my birth date.

"March seventh?" she asked. I nodded. "Shit, that's today. Well, happy birthday. You gonna party tonight?"

"Uh . . . no," I said, taken aback by Crystal's chattiness.

"Why, Lord, honey, it's a Saturday, go have some fun," she said. I started to say that I had church the next morning, plus I didn't go to parties anyway, but she was talking again.

"Make sure you always clock in when you get here and clock out when you go on break." There was a rhinestone-studded purse on the floor beneath the register. Crystal grabbed it and started digging. "You get thirty minutes per shift, but you can break it up into two fifteens or three tens or whatever the hell you want, really." She fished out a pack of L&Ms, stuck a cigarette between her lips, then pulled out another and offered it to me. "You smoke?"

Someone behind me snorted. A man in a backward Subway ball cap and lopsided name tag that read DUSTIN was leaning in the doorway of the prep room, staring me up and down.

"Look at her, Chris," he said. "Of course she don't smoke."

He was right. Smoking was a vice, a sin. But how could Dustin tell? It was my first day on the job. I'd been there all of three minutes.

Crystal threw the cigarettes back in her purse. Dustin headed back to the prep room. Crystal followed, and I followed her.

The room smelled stale, like cigarettes and old bread. I blinked under the fluorescent lights. Crystal grabbed something from a corner closet and shoved it toward me.

"Hat, apron, name tag. Go ahead, put 'em on. Then you're good to go."

I tied the apron around my hips and pinned the plastic name tag to my shirt. It was a men's medium, given to me yesterday after my interview. "The only size we have," Angie had said. "Sorry."

I didn't mind. It was nice and modest, a formless drape that hung almost to my knees. I was glad to be so covered up. Dustin was still studying me, smirking.

At the back of the room, Crystal was untying her own apron. Her long red nails clicked as she fumbled with the strings and shook her hair out of its bun. It fell in a crimson curtain to her waist.

"Colby, get in here," she barked toward the open back door, where another employee was smoking just out of sight. Colby emerged, stamping out his cigarette with exaggerated slowness.

"You mind showing Emilee around?" Crystal asked. "I was supposed to be out of here"—she glanced at the clock above the prep table—"an hour ago."

"Sure," Colby said unenthusiastically.

"Thanks, honey. See y'all tomorrow." Crystal dug around wildly in her purse again, emerging this time with a lighter. She held it to the cigarette in her lips as she darted out the door. A wisp of smoke lingered behind her.

Colby watched the door swing closed. "God, she makes me so fucking anxious," he said.

"Careful." Dustin was talking to Colby but looking at me. "*Some* people might find strong language offensive."

I *didn't* like strong language, but how did Dustin know that, too? Nothing about me, as far as I could tell, screamed "Jesus freak." I was wearing the same uniform—khakis, polo, and embroidered ball cap—as everyone else. I'd taken off my fish necklace, scared of getting it dirty. I hadn't even brought my Bible with me. It was too big to fit in my purse.

Maybe, I thought rather proudly, God's love was illuminating me from the inside out. That *was* the goal, after all, to be the light of the world, a visible beacon of righteousness. Dustin didn't like that, I figured, because he wasn't saved himself. He didn't know what it was like to live a pure, holy life, so he envied those who did.

Instead, what Dustin probably didn't like was the judgment in my eyes: the way I glared at Crystal's and Colby's cigarettes; the way I winced when they swore. These were not the kinds of people I would ever choose to associate with.

Thankfully Dustin was working the afternoon shift, which meant he would be clocking out soon. Colby and I were stuck until closing time. He was eighteen, like me, and still in school—we had a civics class together—so we could only work nights and weekends. He was a shift manager. I, the new hire, was at the bottom of the ladder.

"It's gonna be slow tonight. I can feel it," Colby said. To kill time, he gave me a cursory tour of the restaurant—*That's the dish sink, that's the hand sink, that's where we keep the straws*—and a bored rehearsal of procedures. *Clock out before you take your break. Stack the chairs before you sweep. Don't put onions in the tomato slicer or you're teetotally fucked.* He showed me how to stuff the mophead under the back door to keep the prep room from flooding when it rained. He showed me how to work the stereo, which picked up only a single country radio station. He pointed out each little security camera and its blind spots, warning me to keep my cell phone out of sight. If Angie caught you texting, she'd call you up, cuss you out, and threaten to fire you if it happened again.

"She won't *actually* fire you," Colby said, rolling his eyes. "She just likes having someone to bitch at."

In between the occasional customer and random assignments Colby gave me—stocking the chip rack, sweeping the rugs, scraping dried marinara sauce from the inside of the microwave—I passed the night by finding things to clean. There didn't seem to be much point, though. Everything had a dingy, dirty sheen. The floor tiles, wallpaper, light fixtures, and even the ceiling tiles were the same greasy shade of yellow. In the prep room, the walls, appliances, and floor were stained with dried tomato seeds, teriyaki sauce, and a variety of other unidentifiable splatters that nobody had bothered to properly clean up. My cleaning rag turned a nasty shade of brown in a matter of minutes, and I didn't know where to find another one. I threw it in the trash and resigned myself to boredom: Colby had retreated to the bathroom and wouldn't emerge until closing time.

The Subway sat beside a Chinese restaurant, which sat beside a Dollar General, which sat beside a grocery store in a small plaza near Sam's trailer park on the northern side of town. It was just a short walk across the parking lot from the Mexican restaurant where Sam waited tables. When he was working, I'd spend my lunch break in the booth by the kitchen, helping Sam roll silverware or conversing with the cooks in broken Spanish.

One night in early April, I walked down to the restaurant in tears. I'd been on shift only an hour, but I was so upset that I'd taken my break early and was thinking about not going back.

"How's work?" Sam asked.

I fell into my favorite booth and put my head down on the table to cry. "I'm quitting," I said into my elbow.

"You can't do that." Sam slid into the seat across from me. "What happened?"

I wiped my face with a napkin and recapped the past hour: how I'd let dishwater overflow onto the floor; how I'd burned one customer's sandwich, then squirted the wrong sauce on another. How my series of mistakes had annoyed and exasperated Colby until he could only shake his head in disapproval.

Sam grabbed my hand from across the table. Still feeling bad for myself, I sniffled dramatically and pulled away.

"You can't quit," he said again. "You need that job. And that job needs *you*."

I sniffled again. "They don't need me. They don't even *like* me." It was obvious that Colby, who avoided me outright, and Dustin, who often made snide, backhanded comments about religion, didn't care for me in the slightest. Everyone else was less overt about it, but I sensed they disliked me, too. They worked around me as if I were invisible, leaving me out of their conversations, only acknowledging me to give me orders.

In fairness, the feeling was mutual. I had nothing to talk about with them. I was as repulsed by their sinfulness as Dustin was repulsed by my piety. Crystal had four kids by three different men. Stacey, the assistant manager, had been married three times. Shayla lived with her boyfriend. Trevor had a pregnant girlfriend. Dustin always smelled like weed, and sometimes Colby did, too. They all smoked and had tattoos. They cussed every other word and talked about sex and drinking as casually and as often as if merely discussing the weather.

I had a word for people like them: "unsavory." Sin, I believed, was like a virus, easy to catch and hard to get rid of. I imagined it enveloping my coworkers like a poison cloud. If I got too close, if I breathed in their immorality, my own morals would be compromised.

Sam took my hand again, caressing my fingers. "You don't get what I'm saying. They *need* you there. Who cares if they don't like you? God gave you that job for a reason. He put you there to show Jesus."

I sniffled. Sam got a very serious look on his face. "You can be a light in the darkness. Satan has a hold on that place, but *you* can change that."

I considered what Sam said. It was true: Everyone I worked with was wholly lost to sin. They knew nothing of the joys of salvation, the goodness of God's love. God had given me the job to help pay the bills, yes. What if he'd also given it to me to witness to my coworkers? To lead them to salvation?

I was jolted by the idea. No wonder I'd been having such a miserable time at work. God had given me a serious responsibility, and until that moment I had been completely ignorant of it.

"Let me do it. You're taking too long." Colby yanked the mop from my hands and started dragging it in haphazard zigzags across the yellow tile. They were quick, careless strokes that left the floor more dry than wet.

It was just after closing, the end of another slow night. I'd come back from my conversation with Sam around five thirty to find Colby in the same sour mood as before I'd left. He'd spent the rest of the shift in the bathroom, texting in the fridge, smoking out the back door. Wherever I wasn't. I gave him his space. I needed time to think, anyway, on how to strike up a conversation about God.

I had never been good at sharing my faith. Sam could confidently and seamlessly connect any idea, incident, or conversation to a Bible verse or parable, but my voice shook and my brain scrambled anytime I tried to talk about Jesus. I was confounded by my anxiety—to be a good Christian, I *had* to openly express my beliefs—yet I couldn't shake off the strange discomfort and embarrassment that religious talk inevitably elicited.

My strategy with Colby, I decided, would have to be simple and straightforward. Otherwise I'd get nervous and tongue-tied and lose the emotional impact of my testimony. I wasn't sure what my testimony *was*, exactly, but I knew from hearing countless others that it needed to be delivered as an anecdote about how getting saved had changed my life for the better.

How *had* getting saved made my life better? I started listing the reasons in my head. The most obvious was that I would be spared from eternal hellfire. Others: I always had someone to talk to, someone to listen to me, and I was always being watched over and cared for.

Besides those, I started to sputter out. God hadn't freed me from alcohol, drugs, or fornication like some of my church friends. My lifestyle hadn't been particularly immoral before getting saved. It didn't make me especially happy to live by all of God's rules, if I was being honest, and I couldn't quite articulate the benefits of living by those rules, except to please God.

But what was even the point of pleasing God? I wasn't really sure, except that it was what you had to do when you were saved.

I realized that my logic ran in circles. *Please don't let Colby ask too many questions*, I prayed. *And if he does, please give me the right answers.*

Colby finished mopping. He moved to the appliances next. The oven took a long time to clean, and I realized that now was my perfect opportunity to witness.

I cleared my throat twice and shuffled some chips around on the chip rack.

"Hey," I said nervously, "do you go to church anywhere?"

Colby slowly turned from the oven to look at me. "No," he said, then went back to scrubbing.

My face flushed with embarrassment and nerves. "Well, if you ever want to come with me, you're always more than welcome."

"I'm not really a church kind of guy," he said, this time without looking.

I switched a bag of sour cream and onion with barbecue. "You don't have to go to church to believe in God."

"I guess, but I don't believe in God anyway," Colby replied pointedly.

"Well, that's all right," I said slowly, then paused. *No, Emilee, don't agree. It's not all right!* "I mean, don't you think it'd be nice to, you know, have reassurance about the afterlife? And have someone always looking out for you, you know, and someone to talk to, and . . . yeah." I was faltering, but I pressed on. "God's done a lot for me personally, you know, and you could always give him a try if you wanted to. I mean, he could probably do a lot for you, too."

"*Maybe*," Colby said. The annoyance in his voice was sharp. "But I'm pretty happy with my life, and I'm not going to force myself to believe in something I just don't believe in."

I didn't know how to respond to that. How could you *not* believe in God? How could you be happy or fulfilled without God at the center of everything?

That was the awkward end to our awkward conversation, but I mulled over Colby's response for days after. I couldn't make sense of it. Couldn't understand. God was my whole life. I couldn't fathom how he was no part of Colby's.

17.

Tazewell High School had a tradition of holding graduation on its football field. On a Friday evening in early June, my class took our seats on the sidelines under a graying sky. A light drizzle started falling as the salutatorian, one of my former friends, concluded his speech. The rain increased steadily until, five sentences into my valediction, the microphone shorted out.

It was what Nanny called a "gullywasher": a hard, drenching downpour that came out of nowhere. My graduation cap drooped. The field turned to swamp. The principal herded my class across the stage like cattle in a chute and shoved water-stained diplomas into our arms. We ran for shelter while the crowd emptied the bleachers and fled to their cars.

While my friend Brooklyn shook water out of her cell phone, I stared down at my ruined shoes and cried. I'd been planning my speech for months, since I'd learned my GPA put me at the top of my 115-person class. I was sure this was God's doing: that he'd given me the ability to make good grades so I would be the valedictorian of my class so I would have a platform to spread the Gospel. Which is exactly what I'd planned to do. More sermon than speech, my valediction was a plea for my classmates to submit themselves to God. *Right now, it's uncomfortable to think about facing disappointments or the unexpected . . . but life rarely goes according to the ideals you dream of when you're young. And when that perfect life you once dreamed of evaporates . . . don't try to face it all on your own. The problems of your life are not yours to fix.**

Really, I was preaching more to myself than to my classmates. And I wasn't even following my own advice. I'd disobediently insisted on postponing the wedding, which Sam and I had originally planned for the very next day.

I'd never told Mom or Dad our wedding plans. I'd wanted a secret elopement, a quick severance, before they could talk me out of it or try to stop me. The new plan was to get married the following spring, and I didn't know if I would tell them that either. The distance between us was so wide, and their dislike of Sam so strong, that even normal conversations had become almost too much to bear.

Two days later, Tazewell High held another graduation ceremony. Less than half of my class showed up, but I finally got to finish my speech.

Earlier that morning, I'd been called in to work. The latest health inspection hadn't gone so well. Angie, the owner, had decided that Subway needed a deep cleaning. The task was so momentous that she'd summoned the entire crew. Even though I was supposed to have Sunday mornings off for church—and it was my re-graduation day besides—I didn't protest: It was June 7, exactly

---

*The contents of this speech have been lightly edited for grammar and clarity.

three months from my start date. Beginning today, I would earn my twenty-five-cent raise.

I clocked in at eight and followed the sound of Angie's voice. She was standing in the center of the prep room, dictating what needed to be wiped, what needed to be scrubbed, and which cleaner to use on what surface, while everyone worked around her.

Angie assigned me to cleaning walls. I soaked a rag and started scrubbing the wall behind the prep table. It was covered by a hard, yellow, years-old layer of dried meat-packing juice, vegetable juice, mustard, mayonnaise, and other unidentifiable splatters.

The rag did nothing. Neither did a hunk of steel wool. Oven degreaser only beaded on top of the waxy grime. Eventually, Crystal offered me the razor blade she'd been using to scrape a crust of dirt off the floor. It worked like a charm. I shaved the gunk right off the wall.

Around noon, Angie told me and Colby to take off early and get ready for graduation.

"I'm not going," Colby said. He was moving a shelf back into place. "I already got my diploma."

"Don't you want a proper graduation?" Angie asked.

"You'll regret it," Crystal said. "I wish I would've graduated high school."

"Me too," Stacey added.

Colby shrugged. "I'd honestly rather stay here and work."

"Don't you want to hear the rest of my speech?" I asked him.

Colby made a face. "I'd rather stay here and work."

I sort of wanted to stay, too, now that I was making more money. I'd earned only an extra dollar in the four hours I'd been scraping walls, and with the hours I was working every week, I'd make only an extra four or five dollars per paycheck—but it would stack up quickly, I told myself. Every cent mattered.

Next Friday afternoon, Angie delivered paychecks. I tore mine open as soon as she left, excited to see the difference, however small it was.

As far as I could tell, there *was* no difference. I skimmed over the stub. In the corner was my hourly pay rate, same as it had always been: $7.25.

Angie didn't answer when I called. I left a message asking if she could reprint my check to reflect my raise. A few minutes later, Angie called back. When I answered, she said nothing about my voicemail. Instead, she tersely asked to speak to Crystal.

Though I couldn't make out the words, I heard Angie talking sternly in the receiver. Crystal listened silently, lips pressed together, tapping a pen against the wall. When she finally hung up, she looked at me and sighed.

"Guess she don't have the balls to tell you herself," Crystal said, "but Angie said to tell you that 'your job performance does not warrant a raise at this time.'"

"What?" I felt heat rising in my face. "What does that mean?" Unlike Dustin, who was supposedly sick at least once a week, I never called in. And unlike Colby, who spent more time in the bathroom than out, I never slacked off.

"I don't know, honey. That's just what she said. Don't shoot the messenger." Crystal gave me a pitying look. "She said she'll reevaluate you in another three months, and maybe then you'll get your raise."

"Three *more* months?" I was astounded. "That's not what she promised at my interview!"

"I know, honey," Crystal said, shaking her head. She put the pen in her shirt pocket and pulled out a cigarette. "But promises don't mean shit around here."

A few weeks later, Colby quit. I was the only employee who could cover his shifts. I went from working two and three days a week to five and sometimes six, depending on whether Dustin showed up on the weekends. I often woke up to Saturday morning phone calls from Crystal. "Hey, honey," she'd say, her voice equal parts apology and annoyance. "You mind coming in today? Dustin's *sick* again." I could hear her rolling her eyes.

Even though I was exhausted, I never said no. I figured I might as well earn as much money as possible while I still had time. Come fall, I'd have to cut back my hours. I'd learned that the nearest community college gave full scholarships to local valedictorians, so after a lot of thought and prayer I'd signed up for a few easy-sounding classes. Free tuition sounded like too good of a deal to turn down—even if it was ultimately a waste of time, earning credits toward a degree I most likely wouldn't finish. A pastor's wife wasn't supposed to be a college-educated career woman.

But I wasn't a pastor's wife, and Sam wasn't a pastor. Not yet, anyway. I kept praying and declaring that he would find a church to preach in, but it seemed to me that he would never leave the restaurant. Maybe it *would* be good for me to get a degree and a decent job, I thought secretly, just in case Sam never did.

18.

That summer, I worked the morning shift. I went in at eight to help Crystal with food prep and wouldn't leave until two or three or four, depending on how busy the lunch rush was and whether my replacement showed up.

Most mornings, the brunt of the work fell on me. Crystal was easily distracted. She'd suddenly decide to take a smoke break in the middle of slicing tomatoes, leaving me to finish up. Or, halfway through taking inventory, she'd decide to get lunch at the Chinese restaurant next door, handing her clipboard over to me. Or she'd wash a dish or two before dropping her rag in the water, grabbing her purse, and running down to the Dollar General for a bag of Jolly Ranchers, leaving me to finish the washing. Crystal ran—or at least fast-walked—everywhere, acting instantly on every impulse. I understood why she'd made Colby so anxious.

Sometimes she'd even get distracted in the middle of her distraction, like running down to the grocery store for cigarettes and coming back instead with a handful of scratch-offs. She'd cuss in frustration when realizing that she'd forgotten to get what she went for in the first place. "My brain's damn near fried," she'd yell to no one in particular, then run back down to the store.

Of course, Crystal had a million things to worry about besides work. Her four teenage kids were always getting into trouble. Their fathers, she said, never paid child support, and at least one was in prison. Crystal had been to prison once, too, for something drug related, which she never talked about. She was always behind on bills. The food stamps were never enough. Often at the end of her shift, she would load up four or five footlongs with so much meat and cheese that they were almost too thick to wrap. "Supper," she'd say simply as she crammed the sandwiches into a carryout bag and left without paying. In my eyes stealing was one of the worst sins, but I still knew better than to rat her out to Angie.

One Saturday evening, a big white church bus pulled in to the parking lot. I was working alone—Trevor, my coworker, was on break—and watched in panic as thirty people filed off the bus in my direction.

"Trevor!" I hollered. I darted to the back door. His cigarette smoke lingered outside, but he was nowhere in sight. I sprinted back to the front. The youth group was queueing at the sandwich bar. The line stretched to the door.

I resigned myself to the fact that I'd be making sandwiches nonstop, probably alone, for at least the next hour.

Suddenly the doorbell chimed.

"Lord, honey!" A familiar voice carried above the chatter of the crowd. "You done got swarmed!"

Crystal crossed the room in six-inch heels. She was wearing a skintight minidress and giant hoop earrings that swung violently as she walked. Her eyes were all but invisible under thick layers of liner and mascara. I smelled her perfume before she stepped behind the cash register.

"Where did you come from?" I could only stare.

"I'm on a date." She nodded toward the Chinese restaurant next door. "Saw the bus and figured y'all could use some help. Where the hell's Trevor, anyway?"

The church group had gone bug-eyed. Crystal's heels made her tower over everyone in the store. She seemed oblivious to the attention and worked just as quickly as when she was in uniform, ringing up the sandwiches as fast as I could make them. "You want chips and a drink with that, honey? Extra napkins? All right, it's gonna come to $6.92." Her long red nails clicked and clacked on the register screen. The crowd dwindled.

Soon enough, the store was empty.

Before I could even thank her for helping out, Crystal was gone, too, back to her date. I watched her dart away.

I had never met anyone like Crystal. I didn't know what to think of her. What did it feel like, I wondered, to wear a skintight dress and six-inch heels, especially in front of a church group, without an ounce of shame? What did it feel like to say and do whatever you wanted, whenever you wanted, without anyone to answer or apologize to?

That kind of audaciousness was what the Bible, my pastors, and my own fearful conscience warned against. It was what Pentecostals call a "Jezebel spirit," a vague but all-encompassing term for the brash, shameless, devil-may-care attitude of sinful rebellion that manifests in the unsaved, particularly women. Someone with a Jezebel spirit is especially corrupted by the forces of Satan. Crystal was that spirit personified.

As naive as it was, I thought of people only in categorical terms: There were Christians and Gentiles; the Saved and the Unsaved; the Good and the Bad. There was no room for exception, no in-between. But even though Crystal did and said and *was* everything that I believed made a person bad, she *wasn't* a bad person. She was kind to me, more so than the rest of my coworkers. After all, she'd up and left in the middle of a dinner date to save me from drowning. And it was her day off. As manager, she worked on salary. She wouldn't be paid extra.

I felt a twinge of guilt then. How could I stand there and judge Crystal's morality after she'd so selflessly helped me out? Why did my mind immediately go to judgment instead of gratitude?

I wondered if some things weren't as simple as black and white, even if my beliefs said otherwise.

19.

On top of a hill, the Southwest Virginia Community College campus was a vacuum of sound. All you could hear was the wind and the occasional coal truck Jake-braking through the curve on the highway below. There were endless swells of hills to the north. From the library, you could see over their crests for miles. To the south was one blue rolling ridge that stretched on and on and on as far as the eye could see.

It was a relief to find out that college, at least this one, wasn't as secular as I'd feared. My music theory professor signed "God bless" on all her emails. My precalculus professor was an ordained minister. I made friends with a pair of Apostolic sisters in my American history class. Like my friend Sarah, they kept their thigh-length hair pinned up in cinnamon bun swirls. This made me feel a little less guilty about being in college, working against God's calling for my life. Wasting time and gas money, Sam liked to remind me. I didn't disagree with him—I doubted I'd stay enrolled long enough to declare a major—though a small part of me still felt as if I were accomplishing *something.*

Between five college classes, four church services, and thirty hours of work a week, I was exhausted. So exhausted that in October, I skipped Wednesday night youth group for the first time in my memory.

Sam had a car now, a cheap, junky thing bought with money I'd lent him, and went to church without me. There was a guest speaker, an evangelist named Ryan LeStrange. According to the write-up in our church bulletin, Ryan was an "Apostolic Prophetic Revolutionary."

"I don't like how he advertises himself," I'd told Sam earlier that week. "If you have to tell people you're revolutionary . . . *are* you revolutionary?"

Sam had rolled his eyes. "He started his own ministry, so obviously he's doing something right."

On Thursday morning, after a hard, much-needed sleep, I woke to half a dozen texts.

That sermon was AMAZING, one said. *Ryan is one of the most anointed people I've ever met.* Sam told me Ryan's message was so powerful, so edifying, that Sam stuck around after service to meet Ryan himself. They talked awhile, one on one, about a spectrum of spiritual matters: prophesying, breaking curses, resisting demons.

"He's a true prophet," Sam told me. I had never met Ryan or heard him preach, but if Sam thought so, then I agreed.

A week later, I got a haircut. It was just a trim—"a dusting," the beautician called it—to get the worst of the split ends off. Sam had asked me to stop cutting my hair, so I usually got it done only two or three times a year, and I made the appointments in secret.

That Wednesday, though, I was feeling bolder than usual. Playful. After the trim, I texted Sam a picture of myself in the salon, tucked my still-long hair into my collar, and fluffed it out a bit to make it look as if I'd cut it to my shoulders.

When I went to church afterward, Sam avoided me. It was active and purposeful: When I walked in his direction, he walked away. Then, when I sat down beside him at the beginning of service, he stood up, crossed the room, and found a different seat.

Several of our friends noticed. I saw them watching me, watching Sam. I wanted to cry with embarrassment. I wanted to run from the room. That would only inflict more damage, I decided, so I stayed in my spot for the whole service, praying for forgiveness from Sam and God both.

I'm sorry, Lord. I shouldn't have joked about my hair. I shouldn't have even trimmed it. Please forgive me. Please help Sam forgive me. I'd blatantly defied his authority. Worse, I'd made light of it with my joke.

After service, in the dark of the parking lot, I begged for Sam's forgiveness. I berated myself for my stupidity, my disrespect. My tears flowed as fast as my apologies.

Sam said nothing. He looked down at me, got in his car, and drove away.

I didn't hear from him for two days.

I hated the silent treatment almost as much as I hated disappointing Sam. Still, in my mind, it was justified. Deserved. When would I learn to fully submit? How would I ever make a good wife?

On Friday evening, Sam broke his silence. *Want to go to Walmart?* his text read.

I immediately replied yes, jumping at the chance to smooth out the tension.

But it seemed that there was nothing to fix. Our conversation was normal, and Sam's anger was gone, as if nothing had ever happened, as if I'd never disrespected him. As if he hadn't ignored me for two days.

For most of the car ride, Sam talked about the conversation he'd had with Ryan LeStrange more than a week earlier. Ryan was theologically nuanced, Sam said. That was what made him so revolutionary. Some of his ideas weren't popular. Some of them were pretty radical, even for evangelicals.

"Like what?" I asked.

Sam seemed pleased I was curious. "When it comes to marriage, for example. Most Christians agree that the husband is the head of the household, right? And that he has authority over his wife, right?"

I nodded.

"Well, how do you enforce that dynamic? What does the husband do when his wife disobeys?"

Give her the silent treatment, I thought, but knew better than to say that.

"Most of the time, he doesn't do anything. He lets her get away with disobedience. That creates a problem, because then she thinks she can get away with more and more."

I don't, I thought, but didn't say that either.

"It's the husband's job to correct his wife when she sins. Otherwise she'll just keep sinning. But most don't bother with correction because they don't know how to go about it."

I nodded again, even though I had no idea what Sam was getting at.

"Ryan has a solution. Well, it's not his idea, but he's been practicing it for years. He said it's worked wonders for his marriage."

Sam looked over at me. "Have you ever heard of domestic discipline?"

I remember exactly where we were when Sam said this: on a bridge rounding a curve, less than a mile from the exit we'd take to get to Walmart. For years I would sweat through that stretch of road, recoiling from the echo of a phrase that would never leave my mind.

Sam launched in. He explained the purpose of domestic discipline before revealing what it entailed. The goal, he said, was for a wife to learn submission and obedience to her husband, and for the husband to correct his wife when she disrespected his authority.

"So how are you supposed to make that happen?" I asked.

"Physical punishment," Sam said simply.

I looked at him with raised eyebrows. "Are you telling me Ryan *hits* his wife?"

"Not hits," Sam replied. "*Spanks*."

When I didn't reply, Sam glanced over. He saw the look on my face. "It's not as crazy as it sounds. You don't do it all that hard. The point is to remind your wife of her role in the marriage."

"Can't you do that without *spanking*?" The word felt vulgar on my tongue.

"I can't think of anything that would be more effective."

That *would* have a lasting impact, I thought, being spanked by your husband. I tried to picture Sam spanking me. The imagined feeling made me cringe, and the thought of his hand anywhere near my backside made me feel icky. I tried to put the image out of my mind.

"There's a bunch of information online. You should look it up." Sam stared ahead at the road. There was an expectation in his voice that I didn't like. "Maybe it would work for us."

What did that mean?

I didn't ask.

I saved all my questions for Google instead. That night, I typed "domestic discipline" into the search bar.

There were more articles and blog posts than I expected. Most were years old. Their websites were laughably outdated. The information seemed written by men, for men, referring to women as "the wife," "the female," and "the submissive." I was mildly suspicious that the concept was just a kink disguised as religiosity, or a sneaky justification for domestic abuse. But since Sam suggested it, that couldn't be possible. I read carefully, trying to make sense of it all.

*Obedience is a simple and effective way of getting everything a wife has ever dreamed of—love, romance, intimacy, fulfillment, and harmony.** This was a good selling point, a promise of things I wanted out of my relationship but rarely felt.

Obedience is a simple yet effective technique for building love in a relationship. When a man is obeyed by his woman, he sees and feels a concrete demonstration of her love, respect, and trust for him. I paused to absorb this, realizing I didn't disagree. Obedience was an act of submission; submission was an act of respect. Respect was an act of love.

I was surprised to realize that the more I read, the less bizarre it all sounded.

In its own way, domestic discipline reinforced the marriage hierarchy outlined in the Bible: wise, authoritative, decisive male; misguided, deferential, compliant female. The means of enforcement were a little extreme.

But maybe physical pain was what it would take for me to finally

---

*These quotations have been lightly edited for clarity.

learn obedience and respect. Maybe fear would sear the concept of total submission into my brain. Maybe it would ease the always-simmering strain between me and Sam.

Maybe, I hoped, this was the answer to my prayers.

A few days later, in the living room of Sam's trailer, I bent forward over the arm of the couch.

"Be still," he said. I tensed and squirmed, preparing for the blow.

The first was light, a trial run. The next was harder. So was the next. Four, five, six, seven. I squeezed my eyes shut and gripped the cushion with my nails.

When he finished, I was crying. Not out of pain, but out of embarrassment. I tried to hide the tears from Sam.

He saw anyway. He softened then, and his eyes turned gentle. He sat down on the couch and pulled me into him, cradling me in his lap. "Did I hurt you?" he asked.

"No," I said. It wasn't a lie: The sting had already faded. I wrapped my arms around his belly and tucked my head against his chest.

What I felt was too complex for me to articulate. There was the immediate, visceral feeling of humiliation, of bending over in front of my fiancé and feeling degraded beneath the strength of his hand. Then there was gratitude for the twisted sense of intimacy fostered by the spanking. I couldn't remember the last time Sam had been this tender with me.

Then there was an odd sort of vindication. It was the most confusing feeling of all. I felt that the spanking had righted—at least temporarily—my sinful wrongs, tamed my defiant, disobedient nature. I was Jesus on the cross, shamed and ridiculed, sacrificing my pride and body for eternal sanctification.

But Jesus had not deserved his punishment.

I did.

I deserved more.

Almost every time after, the spankings were my idea. Sometimes I suggested them when I sensed Sam was angry. It was a quick resolution, one I much preferred to ice-cold glares and days of the silent treatment.

Most of the time I asked to be spanked out of guilt. When I'd had a sinful thought or feeling, when I'd rankled against Sam's authority or doubted God's ability to provide, I asked for punishment. I *wanted* Sam to beat the sin out of me. I asked him to hit me hard, too, even though pain was not the true price of righteousness.

Shame was.

20.

That fall, I finally got my twenty-five-cent raise. It showed up unannounced on my paycheck one week.

In January I got another raise. A whopper this time. Angie promoted me from lowly sandwich artist to night-shift manager. Suddenly I was making eight dollars an hour. The raise seemed enormous, especially considering where I'd started and how long it had taken me to work up to it.

The promotion came out of necessity. In less than a year, more than half a dozen Subway employees had come and go. Dustin had finally stopped showing up for work altogether, and for a few stressful weeks we were understaffed until Crystal and Angie went on a hiring spree.

One new employee was a high school dropout. One was a forty-year-old grandmother. One had just gotten out of jail. I was in charge of training them on the night shift. It wasn't a difficult task: I demonstrated how to scour the oven, how to restock the chip rack, how to mop Colby-style for maximum speed and efficiency. Balancing the register was the only aggravation. It was always short by at least four or five dollars. Not a significant amount, of course, but that was the point: If you took only a dollar or two at a time, it was hard to notice, and even harder to catch. I never figured out who was doing it. Or if *everyone* was doing it.

The new hires were easy to train except Jeremy, who was fresh out of jail. ("What were you in for?" I asked. "I put a guy in a coma," he replied without explanation.) Despite that fact, Jeremy was easygoing around me—always joking, goofing off, finding something to be distracted by. He was perpetually high and giggly. The only thing he was serious about was making me laugh, too.

"You never smile!" he'd say. "Lighten up. Loooosen up." He'd drag out the word and flail his arms, mimicking one of those inflatable tube men you see in front of car washes. If that didn't work, he'd try to scare a grin out of me. He would hide inside the fridge and pop out when I opened the door, or he'd contort all six-plus feet of himself into the cabinet under the sink and grab my ankle when I walked by.

I wanted to be annoyed but couldn't. Jeremy was the only person I worked with—really, the only person outside my religion—who tried to be friends with me, so I let him slack off while I did both his work and mine.

Around the time I got promoted, Sam got a new job.

I was amazed. I hadn't heard him talk about job hunting in months. The position was mentoring at-risk elementary schoolers through an after-school drug prevention program run by the Tazewell County Commonwealth's Attorney's Office. It paid ten dollars an hour. I was overjoyed until Sam told me he worked only six hours a week.

"I'll probably go full-time eventually," he said.

Something in his voice told me that wouldn't happen.

We had decided to get married in May, after the semester ended. It was a year after our original date, and postponing again wasn't an option. All the spankings in the world wouldn't pacify Sam's anger, or my guilt for defying God's will.

But I'd just helped Sam pay a big surprise medical bill, depleting what I'd saved since helping him buy his car, and my paychecks averaged only $150 a week. After taxes, Sam was barely making $50. Two hundred dollars a week, $800 a month, $10,000 a year. Even in Tazewell, it was going to be impossible to make ends meet. The thought of this made my chest tight. What were we going to do?

The question was really of what *I* could do.

"Maybe I should finish my degree," I told Sam one day. He wanted me to drop out of college. Part of me wanted to drop out, too, but I knew I needed a better job. "I could be a teacher."

"You're not very good with people," Sam replied.

The words hurt even though they were true. I was too timid to be a teacher.

What else was there, though? We needed money, and fast.

"Maybe I should go to Radford," I said. That was where my mom had gotten her teaching degree. "Or Virginia Tech." They had a teaching program, too.

Sam pressed his lips together and gave me his that's-not-a-good-idea look. He didn't even have to say anything: I already knew both schools were too far away and out of our budget. That was the thing: Making money *cost* money. Money we didn't have.

And because of that fact, because I realized the impossibility and absurdity of our situation, I made a joke. "Maybe I should go to Harvard."

Sam was visibly annoyed now. He did not see the humor. "You couldn't get in."

His doubt stung more than his tone. Of course I couldn't get in. I had no plans to try.

"It was just a joke," I said quietly.

One night after youth service, I walked outside to find Sam, Jared, and Whitney watching a video on Jared's phone.

"I like him," Jared was saying, "since he's not a politician." Sam nodded in agreement.

"Don't you think he's kind of"—Whitney trailed off, struggling to find the word—"*crass*?"

"Yeah, and it's great," Jared said.

"It's hilarious," Sam added. "We need someone who tells it like it is."

I asked whom they were talking about.

"Donald Trump," Jared said. "He's coming to Radford next week."

Over the past few months, I'd heard Trump's name floating in and out of conversations at the grocery store, in the parking lot after church. Soon Trump would win the Republican presidential primary, and then the nomination, and I'd be hearing his name a lot more.

I didn't allow myself to watch TV or browse the internet, and I hadn't cared enough about politics to keep informed, but now I was curious. It was almost unheard of for a presidential candidate to campaign in southwest Virginia. We weren't the kind of people politicians cared about.

The rally was on February 29, a Monday. I decided to go, drawn by the novelty of seeing a real-life celebrity. I skipped my college classes, and Erik, who was a high school freshman now, persuaded Mom and Dad to let him skip, too. It was a seventy-mile drive to

Radford. We arrived three hours before Trump was scheduled to speak.

Though the morning was bitterly cold, the energy was high. Erik and I joined the growing line outside a basketball arena and stood there for two hours, breathing moist heat down our coat collars while a man ahead of us strummed a guitar and sang songs about Trump. Another man offered us orange stickers that said GUNS SAVE LIVES. When the doors finally opened, the line moved as fast as people could run. Erik darted ahead to save us a spot in the bleachers.

Outside the arena, the crowd's energy was palpable; inside, concentrated under a single roof, it was electrifying. As the room filled, the anticipation grew explosive. It rose from the crowd in merry shouts and chants—*Trump*, *Trump*, *Trump*—while the bleachers trembled with the weight of the noise. Everything about it—the atomic energy and sound, the thrill of being part of something so much larger than myself—reminded me of Winter Ramp.

Trump was introduced to the stage by a woman I recognized, a lawyer from Tazewell, and launched into his speech. He talked about how many celebrities and politicians had endorsed his candidacy, and how he was going to build a wall between the United States and Mexico, and how pathetic all the other candidates, both Democratic and Republican, were. He mocked the press, who were corralled in a pen near the stage, and jeered at protesters as they were forcefully escorted from the arena. I watched one woman get dragged from her seat by her wrists. I saw another man get body-slammed to the floor. Trump shouted for security to get them out, smirking as he looked on.

Meanwhile, my heart pounded as if *I* were the one being wrestled or dragged or laughed at, instead of passively watching from the bleachers. Later, I would pray for forgiveness, feeling guilty by association—as if I'd committed a sin by simply witnessing the violence in that room.

Later, on the drive home, Sam would call from work and ask what I thought about Trump. I'd pause, still reeling from the rally, and say I didn't know yet. On one hand, I liked Trump. Or, I felt as if I *should* like Trump. Sam and most of my church friends did, after all, and Trump seemed to support the conservative ideas that aligned with my faith. Plus he'd actually come to my part of Appalachia, which was more than any other candidate had done. At one point in his speech he'd promised to bring back coal "100 percent." The crowd had practically detonated. I'd cheered along.

But I was leery, too, that Trump seemed amused by brutality, and that his political career caused so much contention. Eventually I'd end up telling Sam I was for Trump, even though I was really somewhere in the middle—torn between what I felt and what I thought I was supposed to feel.

I turned nineteen a week later. Soon after, Jared stood up in church and announced that he would be directing that year's Easter play. He had already cast himself as Jesus, but there were a lot of other parts that needed filling.

Sam volunteered us right away. He became one of the soldiers who mocked Jesus on the cross. I became the Virgin Mary. Play practice was twice a week. Between my classes and work, I was always running late, always in a rush. One night I was fumbling with my shoelaces, trying to get out the door. Dad came downstairs with his usual goodbye: Be careful, watch for deer, don't drive too fast. I nodded and stood.

My left hand went to the doorknob. Dad's eyes went to my hand.

"What is that?" he asked quietly.

I looked at my hand, stomach sinking, and realized my mistake.

Several months earlier, Sam had somehow scraped together enough money to buy me a tiny engagement ring. I had been so very careful to hide it from my parents, slipping it on when I left the house and slipping it off when I returned. In public, I flaunted the fact that I was engaged. At home, I was ashamed of it.

I knew I needed to tell them I was getting married. I knew it was wrong to not tell them, that they deserved to know. Still, every time I'd gathered my courage and started to open my mouth, the words caught in my throat, died on my tongue. I knew they would only widen the fracture that had been growing between us for years, maybe to the point of no return. It was an unbearable thought, losing those last shreds of our relationship, the rare moments of warmth and normalcy. I knew I couldn't be both their daughter and Sam's wife.

Frozen at the door, I glanced up at Dad. I expected disappointment in his eyes, maybe even anger, but there was something else instead. Worry. Fear.

Mom, noticing the strained silence, peeked out of the kitchen. The same emotion was written on her face.

Neither knew what to say. I didn't either. There was no changing my mind, and there was no changing theirs. I walked out the door and shut it behind me.

In my car, I berated my cowardice. God's will was far superior to whatever my parents thought about my relationship. Why, then, was I so afraid of their opinion? Why wasn't I brave enough to *tell* them about my engagement?

The fear was a mystery to me then. It was about more than their disapproval, or the potential damage to our relationship.

I was afraid of being wrong.

My parents had the wisdom and foresight I lacked in youth, and every time we disagreed, I ultimately found myself siding with their logic. I couldn't admit my wedding plans because I knew they would talk me out of them. They would tell me I was too young, and that Sam and I were too poor: old fears I had worked hard to suppress, ones I didn't want to grapple with this close to my wedding.

The only way to maintain my power—or sense of it, at least—was by not engaging. It was like that with everything. Silence was my only defense against my parents' wisdom, Sam's authority, God's will.

A few hours later, when I got home from play practice, Mom cornered me in my room. Her face was troubled. My stomach sank again.

"Just wait until you're out of college," she pleaded.

I didn't respond. Mom looked as if she might cry. "You *are* going to finish college, aren't you?"

This time, I didn't have the option of saying nothing. I couldn't stand the pain on her face. "Yes," I answered quietly.

She knew I was lying. She turned and walked out of the room.

Easter Sunday was that weekend. I left for church early that morning, wrapped up in the modest tunic that served as my Virgin Mary costume. A couple hours later, I picked out Mom's face in the very back row. I strained to see Dad beside her, but he wasn't there. He had never missed one of my church plays.

One morning in early April, over Hardee's sausage biscuits and sweet tea, Sam and I set our wedding date for May 21, a Saturday. Pastor Ron, who paid for our breakfast, handed us a list of wedding packages. I nearly choked as I looked at the paper. The cheapest option—a quick vow exchange, no decorations, no reception—was well over a hundred dollars.

"You don't have to decide right now," Pastor Ron said, reading my face.

Maybe I'd exhausted my anxiety, or maybe the only way I could accept reality was to adjust my perspective. Whatever the cause, I felt myself slowly resigning to fate. Sam and I were just going to have to make do with what very little we had, and trust God to miraculously provide what we didn't.

"That's all we need," I said, pointing to the basic package. "Something quick and simple."

Pastor Ron circled it in red pen. "How many guests?"

"Jared, Whitney, Pastor Will . . ." Sam named a handful of church friends.

Pastor Ron raised his eyebrows. "No family?"

"No," Sam and I said at the same time.

Sam hadn't spoken to his grandparents since they'd kicked him out of their house. I'd barely spoken to my parents since accidentally revealing my ring. I left home early in the morning and returned late at night, avoiding them even more than I already had been. We tiptoed around each other and the fact of my engagement in a tense, terrible silence, except for the occasional agonizing moments in which they practically begged me to reconsider, which I always walked away from.

Across the table, Pastor Ron shuffled his papers and cleared his throat. "You know, I'm a parent myself. Sometimes I don't agree with the decisions my kids make."

I expected him to say something about *honoring thy father and mother*, or urge us to postpone the wedding until we earned my parents' approval.

"But," he said, smiling and folding his hands on the table, "a decision made in accordance with God's will is never wrong."

I smiled back. Sam did, too, and took my hand.

"It's God's will," Sam said. I squeezed and smiled wider.

It was.

21.

One night in late April, at the beginning of youth service, Sam disappeared.

We usually rode to church together, but for some reason we drove separately that night. I saw Sam's car in the parking lot. I said hi to him on my way to the youth room, but didn't see him again, not during worship or the sermon or anytime after. His car was still there, so he was, too. I searched the whole building. I couldn't find him anywhere.

When I got home, I called Sam. His phone went straight to voicemail. Next I tried texting him. The messages wouldn't deliver.

Something didn't feel right. Sam usually turned his phone off when he was angry at me, and I couldn't think of anything I'd done to upset him. Why was he avoiding me? And where had he disappeared to?

The next day, I still didn't hear from Sam. The calls and texts still wouldn't go through.

When he skipped service at Lighthouse that evening, I knew something was wrong. He never skipped Thursday night service. Never.

I left church early and went to Sam's trailer. His housemates were gone, but Sam's car was parked in the grass by the porch.

I knocked on the door. No answer. All the lights were off.

I tried the doorknob. It was unlocked, so I let myself in.

Through the dark, I could barely make out Sam's form on the couch.

"What's going on?" I asked. My voice came out in a worried whisper.

"Everything's fine," Sam said.

"Why are you sitting in the dark?" I asked.

Sam didn't reply.

"Something's going on." I stepped inside and turned on the lamp, then sat down on the opposite side of the couch. The room was tense even though Sam was alone. "You have to tell me what's going on."

"Everything's fine," he said again.

I folded my arms.

Sam refused to talk.

I kept prodding, badgering, asking questions. Finally, Sam must have realized that one way or another I was going to get to the bottom of whatever was happening.

Slowly, carefully, he started talking.

This was the situation as he told it to me. Several months earlier, a sixteen-year-old girl in our youth group texted Sam a picture of herself in a bikini. Last night—Wednesday night—she'd tipped off the police that Sam had a nude picture of her on his cell phone ("But she wasn't actually nude," Sam insisted, "and I deleted it as soon as she sent it!"). The police got to the church soon after I left. They seized Sam's phone. Now he was under investigation for possessing child pornography.

I slowly sank back into the couch. For a moment I couldn't speak, couldn't think.

Then my brain went into hyperdrive.

Nothing about the story made sense. Why did the girl have Sam's phone number? Why would she send him that kind of picture? Why didn't he tell anyone? Why would she want to get him in trouble? Why would she call the police if there was nothing illegal about the photo? And if she *had* sent a nude picture of herself—I felt sick thinking about it—why would she admit it? Why would she choose to get herself in trouble, too?

Besides, I hadn't even seen the girl at church last night. If she *was* there, where had she been?

My heart dropped.

Where had *Sam* been?

"I don't know," Sam said over and over. That was his answer to every question. "I just don't know."

None of it made sense. "You *do* know," I whispered.

I kept pushing.

The girl, Sam told me, was jealous. She wanted to date him. She wanted him to break up with me ("But I wasn't interested!" Sam insisted. "I'm engaged!"). The bikini photo was meant to entice him. She was devious, Sam said. Vindictive. Had a Jezebel spirit. With our wedding coming up in just a few short weeks, she must have realized she was running out of time. She called the cops hoping that Sam would somehow get in trouble, and that even if he didn't, maybe I'd get mad, or scared. Maybe *I'd* break up with *him.*

It was as convoluted and dramatic as a soap opera plot, and didn't add up. I barely knew the girl in question, but I couldn't imagine her being as conniving as Sam made her out to be. She was friendly but quiet, and mostly hung around the younger members of our youth group, the twelve- and thirteen- and fourteen-year-olds. She looked their age, too. If Sam hadn't told me she was sixteen, I never would have guessed.

"Why didn't you tell me about any of this?" I asked.

"It's nothing to worry about," Sam said again. "I didn't do anything wrong."

I knew he was lying, but I wanted to believe him anyway.

For four and a half years, most of my adolescence, a quarter of my life, I'd been dating this man. For two and a half years, I'd been planning to marry him. I had literally grown up with him. I had the rest of my life planned around him. I think I knew that pursuing the truth—whatever the truth was—would jeopardize our future together. Maybe end it all together.

I couldn't and didn't want to imagine a life without Sam, so I tried to accept the lie.

"Please come see me tomorrow," Sam begged as I left his trailer.

When I returned in the morning, Sam was wearing sneakers. "Let's go for a walk," he said.

I was surprised, but agreed. There was a trail in the woods near the trailer park. As many times as I'd asked, I had never been able to persuade Sam to check it out with me.

After we got back, Sam made me lunch. That was unexpected, too: Sam never cooked.

Then, after we ate, Sam pulled me onto his lap on the couch. He cradled me, held my head against his chest. Breathed into my hair.

"I'm sorry," he said. His face crumpled, and his belly trembled with sobs. His breath started to come in hot gasps. "I'm sorry," he repeated. "I'm sorry, I'm sorry, I'm sorry."

I remained in his embrace. "Why are you apologizing if you didn't do anything wrong?" I asked. My voice was delicate, a whisper. Yet Sam still detected the doubt.

His arms loosened and he pulled away. "I *didn't* do anything wrong," he said. He looked down at me with pleading eyes. "You have to believe me. Please believe me."

For all his crying, there were no tears.

"I believe you," I said.

But it got harder, then impossible.

Since I had to work and the police had Sam's phone, we continued our conversation through email on Saturday.

I kept probing. Maybe it was easier to confess through writing, or maybe he figured I'd eventually find out anyway, but Sam finally admitted that the girl had sent him multiple photos, not just one.

Then he admitted she'd sent videos.

Then he admitted that the pictures and videos were, in fact, explicit.

It occurred to me with a jolt of horror that Sam might be guilty, and that he might go to jail.

Why didn't you block her from texting you? I asked.

I wasn't thinking, Sam wrote back.

That Sam hadn't put a stop to the pictures and videos indicated interest, I reasoned. He was not the innocent victim of a single unsolicited sext. He had actively, willingly received porn—*child* porn—countless times over the past several months.

He'd wanted it. Clearly.

And yet I didn't want him to get in trouble.

Reading over those emails now is painful. They're terrified, confused, and pitifully, naively optimistic, vacillating between acceptance and denial, anger and forgiveness. In some messages I lashed out: *You're a liar and a cheater and I am disgusted by you.* In other messages I forgave Sam, minimizing his personal responsibility and instead blaming human nature, satanic temptation, and even myself for his sins. I said that I still felt as if God wanted us to get married, that I hoped the police wouldn't find any evidence on his phone.

Even though I finally knew what seemed like the truth, I still didn't want to accept it. How was I supposed to face a reality without Sam? How was I supposed to face a reality *with* him if he was a criminal? A *predator*?

That was not the man I knew. When I looked at Sam, I saw a man of God. I saw his well-worn Bible, his perfect church attendance, his weeping at the altar in divine supplication.

I did not see a predator.

That was the problem: I never had.

Not when he catcalled my fourteen-year-old self on the street.

Not when he developed a crush on a twelve-year-old girl.

Not when he started volunteering in a youth group.

Not when he took a job mentoring at-risk schoolchildren.

Only now when he was being investigated for sexting a sixteen-year-old girl.

And still, I didn't want to believe.

On Sunday morning, I went to church at Deliverance. After service, Pastor Ron called me over.

"Are you doing all right?" he asked.

"Yes," I lied, then spoke in a rush. "Do you know anything about what happened Wednesday? Or what's going to happen to Sam?"

He hesitated. "I can't talk until the investigation is over. But Emilee?" His look turned to pity. "I think you should postpone the wedding."

"Sam might not go to jail," I challenged.

Pastor Ron shook his head. "You should postpone the wedding."

Please, God, don't let Sam get arrested. Please, please, please don't let him go to jail.

I went home, locked myself in my room, and prayed on my floor until work. After I got off, I came home and prayed some more.

That was all I could do—pray. Not getting arrested wouldn't prove Sam's innocence—he'd already admitted *plenty* to me—but a lack of legal consequences felt more tolerable, more forgivable. If he didn't go to jail, if no one else found out about what he'd done, I could still see the chance of a future together.

After a night of almost no sleep, I got up on Monday morning, typed out a prayer, and emailed it to Sam.

Lord, all I ask is that you please, please don't let him be arrested. Please, God. Amen.

22.

There was a phone call.

It was mid-afternoon. I'd just come home from my Monday morning college classes. I didn't recognize the number.

On the other end was a hushed, nervous-sounding Pastor Sue, the new children's pastor at Deliverance. I saw her in passing every week at church, but I had never had a full conversation with her.

"Emilee," she said quietly, "don't tell anyone I called you, okay? I can't have anything to do with this."

I held my breath.

"Did you know Sam got arrested this morning?"

I sat down on the floor right where I was standing. "No," I whispered.

"He called from jail and asked me to bail him out," she said. "I'm not sure why he asked me. I think he didn't want you to know." Another pause. "I can't have anything to do with this," she said again.

Bail was set at two thousand dollars, she told me before hanging up. If I went through a bail bondsman, I'd have to pay only 10 percent. The company would post the rest, and Sam would be free until arraignment.

I burst into sobs. Sam was in jail.

My fiancé was in jail.

For possessing child porn.

Our wedding was in two and a half weeks.

I couldn't wrap my head around it. Everything had happened so fast, and the whole situation was so outrageous, that even after all Sam had done, even after admitting to it, even after being *arrested* for it, a small part of me still couldn't, wouldn't believe it was true.

I never considered leaving Sam in jail. I was angry and hurt, of course, but I worried that if I didn't bail him out, no one would, and that seemed cruel. But most of my savings from the past year had already gone to Sam, for the car and the medical bill and many other smaller things he'd promised to repay me for but hadn't. At that moment I had ninety dollars in cash, the leftovers from last week's paycheck, and a little over a hundred in my bank account. Withdrawing it would give me just enough to pay the bondsman. It would also leave me almost broke.

I paused on that thought. I'd nearly drained my bank account on Sam several times.

Not again, I decided, and drove to Sam's trailer to scour his room for hidden cash.

I searched everywhere, even his pants pockets, and only came up with some change. It seemed less out of sympathy for Sam and more out of sympathy for me, but Sam's housemates, TJ and his brother Ricky, offered to pitch in their spare cash. I added it to my ninety dollars, but it still wasn't enough. They called up another brother, Bill. He said he would cover the rest.

I rode with TJ to Bill's house across town. I promised to repay him and his brothers after my next paycheck.

"Sam can pay it back," Bill said. "He's the one in jail."

I regret that I never properly thanked those brothers for their kindness, especially TJ. Without being asked, he drove me to the bail bonds office on Main Street.

The office was in a dingy brick building across the street from the county jail. It was past regular business hours by then, but a neon phone number buzzed electric blue in the window. I'd started crying again. TJ called for me.

"The bondsman can't make it for a couple hours," he said after hanging up. He leaned against the door, looked up at the darkening sky, and checked the time on his phone.

"I think you should come back tomorrow," he said. Across the street, the jail windows were microscopic, tiny rows of paper cuts in the wall. I wondered which one Sam was behind. "Just leave him for the night. He deserves it."

Does he? I imagined Sam lying on a metal bed in a cold, concrete box, a nameless face in a long, loud row of dark cells. I was suddenly scared for him more than for myself.

The day before, after talking to Pastor Ron, I'd sent Sam another angry email. *If you go to jail*, I wrote, *I'm leaving you*. In my pain, that was easy to say.

Now, after the worst had happened, my anger was unexpectedly melting away, overtaken by a sense of pity and tenderness I knew I shouldn't feel. Even after everything that had happened, I was still clinging to some small absurd hope that we had a future together. I knew it was the wrong thing to want, but I wanted it anyway.

Until.

That night, a thought came to me.

I'd gone to bed as soon as I'd come home, knowing my puffy eyes would make my parents ask questions I didn't want to answer, then lain there for hours, exhausted yet wide awake, trying to tease out signs that Sam was preying on that sixteen-year-old girl. I couldn't recall seeing them even speak to each other. Sam had kept the secret very well. I could've easily never found out.

What if that meant there were others?

I'd never snooped through Sam's phone or social media. I thought that was something that—I realized the irony—only people in unhealthy relationships did. I felt absolutely criminal as I picked up my phone, logged out of my own Facebook account, and typed in Sam's email. I held my breath as I guessed his password.

The log-in failed. I tried another password and failed again. I tried another, and another.

Unexpectedly, it worked.

My heart pounded. This was wrong, very wrong, but I had to know. I clicked on his inbox.

There were dozens of unread messages from just the past weekend, and below those were a hundred conversations going back several years. I looked over the names. Many I recognized, some I didn't, but they were all female. Some had graduated from high school with Sam. Some had graduated with me. Some were years younger. Seventeen. Sixteen. Fifteen. Fourteen.

I clicked on a few conversations to see what Sam had sent, then I wished I hadn't.

I'm so glad I got to see you last night.

We should talk more.

I miss hanging out with you.

I've been thinking about you all day.

Hundreds of these messages. Years of these messages. They stretched back to the day Sam had made his account. Almost the whole length of our four-and-a-half-year relationship.

I put my phone down and stared into the darkness, finally defeated.

Oddly enough, I didn't feel much like crying anymore.

I remember the next morning in numbers.

Ten photos of me and Sam in a collage frame. Two borrowed books. One silver heart necklace (the Jesus fish I kept). One class ring, Sam's. These were things he'd given me that I didn't want in my house anymore. After my parents left for work, I gathered it all and threw it in the passenger seat of my car.

One hundred dollars in store credit for returning my wedding dress. I printed a return label, stuffed the dress back in the box it came in, and dropped it off at the post office.

One hundred fifty dollars for my engagement ring. I drove from the post office to the jewelry store and sold it back to the jeweler who'd sold it to Sam months earlier.

Seven minutes between Sam's trailer and the bail bonds office. I picked up TJ and Ricky, who had very kindly offered to go with me. *So you don't have to be alone with that fucking pervert*, TJ said.

Two hundred dollars, mostly in wrinkled fives and ones, to pay the bond. I counted it out to a sour-faced woman in a turtleneck. In return, she handed me a stack of papers too thick for a staple. A thousand signatures later, after signing a million pages of terms and conditions I didn't bother to read, I was ushered to the waiting room.

TJ and Ricky sat across from me in mismatched chairs, scrolling through their phones and flipping through months-old gossip magazines. The blinds, floor, and even the air were dusty. I watched the pale particles float lazily in the gray light. Outside, rain puddles gathered in the street from another downpour.

Finally I saw Sam crossing the road. He was followed closely by a police officer, who kept a hand on Sam's shoulder. When they walked in, I realized Sam was in handcuffs.

The officer released the cuffs with a cold clink and left without saying a word. The sour-faced woman beckoned Sam to her desk to sign paperwork. When he put down the pen, she told him he was free to go.

Sam walked toward me. His shirt was wrinkled, his face greasy. He'd pulled his gritty hair into a haphazard ponytail. Though he wore flip-flops, his feet were as black as if he'd gone barefoot.

TJ and Ricky stood up, creating a wall between me and Sam. Even together, they were no match for him—the brothers were barely taller than me, and Sam towered over us all—but Sam stepped back anyway. I walked out the door.

Nobody spoke until we got to my car. Sam paused on the sidewalk, looking down at the picture frame in the backseat.

"Are you breaking up with me?" he asked.

I didn't respond.

Back at the trailer, I stayed in the car. The brothers got out, understanding I wanted a moment alone with Sam, but hung out on their porch, watchful.

Silently, I pushed Sam's things toward him. He leaned away, opened his door, and stepped out.

"Keep everything," he said.

"I don't want it."

He shut the door harder than necessary and came around to the driver's side.

I opened my door now. I took Sam's class ring from my cup holder and held it toward him, but he wouldn't open his hand. "Keep it," he said again. I could feel his anger growing.

Somehow, it didn't scare me anymore. I held the ring out, refusing to budge.

We'd never faced off like this. Sam glared at me for a moment, then tried a different approach. "Please just keep it," he repeated, gently this time. He stepped closer and softened his eyes. They begged sympathy, forgiveness. Something I was no longer willing to give. "Maybe one day you'll want to remember me."

I've never been prone to sudden rage, but that brought me to the edge of explosion. I yanked my car door shut with all my weight. Sam yanked it back open and grabbed my left hand. I jerked away.

"Where's your ring?" he asked in a deadly whisper.

I didn't reply.

Another shift. Sam's face broke. He sank down, shorts hiking up to his thighs, bare knees on wet pavement, and startled to sniffle.

"Please," he started, grabbing again for my hand. I jerked away once more.

"Quit it!" I said. "You're embarrassing yourself." Embarrassing me, I meant. We were at the edge of the driveway, right beside the road, and people were slowing down to look as they drove by. A neighbor was watching from her front porch.

I shifted my car into drive and let it slowly roll forward. Sam jumped up, startled, and stumbled backward.

"What are you doing?" he yelled.

"I'm leaving you," I yelled back. Inside my brain was a jumble of things I wanted to say, accusations and insults and all sorts of mean, furious words, but they fumbled and died on my tongue before I could get them out. Instead, I grabbed my car door and slammed it shut again.

I heard myself apologizing before hitting the gas. I didn't know if Sam heard me, but hoped he hadn't. He stood where I left him as I pulled onto the road.

Part TWO

23.

The going was slow, even slower around the curves. Dad watched the edge of the road, careful to keep us from pitching over the side of the mountain. A line of cars trailed behind. "If coal trucks can do it," he said, "so can a U-Haul." Mom gripped her seat belt with both hands.

Years had passed since Nanny had last heard from Concoal, and she hadn't seen a dime. A decade of holding out for nothing. Keeping up the house alone had been hard on her. She'd done all the mowing and weed eating; all the wood chopping and fire building. She'd vacuumed water out of the basement every time it rained. One day she woke up with an oak limb coming through her bedroom ceiling and decided she'd try her luck. The FOR SALE sign went beside the mailbox.

The house was on the market for more than a year before she got an interested buyer. He was a logger, and cared less about the house and coal than the forty acres of timber out back. Nanny sold for cheap. My parents and Erik and I helped her move to Tazewell, to a duplex on a sunny, level lot, in mid-May.

The weather on moving day was hot and exhausting. We heaved boxes and furniture around in a weird, sweaty silence. Interacting with Mom and Dad, even being in the same vehicle as them, was painful after years of tension. After almost marrying a man they hated.

My parents and I were strangers now. I realized this as I looked at them, actually looked them in the eyes, for the first time in what must have been three or four years. Mom, who had once loved Deliverance, never went anymore: the deeper I'd gotten into church, the more she'd pulled away. Dad was about to start a new job at a rock quarry. It came with a pay cut, but at least he had a job. The company that owned Knox Creek Mine had gone bankrupt, and the mine would be idled in July.

All this had barely registered before. Sam and God had taken up all the space in my mind so that everything else, even the lives of the people I'd lived with, had faded into the background of my consciousness.

A few days earlier, the night after bailing Sam out of jail, I'd cried in my parents' kitchen and apologized to them both. "You were right about him," I said.

Mom cried, too. "I wanted you to see who he really was," she said, "but I didn't want it to happen like *this*."

Me either.

Me either.

I don't remember much about the days following the breakup. The world carried on, kept spinning, kept going. I carried on, too, in a stumbling, shell-shocked way. I went to school. Went to work. Went to church and sobbed into my hair and hands for an hour.

Now I was moving Nanny out of her house, the house and holler of my favorite childhood memories, and I felt nothing at all. Not as we loaded the U-Haul. Not as we pulled out of the driveway. Not as I watched the top of the mountain disappear in the mirror, wondering if I would ever set foot in that once-magical place again.

Thank you, God, for not letting me marry that man. For the first few days, this was my prayer. I'd come so close to catastrophe.

Then the numb gratitude evaporated, and anger took its place. I'd come *so close* to catastrophe. All I could scream-pray was *Why? Why? Why?* Why had God allowed this to happen? Why had he allowed me to waste so much time with Sam? Why had he commanded me to *marry* him?

There were moments of no feeling, a disbelieving awareness that the biggest part of my life was no longer part of my life at all, save for a stream of daily emails I didn't reply to. Some were pleading. *Please talk to me. I miss you. I need you.* Some were threatening. *I'm not leaving you. I still love you, and I know we are meant to be together.*

Mostly I felt anger. Actually, "anger" was too soft a word. It was a waking, sleeping, brain-on-fire burn, a grief so raw and ragged that I could think of nothing else. My prayers were raging tantrums, silent screams that consisted only of emotion too fresh to articulate. It would have been a sin to say the words I wanted to say, anyway: *If you loved me, you wouldn't have let this happen.* I wasn't supposed to make accusations that questioned God's goodness.

And that made me angry, too.

If anger was a sin, then this feeling was absolutely profane. Yet I didn't try to not feel it. I didn't even ask forgiveness for it. Anger was my only illusion of power. Beyond that, it filled the hole of Sam's absence.

In my fury, I decided I needed answers. I suddenly had to know everything about whatever had gone on between Sam and that sixteen-year-old girl. I wanted the whole, real truth from the people who knew it: the pastors and leaders who had been at church when the police came, who'd been roped into the investigation.

That Wednesday, I went to church early and cornered anyone who might have answers.

Pastor Ron looked nervous when he saw me coming. "I can't say anything until this plays out in court," he said.

Pastor Will wouldn't talk either.

Or Jared.

Or Whitney.

When Pastor Sue saw me coming for her, she turned and walked out the door she'd just entered through.

I started to wonder what was going on. I wasn't asking for conjecture, only what everyone had seen and heard with their own eyes. What kinds of questions had the police asked? What had Sam done and said? What had happened to the girl?

Gossip usually carried through the church at the speed of light, but not this time. Nothing could have been louder than that silence. I realized I was the only one saying Sam's name. I was the only one talking about what he'd done. All of my questions were met with nervousness and deflection, as if the incident shouldn't be spoken of at all. As if such a thing couldn't happen within our church.

As if I shouldn't even acknowledge that it had.

It seemed counterintuitive to try to heal in the church where Sam had betrayed me, but I went anyway, and as often as possible. (Sam no longer attended Deliverance. I heard he still went to Lighthouse, though, so I stopped going there.) At first I was frustrated that everyone refused to talk about Sam, but that soon turned to gratitude. I, too, wanted to pretend I had never known him.

I threw all my energy into worship and prayer, trying to understand where it had all gone wrong. *Speak to me, Lord.* I thrust my arms high in the air and let the tears flow. Had I misunderstood God's will? Had I misinterpreted all the dreams, visions, and divine coincidences that urged me to get married? Was Sam's betrayal some kind of punishment for my sins?

For all my praying, there was no response.

I didn't give up. One night at youth group, I started speaking in tongues. That night, unlike most others, the tongues came easily.

I could barely hear my own voice over the worship music. The drumbeat echoed on the high, dark ceilings. For a moment I thought I felt the Holy Spirit in the room. I kept speaking. I was sure I was on the verge of hearing God.

Suddenly a stray note died in the air.

Jared walked away from the keyboard he was playing. He went for a standing microphone at center stage, grabbed it with both hands, and began speaking, then shouting, in tongues. The drummer let the beat die. Jared's voice jarred the now-silent room.

I opened my eyes a sliver. Jared's eyes were shadowed. Troubled. It was as though he'd seen something he didn't want to, some demon or devil lurking among the crowd.

He stopped speaking and locked eyes with a girl maybe eleven or twelve years old in the third row. I'd never seen her at our church before. Jared raised an arm and pointed at her, hand trembling.

"God can free you!" he shouted. He leaned into the microphone, finger trained on the girl. Her eyes were wide, but Jared's were wider, burning with unidentifiable emotion.

"You can't keep living in sin!" There was an intensity in his voice that I rarely heard even in church. "You can't keep living in evil!"

The girl went white.

Jared kept pointing, breathing hard into the microphone. It was the only sound in the room. The rest of us were silent, on edge. The air seemed as if it might shatter.

We heard Jared inhale as he opened up his mouth to speak. He opened his hand palm-first and screamed, "I command Satan to BE GONE FROM YOU!" He shoved at the air in the girl's direction.

Her eyes rolled back in her head. She collapsed face-first into the folding chair in front of her.

The sickening sound of dead weight hitting metal, then concrete. The awkward crash of the chair. Screams, then a flurry of motion.

Pastor Will and the other adults ran to the girl. We rolled her onto her back. Blood gushed down her face, into her hair, onto her shirt. She'd bitten through her lower lip during the fall. Someone dialed 911.

Jared remained onstage, back to speaking in tongues. He looked down at us as we tried to stop the bleeding with paper towels.

The girl came to before the ambulance arrived. She was terrified, having no sense of where she was or any recollection of coming to church that night. She'd wet herself, too, and started crying when she saw the dark spot on her jeans. She cried harder as she was placed on a stretcher and wheeled out of the church.

I held the door for the paramedics. The flashing red lights colored the dark sky long after the ambulance was out of sight.

When I rejoined the youth group, the room was unsettled. Everyone was tense. Only Jared, who was now sitting quietly in the front row, Bible open on his lap, seemed unbothered.

Pastor Will tried to carry on the service as normal, but he looked more than a little shaken himself. "Let's pray really quick for, uh . . . let's pray for . . . let's pray she'll be okay."

He didn't even know the girl's name.

I bowed my head. *Lord,* I said quietly, *I hope that girl is all right.* For some reason it felt wrong to pray out loud, even in a whisper, so I prayed silently. *Make sure she's all right.* That still felt wrong.

I'd seen hundreds of people collapse as they cried out to God, but never an unsuspecting preteen during her first visit at an unfamiliar church. I didn't understand what had happened. Had she been exorcised of a demon, or simply overwhelmed by the Holy Spirit?

Whatever it was was certainly proof of God's power.

But why had he done that to her?

She was a child, too young to be "living in evil" like Jared had accused. Nothing warranted the embarrassment of being called out, then *passing out*, in front of a crowd of strangers. Nothing warranted blood or pain or a hospital visit.

Why did you do that, Lord?

Utter silence. Another unanswered question.

The more time I spent in church, it seemed, the less I understood God.

24.

There was a heat wave in June. Down the plaza from Subway, the Dollar General's air conditioner conked out. Since Timbo, the manager, kept making empty promises to fix it, his sweaty, red-faced employees made regular trips over to Subway to get a few minutes of relief.

"Timbo! When are you gonna get that goddamned A/C fixed?" Crystal would yell. Lately Timbo had been lurking around our back door when Crystal was on shift. "Your cashiers are spending more time over here than there."

"Any day now," he'd say with a big lying smile. Every one of his teeth had rotted into mottled black stumps.

I was glad Timbo only came prowling when Crystal was around. He had beady black eyes, a raspy voice, and a hair-raising squeal of a laugh that set me on edge every time he poked his head through the back door.

For the past few weeks, ever since Timbo had started hanging around, Crystal had acted off. She'd run to the bathroom after their encounters, then come back out with her usual nervous energy all but gone. She'd move and talk so slowly it seemed as if she might fall asleep, and was somehow even more unfocused and forgetful than before.

Occasionally, though, her mood did a one-eighty. Then she became absolutely, inconsolably enraged. It was a ten-alarm fury that I'd never seen in her, or anyone, before. Little things like the phone ringing or the receipt printer jamming up could send her into a screaming, cussing, crying fit. Even if there were customers out front, she'd tear through the prep room in a holy rage, banging her fists on the walls and tables, shouting a mile-long string of obscenities, grabbing whatever was in reach and throwing it as hard as she could across the room. Then she'd fall against the wall, collapse to the floor, and sob wet black streaks down her face. After a while she'd calm down and apologize on repeat before disappearing into the bathroom or out back by the dumpster.

Or next door to the Dollar General.

I figured out what was happening before I got a glimpse of the pills in her purse one day. Surely my coworkers knew, too, but we never talked about it to Crystal or each other. None of us knew what to say. We all just worked around her in silence, tiptoeing around her unpredictable moods.

Those scorching few weeks unsettled everyone, not just Crystal. Jeremy got into a fistfight with his housemate that got them both evicted. Trevor brawled with his girlfriend and came to work with blood still dripping from his nose. There were more fights between shoppers up and down the plaza, at the grocery store and the Dollar General and right out in the middle of the parking lot. The police were on constant patrol.

I didn't know if it was the heat, the atmospheric tension that had stoked everyone's temper, or the fact of my breakup—although it was probably all three—but I, too, was unusually on edge, as if I had ants in my blood. I was horrified that I'd almost married a predator, disoriented by how quickly my life had fallen apart, and scared that I didn't know what the future looked like anymore. I couldn't delineate those emotions, though. Anger was the easiest thing to call them, and the easiest thing to feel.

As the weeks passed, my anger manifested as a reckless need for revenge. One day I bleached my hair blonde, knowing Sam liked my natural brunette. I bought shorts and tank tops and other clothes he would have been shocked to see me wear. I started rimming my eyes in dramatic black liner and dusting my cheeks with shimmery blush.

Then I started talking to another man.

His name was Chandler. He messaged me on Facebook after seeing my relationship status change. I don't remember anything about our conversations, or what was going through my head when I agreed to go on a date so soon after my breakup, especially with someone who was so unlike me. Chandler told me he was not at all religious. And even though I knew I could never be in a relationship with an atheist, I uploaded a photo of us—heads together, smiling—to Facebook the morning after our date. I wanted Sam to see that I didn't belong to him anymore.

Next Sunday, I got odd looks at church. Most people didn't know that I'd broken up with Sam. The few who did knew why, and kept the secret well.

"So this new guy," Pastor Ron's wife said to me. "Is he a Christian?"

I hesitated, embarrassed by Chandler's apostasy, but decided not to lie. "Not really."

She pressed her glossy lips into a thin flat line. "Well, honey, it will never work out then."

I bristled a little, but I already knew that. I knew it before Chandler told me he was an atheist. I knew before he hugged me and slid his hand down to my lower back, and before he sat so close to me on the lakeshore that our thighs touched, and before we waded into chest-deep water and he slipped his thumbs under the waistband of my new bikini bottoms. "Wrap your legs around me," he'd said breathlessly, head barely bobbing above the surface. I'd draped my arms around his shoulders and nervously kicked my legs back instead, floating on my stomach, to keep plenty of space between our submerged bodies.

Of course it wouldn't work out. I was just a few weeks out of a four-and-a-half-year relationship. I didn't want to date Chandler. I didn't want to date *anyone*. I just wanted—*needed*—to feel wanted.

Still, when Chandler invited me back to his apartment that evening, I nervously declined. "I don't believe in *that* before marriage," I mumbled, too timid to say the word "sex" aloud.

He gave me a strange look. I quoted some Bible verses to justify my position. "It's a sin," I tried to explain. "I'd feel guilty."

"The concept of sin is a weapon," Chandler said. He sounded as if he'd given this a lot of thought. "Sin justifies punishment. Punishment creates fear. When people are afraid, they can be controlled. And when they're controlled, they're oppressed."

"I'm not oppressed," I replied.

He said nothing for a while. We sat in the sand, watching the treetops turn golden in the June sunset. "I don't get why you'd believe in a God that makes you feel guilty about every little thing."

"I *don't* feel guilty about everything," I said.

That was a lie. I felt guilty about Sam's crime, as if it were somehow my fault. I felt guilty for leaving Sam. I felt guilty for going on a date with someone who wasn't him, and even guiltier for going on a date with a non-Christian. I felt guilty for having a body that could be touched and looked at. The guilt was so strong that it almost felt like fear. As the lake air cooled, I became electrically aware of my bare thighs and shoulders. So many goose bumps. So much flesh on display. The weight in my chest swelled until I finally jumped up and said I had to go.

The drive home was dark. I turned up the radio, which was tuned to Christian rock, to fill the silence, frustrated at something I couldn't identify.

Guilt had always been necessary to maintain the integrity of my faith: It guided my conscience between good and bad, right and wrong, sin and righteousness. Guilt was the mouthpiece of the still small voice inside my head. Without guilt, how could I know I was living within—or outside—God's will?

Chandler was right, though. Guilt had made me afraid of God. Of *life*. It kept me on high alert, hyperaware of any potential sin and its infinite consequences. Guilt followed me everywhere, a thundercloud of punishment, lightning bolt ready to strike at any moment.

A few weeks later, on a hot Wednesday evening in early July, I found myself speeding around mountain curves faster than I wanted, trying to keep up with the yellow Camaro in front of me.

Lucas was a pastor's son. I'd seen him play guitar a couple times at Deliverance, which was where we'd met. A week earlier, he had asked for my number after service. Because I'd just told Chandler I couldn't see him again, and because I didn't know how to be alone, I gave it to him.

Most Wednesdays and Sundays, Lucas led worship at his father's church. That was where we were headed for our first date. The church was an old one-room building on a precariously steep mountainside. I parked behind Lucas's car and double-checked my emergency brake before stepping out. He'd warned me that service could go on for hours and hours, and that I ought to drive myself if I didn't want to stay late into the night.

I didn't know much about Lucas. He was a little older than me. Had never been to college. Christian, of course. (Pastor Ron's wife would be pleased.) I sensed he wasn't too strict about it, though. He had a breezy personality and a cherry-red electric guitar, and he played it with what I suspected was a passion more for good music and less for God. Once after service I'd heard him picking out a Led Zeppelin song. And when I'd met up with him in a grocery store parking lot half an hour earlier, he'd walked up and hugged me tight, wrapping me up in a confident, sensual embrace that forced our bodies together.

I tensed, but let it happen. Let it linger.

We walked up to the little church. Lucas held the door open and followed me inside. The single room had no windows and was lit only by wall sconces. As my eyes adjusted, I made out a few figures in the pews nearest me. There were four or five women, all with bare faces, long denim skirts, and hair that was either braided to their knees or swept up in big swirling buns.

"I didn't know you were Apostolic," I whispered to Lucas. Apostolics are some of the most fundamental evangelicals: Outward displays of modesty are requirements, not suggestions. Especially for women.

"Welcome, welcome, welcome!" said a woman in the back pew.

She jumped up and hurried over, then looked me up and down. "Lucas told me he was bringing a girl."

"Emilee, this is my mom. Mom, Emilee," Lucas introduced us.

His mother shook my hand with a forceful grip and stared down at my jeans, which had holes in the knees. She gave Lucas a look I couldn't decipher, then insisted I sit beside her for service.

Lucas joined his dad and another woman onstage for worship. He strummed a few notes on an acoustic guitar—his electric one was nowhere in sight—and the woman beside him started singing. The hymn started out slow and reverent but quickly picked up. Lucas squinted his eyes and strummed faster. Soon he was scraping at the strings so hard I wondered if they would break.

The woman's voice rose, mirroring the guitar. Her words blended from English to the unrecognizable. In between tongues she wailed "Jesus, Jesus, Jesus." Lucas's father and mother and all the other long-haired women in the pews had descended into worship, lifting their arms up high, shouting and crying and jumping to the frenetic beat of the wild, wordless song.

Trying to blend in, I closed my eyes and raised my arms. It was impossible to concentrate. I was too aware of the holes in my jeans, my heavy-handed eyeliner, and my bright blonde hair.

Apparently everyone else was aware, too. "Let us pray for you, sweetie," Lucas's mom yelled above the music. She grabbed me by the wrist and pulled me toward the altar. I followed her lead, worried it would be rude to resist, but tried to shoot Lucas a "help me" look.

In an instant I was surrounded by the rest of the congregation. They laid their hands all over me, praying loudly for God to save my soul.

I'm already saved, I thought angrily.

But just a few short months earlier, I too would have judged someone who looked like me. If a bleached blonde in ripped jeans and heavy makeup had walked into my church, I would have assumed her faith to be nonexistent at worst or halfhearted at best. After all, if your outward appearance didn't reflect your inward piety, how could you call yourself a true Christian?

That thought would have passed through my brain unchallenged anytime before, but at that moment I paused on it. How silly, I realized, to judge someone's faith by their hair, face, and clothes. I looked different now, but I was still saved. I still had faith.

Sort of.

Over the past few weeks, my idea of God had morphed into something unfamiliar, something I couldn't quite visualize or explain. The God who had once thrilled me and terrified me, who'd given me visions and dreams and overwhelmed me with his heavy spirit and spoken to me in loud, powerful voices, seemed less real to me now. Despite my raging prayers and questions and a hundred thousand "whys," God had not spoken to me once. Not in a still small voice, not in big booming shouts. Not through visions or verses or songs or dreams.

For years, I'd had an intimate and constant stream of communication with God. Now he was silent, and I was mad, and all the microscopic cracks in my faith, all the quiet doubts and fears, were growing.

Still, I pressed on. I went through the motions of worshipping. I closed my eyes and tried to pray. I tried to force any old feeling of devotion. I tried to make out the whisper of God's voice in the gaping silence.

As if on cue, Lucas's mom pulled my arm high into the air as if she were announcing a victory. She cried, "Speak to her, Lord, speak to her!" then dropped to her knees. She stretched out her arms and grasped at the air, praying in intercession for the salvation I already possessed.

I stretched my arms out, too, but for a different reason. I didn't need salvation. I just needed a word. A sign. A feeling. Anything to prove that God was still there, still listening to me.

I stretched my arms out, grasping for any crumb at all.

25.

"Hey, where's your ring?"

Jeremy sat on the counter in front of the microwave. He was supposed to be finishing up the day's dishes.

"Sold it," I said. I was crouched in front of the open oven, steel wool in one hand, degreaser in the other. Ten minutes of spraying and scrubbing had barely made a difference on the greasy orange glass.

"Sold it?" Jeremy echoed. "Ain't you supposed to be getting married?"

I sighed. Sam had gone to jail only two months earlier, but it felt like a lifetime ago. "Not anymore."

"Well, shit," Jeremy said. "What happened?"

I was surprised by Jeremy's attentiveness, that he'd ever even noticed my engagement ring in the first place, let alone that I wasn't wearing it anymore. Even when he wasn't high, he was usually off in his own world, humming or daydreaming or doodling on the back of the notepad we used for catering orders.

"Sam went to jail," I said, still scrubbing. "For child porn."

I was too embarrassed to disclose that fact to most people, but for some reason I told Jeremy without hesitation.

His mouth hung open. "You're shitting me."

"I wish."

Jeremy's face hardened. He balled up the dishrag in his fist and squeezed. "I fucking hate motherfucking pedos, man. Scum of the earth," he mumbled. I'd never seen him look so serious. After a moment his voice got softer, and his eyes followed. "I hate that that happened to you."

"Yeah. Me, too." I started to say something about how it was part of God's plan, but didn't. I'd heard that phrase a thousand times over the years: *God uses all things for your good.* I wasn't sure I still believed that. In the dark reverence of a church sanctuary, it was easy to glorify pain, assign it a divine purpose. I was trying to cling to the idea that there was a reason for my hurt and heartbreak, that I was becoming stronger, but I wasn't convinced. So I said nothing and kept scrubbing.

Jeremy still seemed bothered. He sat on the counter and swung his legs, passing the balled-up dishcloth from one hand to the other, while he stared out the storefront window into the dark. It wasn't like him to be so quiet. Finally I asked what was on his mind.

"There's somewhere I wanna take you," he said.

"Where?" I asked.

"It's a surprise," he said, hopping down from the counter with a clunk. He always wore steel-toed boots to work. "It'll be fun. Let's hurry up and get out of here."

And for the first time ever, Jeremy washed all the dishes without my prompting.

After we locked up, we headed toward the parking lot. It was empty except for our cars. My old Subaru was nothing to look at, but Jeremy's Honda was comically hideous. Every surface—hood, roof, trunk, and doors—was banged and scratched and dented, as if someone had beaten the car with a baseball bat. It was spray-painted matte black, but the patchier spots revealed the original silver underneath. The hubcaps were missing. The tires were so bald that the wires peeked through. The back windshield was busted out and covered in purple Saran wrap.

"I call her the Baby Car," Jeremy said. He ducked through the driver's side window feetfirst, explaining that the door was permanently jammed. "Because she's so tiny." His knees splayed to each side of the steering wheel. "Death trap" was the phrase that came to mind, but I stooped inside anyway.

Jeremy stuck the key in the ignition. Before he turned it, he warned me to cover my ears, saying something about a straight pipe, which meant nothing to me. I cupped my hands over my ears. He turned the key. The engine came to life with a violent shudder and monstrous ripping roar that made me jump in my seat. Jeremy grinned so big I could see all of his teeth. The Baby Car quaked as it idled, and when he shifted into first gear, it gave an explosive lurch forward.

"Where's the seat belt?" I yelled over the noise.

"What?" Jeremy yelled back.

"SEAT BELT!"

Jeremy grinned bigger.

We rolled out of the parking lot and onto the road. When Jeremy hit the gas, the car somehow got louder. He saw the look on my face and threw his head back in a laugh I couldn't hear.

The sun was long set and the town was dead, but I still felt conspicuous in that ugly, blaring hunk of metal. A couple months earlier it would have been unthinkable for me to be in a car alone with a man other than my fiancé. Now I was tearing through the night at full volume and full speed—Jeremy hit the highway doing eighty—and no one knew where I was or what I was doing. I had no one to answer to. No one to make me feel guilty and dirty and sinful for having a male for a friend or riding in his car. Liberation seized my heart. I felt free and wild and terribly strange, doing something that would have once brought great consequences but now brought none at all.

We passed Lighthouse, which I hadn't been to since the breakup, and then onto a stretch of empty highway. Far from houses and people now, Jeremy flipped a switch on the floorboard and brought the subwoofers in the trunk to life. The mirrors and dashboard vibrated. I could feel the bass in the pulps of my teeth.

Jeremy hadn't stopped smiling. "HAVING FUN YET?" he yelled. I nodded and felt myself smiling, too.

Jeremy got off at the next exit and headed toward the lake. The road was narrow and winding and he took the curves way too fast, but I couldn't bring myself to feel afraid. I let my long hair out of its modest bun. It whipped around in the rush of air, tangling into yellow knots, and I stuck my head out the window to let the cool wind assault my face.

Soon I started smelling water and fish. Jeremy slowed down when he hit a gravel road. He parked close to the lakeshore, right by the dock. When he cut the engine, the silence was so sudden and loud that my ears rang. Without the car's vibrations to dictate my heartbeat, my chest felt hollowed out, abruptly and achingly empty.

For a while neither of us spoke. Slowly the frogs, which had been startled to silence by the noise, started peeping again. The black lake water lapped softly at the grassy shore. It was a cloudless night.

"Let's look at the stars," Jeremy whispered, climbing from his seat to the hood.

We reclined against the windshield and looked up at the sky. It was still weird to be in such proximity to someone who wasn't Sam, so I gave Jeremy a wide berth, scooting as far as I could to the opposite side of the hood. The stars above us were as bright as the moon. Jeremy pointed out constellations. He traced them slowly with a tattooed finger. I followed along with my eyes.

"What else do you think's out there?" he asked after a while.

"What do you mean?" I said. "Like aliens?"

"No," he said. "Like God."

"Oh." That caught me off guard. I hesitated. "Why do you ask?"

Jeremy put both hands behind his head. His eyes were far away, beyond the sky.

"You seem like you would know," he said. He turned his face to me after a moment, to the Jesus fish necklace resting on my chest. Even though it was a gift from Sam, I couldn't bear to part with it.

Jeremy went on. "I think about it a lot. I mean, there's gotta be something, right? The universe is so big and we're so small . . ." He trailed off into deeper thought. "There's gotta be something," he said again finally. "Something bigger than us. I just don't know what it is."

I wasn't sure how to respond. I hadn't been expecting Jeremy—Jeremy, who was always high and giggly and lost in some faraway dreamworld—to pose a serious theological question. How did I explain God, creator and keeper of the universe? How did I explain God at all?

Despite a lifetime of church, I'd only ever had an abstract understanding of God. And now, after everything that had happened, after weeks of pain and fury and unanswered questions and prayers, I was completely unsure of who he was, what his role was in my life or anyone else's.

"There's something," I affirmed very slowly. "But I'm not sure what it is either."

It was the first time I'd ever doubted God's existence aloud.

I half expected a lightning bolt to strike me dead that instant.

But the cloudless sky stayed dark and quiet, and my blasphemy went unpunished. Jeremy laughed a little.

"I figured you'd give me a whole damn sermon," he said. He scooted a hair closer to me. "Maybe you're finally loosening up after all."

I held my breath nervously, the way I always did when my coworkers got too close. It was a knee-jerk reaction to keep from breathing in their sin. An *absurd* reaction, I realized then. I exhaled and then inhaled again, long and slow, as if to prove to myself that nothing bad was going to happen by breathing the same air as Jeremy.

The cool lake air filled my lungs. It was fishy and salty, sweet and biting. There was another smell, too, fainter—weed and old carpet, engine oil and cherry air freshener. The scent of Jeremy's car and clothes. It was oddly soothing. I wanted to bottle it up. Take it home. Maybe even wear it myself.

I scooted an inch closer to Jeremy and breathed in deeply once more.

A few days later after a Wednesday night youth service, I went up to Pastor Will and asked for prayer.

"I need to hear from God," I said vaguely. That was nowhere near the extent of what I really needed.

Since I'd admitted my doubt to Jeremy, it had grown and grown and grown, taking up more and more space in my mind until I hadn't been able to think about anything else. Now it was unrestrained, a wild, creeping thing.

That Wednesday night prayer request was a desperate attempt to find something to still believe in. A God who was good in spite of all the terrors he inspired. A God who, in his incomprehensible wisdom, had orchestrated my life down to the very second, good parts and bad, for some great divine purpose. A God who was still in control.

Beneath that, and perhaps more urgently, I was searching for a connection to who I'd been just a couple months earlier. I felt severed from the core of what I'd unconsciously started to think of as my "old life," which had revolved entirely around Sam and God. Without them, who *was* I?

Pastor Will stood in front of me and laid a hand on my head. Jared and Whitney and a few other youth group volunteers I was friends with circled around me, laying hands across my back and shoulders. At first their prayers were whispers, delicate and barely audible, but they grew louder with each sentence, until I was surrounded by half a dozen shouting voices commanding a renewal of the Holy Spirit inside me.

While the prayers flowed, I squeezed my eyes shut and tried to talk to God. I tried to force my own prayer, but my mind remained empty, as if I'd forgotten how to speak English. Surrounded by the most faithful people I knew, I felt more aware than ever that my own faith was beyond retrieval. Frustration rolled over me in a hot wave. I started to cry.

"Thank you, Father, for remaining steadfast in Emilee's life." Pastor Will mistook my tears as a sign that God was working inside me. "Even when she can't hear you, I pray she always knows you're there."

The voices descended into a chorus of "amens" and the hands fell away. Whitney hugged me. Jared offered me a tissue.

"It's going to be okay. God is always with you," Whitney said. She paused, then spoke again more quietly. "I'm sure things have been hard lately."

The subtle allusion to the breakup was more than anybody else had given me. Surprised, I could only nod.

"Sometimes it's hard to hear God when you're living outside his will," Jared added. I sat down on the stage and wiped my face. He and Whitney sat down on either side of me. Pastor Will and my other friends took seats in the front row. "It's like a check-engine light. Except instead of a neon sign, you feel overwhelming silence. You feel so, so far away from God. That's because he's trying to get your attention."

I nodded at Jared. Overwhelming silence was *exactly* what I felt. It was an awfully cruel way to get someone's attention, I thought. Yet I couldn't say it hadn't worked: I'd been thinking about God—raging at, pleading with, and doubting him—nonstop. It was just like when Sam gave me the silent treatment. I would stay on edge for days, worrying about what I'd done wrong and how to fix it. How to be better next time so I wouldn't have to face the torturous silence again.

"What am I doing wrong?" I asked Jared.

"You just have to keep praying until God tells you," Jared said. "And in the meantime, you have to examine your life. Are there areas you've been disobedient? Has God told you to do something, but you've defied him?"

"He hasn't talked to me at all lately," I said. I was embarrassed to admit that, worried it revealed my lack of faith.

Jared considered this for a moment. "Your soul is volatile right now," he finally said in a pensive voice. I looked over at him. He was gazing toward the back of the room, eyes growing distant.

I knew this look. It always came over him when God was revealing some kind of wisdom or knowledge. It was the look he'd had weeks earlier when exorcising evil out of the preteen girl.

After another moment, Jared turned to me suddenly. A change had fallen over his face. It was as if he were gone and somebody else were behind his eyes.

Jared opened his mouth slowly, then issued his command.

"God will return to you when you return to Sam."

I said nothing.

I could think of nothing to say.

It was one of those moments in which time moves both fast and slow. I was shocked first by hearing Sam's name aloud—hearing someone within those church walls acknowledging that he'd actually existed—and then at the actual statement itself. How could Jared suggest such a thing? He knew about the sixteen-year-old girl. He knew what Sam had done, all the secrets and lies. He'd been present for the entire police investigation. He knew more than he would ever tell me.

How could he suggest I go back to Sam?

How could God?

I didn't know whether Jared was speaking as himself, or if God was speaking through Jared, or if I even still believed God spoke through people. None of that mattered, though. What mattered was this idea that my cold, dead faith could only be renewed by returning to God's will. Which meant—if Jared could be believed—marrying a man who had preyed on me, controlled me, lied to me, cheated on me. Hurt me beyond reckoning, or forgiveness.

"I don't know if that's what God wants," Whitney protested softly, speaking more to Jared than to me. He cut his eyes at her and she fell silent.

For a few miserable seconds, I waited for someone else to speak. I waited for someone to suggest a more reasonable solution to regaining my faith. Pastor Will and my friends only watched wordlessly, gauging my reaction, and I realized that this was the consensus: My faith was suffering because I hadn't married the man God had told me to.

Suddenly I felt very far from myself. I felt I didn't know this place, these people. I felt I'd never really known them. Just as I had never really known Sam.

I couldn't go back to him. Not running, not walking, not crawling. I couldn't. I wouldn't. I was too far gone now, too uncontrollable, changed on the outside and changing on the inside in ways I couldn't explain.

I was changed enough, at least, to not even consider the option.

26.

Twelve o'clock, the lunch rush. When I walked into work, there was a line to the door. Stacey, who was supposed to have the day off, was standing at the register.

"What are you doing here?" I asked as I clocked in.

Stacey gestured toward Angie in the back.

Angie never visited the store in the middle of the day. Laid out on her office desk was a spread of cash, a stack of receipts, and a calculator. She punched at it with a hard face, then looked up at me.

"Has the register been short at night?" she asked.

"Sometimes," I said slowly, worried she was going to accuse me of stealing. "But I always call Chris when it's off. She says she'll figure it out in the morning."

"Mm-hmm." Angie nodded, looking down at the bills in front of her. "That explains it."

Angie told me what had happened. That morning, Shayla, one of my coworkers, found Crystal crying on the floor. Crystal jumped up and disappeared. When she returned an hour later, she was stumbling, slurring her words. A customer came in and ordered a salad. Crystal grabbed a salad bowl and a handful of lettuce. Eyes closed and hands shaking, she dropped the lettuce onto the floor.

That was when Shayla called Stacey. Stacey came in and noticed cash was missing from the register. That was when Stacey called Angie.

Angie came right away. She walked in, took one look at Crystal, and made her go sit in the prep room out of the customers' sight. Then Angie counted the register, found it was short, and counted the safe under the register. That was where we kept large bills and nightly deposits. Only Angie and Crystal had a key to it.

It was short by four hundred dollars.

Angie promised to not call the police if Crystal returned the money. But the money was already spent, and Crystal wouldn't say what she'd spent it on.

Angie knew, though. We all knew.

So Angie fired her on the spot. Crystal flew into one of her rages—I could see where she'd thrown some utensils onto the floor and nobody had picked them up—and Angie called the cops.

Before they arrived, though, Crystal went tearing through the dining room, shouting and crying and swearing in front of a line of customers, then out the door. She stumbled to the end of the parking lot, then started down the road.

A silent air of sadness, and a fainter one of guilt, hung over Subway for the rest of that day and several after. Weeks earlier, when Crystal had started acting strange, we all knew what was going on. We knew but didn't want to believe it, didn't want to acknowledge it aloud, because the truth was hard and terrible. Crystal had four kids to take care of and a job she needed to keep. She'd been to prison for this kind of thing before. So we hoped it wasn't true, even though we all knew it was.

And we'd done nothing about it. Just watched her spiral, crash, and burn.

But what could we have done? Staged an intervention? Tried to make her stop?

I didn't know. I wish I'd known. I wondered how far she'd made it down the road. Where she was headed. Where she'd ended up.

It was sad not having Crystal around, but I didn't miss her chaos. Angie appointed Stacey our new manager. From the start, she kept the store running more smoothly than Crystal ever had. Plus she did it without all the crying and screaming.

Stacey was short and blonde and had a gritty smoker's laugh. She was the single mom of two teenage boys, and like Crystal she'd been to prison once, although I never knew what for. Whatever she'd done in her past seemed to haunt her. Every time a customer came in stumbling or jittery or with raw red sores on their arms and faces, Stacey would give them a look that encompassed disapproval, pity, and unease, as if she recognized her past self in their glazed eyes and feared returning to it.

Otherwise, she was rarely serious. She put up with Jeremy's antics and even joined in on them. On slow days they'd run around the store playing hide-and-seek tag or making Santa beards with the stiff white soap bubbles that floated on top of the dishwater.

One slow afternoon, Jeremy challenged Stacey to a napkin-throwing contest. He dragged a big black trash can to the middle of the dining room. He and Stacey grabbed napkins from the dispenser by the cash register, balled them up tight, and aimed.

"Wait! Let me try," I said. They both looked surprised. I had only ever watched their games from the sidelines, never joined in.

Stacey threw first and missed. Jeremy threw next and missed. I threw last. My napkin ball hit the lip of the trash can, then unexpectedly bounced in.

"AYYYYYYE!" Jeremy yelled.

"Michael Jordan!" Stacey said at the same time.

They both offered high fives. My palms met theirs, and for the first time I felt as if I belonged.

For months I'd worked mostly night shifts, and most of those I'd worked with Jeremy. He was a slow worker when he actually did his work: Even though Subway closed at nine, we usually didn't finish cleaning up until after ten. The more we worked together, though, the less I cared. He'd blast his music over the stereo, introducing me to artists I'd heard of but never allowed myself to listen to: Pearl Jam, Matchbox Twenty, Eminem. I reveled in their secularity, in their divergence from the stale Christian rock I was so used to. Even the most tedious parts of our job went by faster when we shared the language of music.

Jeremy and I had so much fun at work that it became hard to say goodbye. After locking up, we'd walk to the red caboose at the playground down the street, then climb through the broken window and hang out inside. Or we'd sit on the bridge near the soccer field and toss rocks into the creek below. Or we'd hop in the Baby Car and go riding, taking the back roads to avoid the town cops, who were always pulling Jeremy over for his earsplitting exhaust.

The lake was where we usually ended up. It was my favorite place and Jeremy's, too. We were the only ones out there that late, all but for a handful of night fishers, who bobbed along silently, invisible except for the yellow specks of their lanterns. The only other light came from the moon.

Sometimes we sat on the dock. Sometimes we sat on the shore and let the black water lap at our toes. Sometimes we wandered way back into the woods, arms outstretched, feeling our way through the trees and the night.

And we often came back during the day. When we had the same day off work we were almost always out by the water, walking the overgrown trail that circled the lake or stretched out on the grassy levee that held it in. An old maple tree stood by the water's edge. Jeremy and I carved our initials into its trunk one morning while the wood was damp from the previous night's rain.

"That's the trick," Jeremy said, adjusting my grip on his pocketknife. He put my thumb near the tip of the blade and guided my hand with his own. "You gotta wait till the wood's soft, and you gotta make little cuts. No big, broad chunks. Just slow . . . and . . . steady."

I didn't know what I was doing or why I was doing it. Why I rode around in that loud car, or stayed out late with a boy who smelled like weed and sunshine, or followed him into the forest in the pitch-black of night, or carved my initials beneath his on a tree. It was reckless, at least by my standards.

My old standards, that is. A few months earlier, I avoided spontaneity and anything that even hinted at the possibility of sin. Now I never knew where Jeremy and I would end up or what we'd get into, only that we'd be out way too late and long.

I craved those moments more than anything.

And I craved Jeremy, too. Loose and wild in the world, he was bound to nothing and no one. He surfed couches and slept under the stars. He collected terrible tattoos from his friends' basements and the county jail. He lived life not in the moment but in the second.

"I'm not scared of anything," he told me once. We'd hiked to the top of a mountain and were sitting on the rocky ledge of an overlook.

"Why?" I asked, looking out over the valley below.

"Why not?" Jeremy said. "I got nothing to lose." He swung his feet carelessly, as if there weren't a hundred-yard drop beneath us.

That was why I liked him. Why I couldn't get enough of him. Jeremy was not cautious or careful or reverent. He was the opposite of everything I'd ever known, my old self included.

27.

"In. Hold. Out." Jeremy sucked in a big gulp of air, held it for a second, then exhaled loudly. His chest rose and fell dramatically, the motions exaggerated, but I tried to mimic them exactly.

When the hot, dry smoke scorched my throat and lungs, I couldn't resist a cough. I passed the joint back to Jeremy and bent forward, hacking at the grass.

Once upon a time, I'd unironically called weed "the devil's lettuce," convinced that it was contrived by Satan himself to lure lost souls into addiction and suffering and the most unspeakable, unimaginable sin. A portal straight to hell. That was ridiculous to me now, sitting there in the grass and puffing with decreasing difficulty on the joint Jeremy had rolled for me. I told Jeremy and he laughed and I laughed and we laughed together until we were howling, and I got so lightheaded that I had to lie back, and the light breaking through the canopy of tree leaves above me sparkled like stars.

I spent every day with Jeremy. At work and off work, we were inseparable. We pushed a hundred on the highway and kept the back roads hot, drifting through every mountain curve. We swam in the river, smoked by the lake. One night we parked near the dock. "Listen to the silence," Jeremy whispered. "You can hear the earth breathe."

I could. I was spellbound by the pulse of the night, and the tender heart beating next to mine. I leaned into Jeremy, nuzzling my head into his neck. He put a hand on my cheek and pulled my face to his. His lips were soft and warm, working gently and urgently against mine. I kissed back, pressing myself into him desperately, releasing something that had been building for months.

And then we were tumbling on top of each other in a scramble to the backseat. Our clothes seemed to fall off without either of us making an effort to remove them. I had a flash of a thought, a recognition of imminent sin, but it evaporated before the guilt went to my head, and didn't return.

We took up every inch of the cramped backseat. We breathed into each other's hair, stuck to each other's skin. We were so wrapped up in the miracle of us that we didn't hear a car park nearby. Its headlights blazed into the backseat. Jeremy rolled onto the floor and I flattened myself against him. We stayed low, giggling and sweating, as car doors slammed. Footsteps crunched in the gravel. My heart pounded against Jeremy's. The footsteps passed within inches of our heads, then continued on toward the dock until we couldn't hear them anymore. Once we were safe, we released our breath in an explosion of giggles.

The guilt I expected after never came. Neither did the lightning bolt of punishment or any other consequences I'd been taught to fear. If Pastor Ron could be believed, my soul was now eternally and inextricably tied to Jeremy's.

I decided I was fine with that.

For the rest of the summer, the world was made of me and Jeremy and nothing else. It was us, only us, on foggy early mornings; hot, lazy afternoons; nights so late that Jeremy's car was the only one on the road, unless Dad hopped in his truck and came looking for me.

He was worried and so was Mom. I never told them what I was doing or whom I was with, but I knew they knew. They gave me anxious, bewildered looks, which I was familiar with but in an entirely different context. In early spring they'd watched me spend every free moment in church and with Sam. Now, in late summer, they watched me spend all my time with *that stoner kid.* I jumped from one bad influence to another in just a matter of months. It was a drastic change in a very short amount of time.

One morning I took off without telling Mom or Dad where I was going. I ignored their phone calls all day, and I would have stayed gone longer if I hadn't remembered last second that I was scheduled to work that night. Already late for my shift, I darted home just long enough to grab my uniform. I'd been sitting in a haze of smoke for hours, and the smell of weed was in my clothes and hair.

Mom was watching for me at the door. "I don't know who you are anymore," she said as I pushed past her.

I didn't reply. I didn't know either.

For months I had simmered. Now I was boiling. I was wired all the time, absolutely electric even though I barely slept. I could barely focus. Barely sit still. Weed, Jeremy had promised, would mellow me out, but I found that even the tiniest bit had the opposite effect. Everything I felt, I felt intensely. I felt reckless and impulsive and often apocalyptically angry. I was so ashamed of who I'd been and who I'd almost become: a college dropout; a teenage wife; a slave to God, church, doctrine, husband.

I went wild to keep from remembering that girl, and to try to become someone else. Someone entirely new.

28.

At the end of the summer, I quit Subway.

"I can't believe you're leaving me!" Jeremy said when I handed in my notice. My new job, which I'd applied for impulsively, was at a gift shop, and paid fifty cents more per hour.

"We'll still hang out," I promised, wrapping my pinkie around his. "Every chance we get."

"Every chance we get," he repeated.

And for a while, we did. But I signed up for more community college classes, and our schedules no longer aligned. By the time the leaves turned in late October, I was filling my free time with other men.

I was ravenous for attention. Had a pathological need to be wanted. Years earlier, I'd tied all of my value up in Sam, crafted my whole self around him, and now I was desperate for someone else to tell me who I was and what I was worth. So deep was this belief that I didn't consciously know I held it, except for its obvious hold on me. I could not be alone. I *could not* be alone.

So I gave my attention to every man who gave me even an ounce of his.

One worked at Pizza Hut. One was a high school history teacher. One, Taylor, played the bass guitar on Deliverance's worship team.

I didn't want anything to do with that church or anyone who was associated with it, but Taylor knew very little about what had happened between me and Sam.

"Wait," I asked him one night on the phone. "You don't know why Sam got arrested?"

"Not the details," Taylor said.

"You never heard he was preying on a girl in the youth group?"

"No one talked about it much."

Apparently Pastor Ron never informed the congregation about what had happened, even though the investigation had concluded and the case was long closed. It was truly as if Sam had never gone to Deliverance. As if his very existence had been erased from the collective memory of the church.

I don't remember how I found out, but Sam's charges were quietly dropped late in the summer. I didn't, and still don't, know why. Over the years I've heard many rumors. One was that Sam's cop friends, including a few who went to Deliverance, pulled some strings. Another was that the sixteen-year-old girl's foster parents didn't want to get involved in potential years of court proceedings and asked for Sam's charges to be dropped. Another was that Sam's prosecution would have caused a major scandal for the commonwealth's attorney. Sam's elementary school mentoring job—which he lost upon his arrest—was sponsored by the county prosecutor. If Sam's name and charges had made headlines, if people found out the prosecutor had employed a child predator in local elementary schools, the prosecutor, who was planning to run for reelection, would have been doomed at the polls.

When I told Taylor about Sam, he went quiet on the other line. "I can't believe he got off the hook."

When I told him about the last time I'd been to youth group, when Jared suggested I get back together with Sam, Taylor got even quieter. "How could he say that?" he whispered.

I dated Taylor not because we had much in common but because he made me feel justified in leaving both Sam and church. It was what I needed even months after the breakup: assurance that I'd done the right thing in spite of what others thought and what God had seemingly commanded. At least *someone* at Deliverance saw things the right way up.

We were too mismatched to last, though. Taylor knew what he believed, and I did not. I was becoming less convinced of God's existence all the time.

Taylor persuaded me into going back to church a few times. Merely sitting in that room felt like a charade. It was painfully strange to be in the place where I'd once burned with passion for God, spoken in tongues, jumped around, and wept on the floor, and feel absolutely nothing. No fervor. No ecstasy. No sense of the Holy Spirit. Nothing. I felt flat inside. Dead.

There was a service that fall. I remember the sermon because it was the same one I'd heard preached a thousand times: Jesus was coming back soon, the end times were near, get saved now or your soul would be lost to eternal hellfire. It was the sermon that had inspired the old fear that I no longer felt. Everyone around me was affected, tearful and awestruck, nodding in agreement with Pastor Ron's words of warning. Shouts of "amen" and "hallelujah" rolled across the congregation. And when the music picked up at the end of service, everyone leaped to their feet to sing their praises to God.

I felt a little spark of something then, but it was only a sense of what I'd lost. I told Taylor I was never going back to church. A few days later, we broke up.

By November, there were three or four signs in every yard in my neighborhood, including mine. Dad had never liked any politician in particular, but he let the signs go up anyway because our neighbor had about a hundred to spare and Dad certainly wasn't voting for the other candidate, and to *not* put up signs implied otherwise. They were all over, everywhere you looked. MAKE AMERICA GREAT AGAIN, some said. Others said, TRUMP DIGS COAL.

I'd waffled about voting for Trump for months. Ultimately, and somewhat guiltily, I didn't. Even though he was the only candidate in decades who'd promised to help Appalachia, I couldn't not think about the rally and its violence, and all the crude, terrible things Trump had said since. Later I'd make friends from big cities who'd tell me they wept in front of their TVs on election night, shocked by the results. I didn't even watch. I expected Trump to win just by how popular he was among everyone I knew.

Choosing not to vote for Trump was one of the more deliberate choices I made around that time. As fall turned to winter and winter turned cold, I fell under another hot spell of recklessness. I started making sudden, haphazard decisions I couldn't explain. I chopped off seventeen inches of hair. I went on a date with a car salesman who was eleven years older than me. I scheduled a date with a man who had five face tattoos. I switched my college major once, twice, then back again in the course of a week.

I hadn't planned to make it so far in community college, but after breaking up with Sam, I'd kept taking classes because I didn't know what else to do. Dropping out had crossed my mind, but that was what Sam had wanted me to do, so I'd done the opposite. Now I was three months from earning an associate's degree. Sam hadn't wanted me to get my bachelor's either, so in February, I submitted transfer applications to Radford, Virginia Tech, and a couple other in-state schools.

The process of applying conjured up the memory of my conversation with Sam, when he tried to discourage me from every career and college I considered. *You're not very good with people. You couldn't get in.* I hadn't thought about those words in months, but once I recalled them, they wouldn't leave my mind. The more I thought about them, the angrier I got. It wasn't just what he'd said that enraged me; it was that I'd accepted it. *Agreed* with it.

For months I'd told myself that I'd continued my education out of spite. But proving Sam wrong was not the whole of my motivation. There was something else: a growing feeling that the unknown was not as scary as before; that change was needed, even vital. I had never considered leaving Tazewell before. But I started to realize that I might never, if not for college.

I figured my grades were good enough to get into at least one state school. I figured the odds of getting into Harvard were next to none. And even if I did somehow get in, I wouldn't be able to attend anyway: Tuition cost ten times what I made in a year. Still, on the night of the March 1 deadline, I filled out a transfer application. *Choice is a strange, precious thing,* I wrote in my personal statement, comparing the array of bread, meat, and vegetables on a Subway sandwich bar to the many directions one's life could take. The conceit seemed silly, but time was short and I couldn't think of anything better. *My lunch is no longer determined by anyone but myself.*

I submitted that essay first to Harvard, because of Sam; then, impulsively, to Yale, which was the only other Ivy League school I had heard of; then to Columbia and Brown, because Google told me they had the highest transfer acceptance rates of all the Ivies. It was a total shot in the dark.

"I just want to see what happens," I told my community college adviser.

"I wouldn't even bother," he told me, but he signed off on my applications anyway.

29.

I was on fire.

It was morning. I was home alone. Something inside me broke.

Around others, I could keep my sorrow contained. When I was alone, the remembrance of Sam's betrayal and the loss of my faith sometimes came on like a heart attack. It pounded in my chest. Pulsed like lightning down my arms. It electrified my fingertips, weakened my elbows and knees. I would buckle into a protective ball, berating myself all the while. *What is wrong with you?* I'd silently shout. *Get* over *it already.* I clawed at myself. I screamed. I bent over and sobbed into the rug, leaving splotches of snot and tears.

Rocking on the floor, knees to my chest. I hated myself for allowing the pain of the past to affect me so deeply. I breathed in punctuated gasps as I stood and stumbled, lightheaded, to the bathroom, and poured an entire bottle of Advil into my hand.

All those pills, round and deliciously red. I wondered how long it would take to swallow them. How many I could down at a time. The thought had crossed my mind before, but I had never gone so far as pouring the pills into my hand. I stared at them. I imagined the ferocious sadness in my chest dulling to an ache and then to nothing at all. I imagined the high tide in my heart falling back to the sea. The calm was so tempting that I stopped crying. I could almost feel my brain tingling with blessed numbness.

And then, panic.

The pills in my hand came into a sudden sharp focus. With the clarity of terror, I dumped them back into the bottle, shoved the bottle back into the cabinet, and retreated from the bathroom. Trembling and frantic, I leaped into bed and wrapped myself under the blankets, a child protecting herself from her own scary shadow. I cried now out of fear.

I don't know who you are anymore, Mom's voice echoed in my head.

I didn't know either.

I knew who I had to be, though. An hour later, completely spent, I got out of bed, combed my hair, and drove to work. I plastered on a customer service smile and spent the rest of the day forcing as much cheer as possible to compensate for the near-fatal sadness of the morning. I regarded emotion as a balancing act: One extreme emotion required correcting by the opposite emotion. Once I returned to equilibrium, I could almost convince myself that nothing was wrong with me.

But I was scared of myself now. A few days later, I called the only mental health clinic in Tazewell County.

I felt guilty scheduling that appointment. I recalled long-ago conversations with Sam about my sadness and anxiety. *You don't need medication*, he'd told me every time I wondered if I might. *Just pray harder. Just trust God*. Part of me still believed mental illness was a sign of weak faith, which now I was surely guilty of. Yet I couldn't find the words to pray for relief, and I didn't trust God to help me anymore.

I didn't know if *anyone* could help. I wasn't even sure I wanted it. The idea of talking about my feelings was embarrassing. The day of the appointment, I parked at the gas station next door so nobody would see my car outside the clinic, and I wore a hoodie so nobody would recognize me walking in. I prayed I wouldn't see any familiar faces in the waiting room.

A woman in yoga pants called me back. She was an intake counselor, she explained, and was going to screen me to determine whether the clinic would accept me as a patient. "We're way overloaded as is," she said.

She led me into a doorless kitchenette and asked me to sit at a dining table, explaining that all the other rooms were occupied. As we settled into our chairs, a clinician walked in, grabbed his lunch from the fridge, and stuck it in the microwave behind me.

The intake counselor looked down at her clipboard, pen in hand, and began to fire off questions that I mostly answered no to. Did I take any medications? Had I ever sought counseling or psychiatric services? Had I ever been diagnosed with a mental health disorder? Had I recently suffered a traumatic event?

"I'm, um, getting over a breakup," I said. It sounded stupid and trite, and I was immediately embarrassed for saying it.

"Do you want to talk more about that?" the counselor asked.

I stumbled over my words. "He just . . . wasn't who I thought he was. He lied to me." *Understatement of the year,* I thought, but I was too ashamed to tell the full truth.

The counselor moved on to the next question.

After a while, she got to questions I started answering yes to. "Do you feel sad?" *Yes.* "Do you feel worthless?" *Yes.* "Do you have crying spells?" *Definitely.*

"Have you ever thought about taking your own life?"

I hesitated on this one. It was the most serious question with the most serious answer. I didn't know what would happen if I admitted to it, but that was why I was here. I took the chance. "Yes."

"And do you have a plan for how you would do it?" the counselor asked.

I pictured the heap of Advil in my palm. Just then, a couple of clinicians laughed in the hallway, and I remembered with a fresh burst of shame that this room had no door. "No," I lied.

The counselor wrote on her clipboard.

There were other questions I lied about. I was asked if I had ever had hallucinations, heard or seen things that didn't exist. I considered the voices and visions I'd attributed to God. They were too clear to deny, but to what did I attribute their existence now? How could I explain them?

I answered the rest of the counselor's questions flatly, quickly, suddenly desperate to be anywhere but that exposed kitchenette. I was almost relieved when she told me that my symptoms were not severe enough for the clinic to accept me as a patient. I cried as I drove home, weak with embarrassment and guilt. *This is what you get for not relying on God*, I thought in Sam's voice. *Should have had more faith!*

The morning after my appointment, I opened the bathroom cabinet. In the center of the middle of the shelf, screaming for my attention, was the bottle of Advil. I remembered the sickening roundness of the pills in my hand. The memory was both repulsive and tempting. I moved the bottle behind other, taller ones so I couldn't see it. Then I made an appointment at the nearest counseling center.

It was in Richlands, about half an hour's drive. I scheduled this appointment, like the last one, in the middle of a workday, so my parents didn't know I'd gone. I walked into a thankfully empty waiting room and approached the receptionist's window.

"Emilee!" the voice behind it said.

I startled at my name, and then at the face that spoke it. The receptionist was Pastor Sue, the woman who had called to tell me Sam was in jail.

I stood there, dumbfounded.

"How are you *doing*?" she asked. She passed me a clipboard of paperwork and gave me a pitying look that said *I think I know why you're here.*

I fumed as I filled out my intake forms, although it gave me some small satisfaction that we'd come face to face after Pastor Sue had avoided me for so long. I was certain she knew things about Sam's crimes she never told me. I glared at the window, which she had shut and moved away from.

After a few moments, Pastor Sue called me back to the therapist's office. She shut the door behind me.

"How are you, Emilee?" the therapist asked.

I stared, doubly dumbfounded. I might have seen the absurd hilarity of the situation if I hadn't been so paralytically depressed. The therapist's name was Tony. He'd gone to Deliverance for years. Until recently, he'd given guest sermons when Pastor Ron was absent. I recalled the scandal under which he had been asked to stop preaching: Tony had cheated on his wife.

I stayed for the session. I don't remember much about it except for having the profound sense that God, if he was real, was mocking me. Tony remembered me. He remembered Sam. He remembered Sam and me as a couple. I couldn't tell how much he knew about our breakup.

Either way, I knew I would not be back.

At the end of the session, Tony riffled through an assortment of pamphlets on his shelf and handed a few to me. "Give these a read," he said. "I think they can help you."

I shuffled through them as I walked out of the office. They were Bible tracts with a vague mental health focus. My eyes landed on an italicized sentence that said *Jesus can cure your depression.*

I crumpled the pamphlets into my purse, making a mental note to trash them when I got home, and sped out of the parking lot, wondering whether I'd been to counseling or to church.

30.

The email was two days old by the time I saw it. *I am a Harvard College alumni interviewer,* it read. *The college reached out and asked me to try to interview you this week.*

Completely stunned, and terrified I'd already missed the opportunity, I responded immediately: *I am available any time.* The interviewer scheduled a meeting for the next afternoon.

It was so unexpected, so last minute, that I had no time to prepare. When I woke up in the morning, I realized I had no dress clothes except for a couple of old, out-of-season church dresses and grease-stained work khakis. I squeezed on my darkest pair of jeans, five years old and two sizes too small, and headed out the door.

The drive to Roanoke was supposed to take two hours, but I was on the road for three. It was only the second time I'd driven on the interstate. It was the first week of April, and the rain was nonstop, steady drizzles punctuated by hard, sudden downpours. I crept along in the right lane. My windshield wipers beat a hundred miles an hour. Trucks whizzed by me as if I were sitting still.

When I made it to downtown Roanoke, I drove in circles trying to find a place where I wouldn't have to parallel park, which I'd never learned to do, and ended up in a lot almost half a mile from the address my interviewer had given me. I headed in that direction, then, disoriented, wandered around for a while until I realized I might not even be on the right street. When I stopped a man and asked for help, he laughed. "You're looking for that right there," he said, pointing to the giant Wells Fargo Tower two blocks down.

Inside, I headed toward the elevator as if I knew what I was doing, though my hand shook as I pressed the button to the fourteenth floor. Alice, my interviewer, was an attorney. I didn't know any attorneys, especially ones who had graduated from Harvard. I pictured Alice as one of the sharp-tongued, cold-eyed, turtlenecked law students in *Legally Blonde.* She was going to take one look at me and see right through my false confidence. She was going to know immediately that I wasn't Harvard material. She was going to wonder why Harvard had ever considered me. She was going to resent me for wasting her time.

Upstairs, though, Alice was the opposite of what I expected. She introduced herself warmly, with a kind smile. She led me to her office. It was cozy and bright despite the dreary cityscape outside her window. Below was a long, wide stretch of rail yard. A single train, its cars rusted and empty, sat on the middle track.

Alice saw me looking. "You have coal trains back home, don't you?"

"There's a track in front of my house," I said. "It used to stay busy day and night."

"Not anymore?" she asked. I shook my head.

Instead of talking about Harvard or asking about my academic history, Alice wanted me to tell her about my home. "You're the first person I've ever interviewed from *rural* southwest Virginia," she said, leaning toward me in interest. She told me she was from the Washington, D.C., suburbs. To her, Roanoke was microscopic; to me, it was huge.

It was the first time I'd ever spoken about coal country with someone who didn't know much about it. I told her about the collapse of the coal market, the struggling economy, the opioid crisis. The lack of quality mental health care.

After a few minutes, I started to realize all my talking points were negative. Worried I might not be making the best impression, I tried to steer the conversation back to the positive. Tazewell was a close-knit community, I told Alice. I found comfort in its familiarity, in the lay of the land and most of its people. Then I started to worry she would think I was so tied to home that I would never be able to leave, that I would never be able to adjust to life at Harvard.

As our interview tapered to an end, I realized how hard I'd tried to make a good impression. How much I *cared*, even though I told myself I shouldn't. In spite of my insecurity, and in spite of the infinitesimal chance of actually getting accepted, I understood—subconsciously, at least—that the opportunity wasn't something to let slip away.

I was afraid to ask Alice if she knew anything about Harvard's financial aid because I suspected the answer wouldn't be what I wanted to hear. But before I allowed myself to get my hopes up, I had to know.

Alice smiled. "They're incredibly generous with financial aid," she told me. "If you get in, they'll make sure you can afford it."

As I walked out of Alice's office, I felt something like happiness, which I hadn't felt for a while, and hopefulness, which I hadn't allowed myself to feel until just then. There was anticipation, too, but a different kind than I'd ever known.

The last thing I'd looked forward to was getting married. That was like waiting for a door to close: My wedding vows would have been an official dedication to God and my husband, a hard severance from the rest of the world. Waiting for Harvard's decision letter felt the opposite.

Before I left, the receptionist flagged me to her desk. "Do you have your parking ticket?" she asked.

I didn't know why she wanted it, but I handed her the white stub anyway. It was the first time in my life I'd ever had to pay to park. I feared she was going to tell me I hadn't done it right.

Instead, she just squinted at the ticket. After a moment, she handed it back to me. "I don't know where this lot is," she said, giving me a funny look. "If it was ours, I could've validated your parking."

"It's okay," I told her. And it was, because I didn't know what that meant.

A month later, I got an email from Harvard. Wait-listed.

According to my frantic googling, that was as good as getting rejected. I knew my chances hadn't been good—there were usually fifteen to sixteen hundred transfer applicants, and only about a dozen were accepted—but I'd gotten my hopes up and was extra disheartened now.

To distract myself from my disappointment, I went back to Subway. I kept my other job, too, so between them I worked fifty-hour, seven-day weeks. I was glad for the extra money. Unexpectedly, in early May, Columbia University sent me an acceptance letter. Beyond stunned, I committed impulsively, even though a single semester of tuition would wipe out my savings, and I didn't know the first thing about getting a loan.

I decided to worry about that later, though. I had to get out of Tazewell.

It surprised me, how strong and sudden the urge to leave was.

Before my conversation with Alice, it had only been a spark, a notion, small and undefined. After, it was a bonfire, gas to my engine, propelling me forward with new ambition and purpose. Leaving meant extracting myself from the people and places I'd let define me, and defining myself on my own terms.

I wanted that. Needed that.

Until a fresh, fierce wave of depression rolled over me in June.

It seemed to come from nowhere. This time it was less of a wild rebellion and more of a constant, bitter annoyance—at my two jobs and the exhausting workweeks; at impassive objects and scenery, the perpetual sameness of the roads and mountains. I even became frustrated with Jeremy, who was often silent and bleary-eyed and not like his old self at all. Sometimes he smelled like liquor, which I'd never smelled on him before. We spent a couple stray evenings together after work, but whatever spell had once bound us together was broken. He was different now. So was I.

I was startled by the reversal, how quickly I'd turned inside out. Suddenly I couldn't even muster excitement for New York. Moving away, getting a college degree, proving Sam wrong—it all sounded so inexplicably empty. I felt myself sinking, being swallowed up by a force I couldn't name. It gave me the sense I was living in one of those dreams where you run and run but don't get anywhere, where your feet are moving, but the ground beneath them isn't.

31.

The call came as I was headed out the door to a twelve-hour workday. An admissions officer with a prim, cutting accent told me that no, she was not joking, that I had really, actually, truly been accepted to Harvard.

Harvard.

Harvard.

Harvard.

The word resonated in my mind until it didn't sound like a word at all. The officer told me that I'd been accepted as a sophomore, that only half my credits would transfer—but how lucky was I to get three years at Harvard instead of just two? On top of that, the college was offering me almost full financial aid, just as Alice had promised.

I stood on my front porch and thanked the woman, too stunned to cry, both numb and reanimated. It was the same feeling I'd had when I found out about Sam going to jail: This was not real life, this was not happening, this could not be happening to me. People like me did not go to Harvard. People like me went to work twelve hours between two jobs, which was exactly what I did when I got off the phone.

The next few days were rushed and blurry. I had less than a week to accept my offer of admission, but I did so immediately, without any debate or consideration. It wasn't even a question.

My official offer of admission came in a glossy envelope a few days later. I posted a photo of it to Facebook, then, in a final act of spite, emailed the picture directly to Sam. His knowing was more important than the rest of the world's.

Right away I started getting congratulatory texts and calls. They came from friends and acquaintances; coworkers past and present; relatives I didn't know exactly how I was related to. A few came from people I didn't know at all. One, a reporter at the local news station, wanted an interview. So did the editor of the county newspaper. "No one from Tazewell has ever gone to Harvard," she told me. We met up at the Hardee's where a little more than a year earlier I'd planned my wedding. "This is a big deal."

My parents weren't the type to make a fuss, but I'd never seen them so excited. Dad spent hours on the internet memorizing Harvard's history, admissions statistics, and notable alumni. Mom ordered the whole family Harvard T-shirts and car decals.

It was surreal. It was more than surreal. There wasn't a word for what it was. The feeling, whatever it could be called, was amplified since I had no frame of reference to imagine Harvard by, only idyllic online snapshots of the campus in springtime. In July, my uncle Danny and aunt Lee Anne decided to forgo their beach vacation and take me and my parents to visit Cambridge instead.

It was a quick, hastily planned trip. We spent more time driving than we did in Massachusetts. Our agenda consisted of wandering around the Harvard campus and Boston at large, getting a feel for the place I'd be spending the next three years. On our first morning, we ventured onto the subway and rode for hours. We jumped from the Red Line to the Orange Line to the Green and explored the city in every direction, aimless. None of us had been on a train before. We gripped our seats when it picked up speed. "Feels like this thing's gonna fly off the rails," Dad said through gritted teeth.

When we finally tired of riding, we realized we had no idea how to get back to our hotel. Lee Anne called the front desk and asked the clerk for directions. The rest of us stood by the busy turnstiles of the Park Street station, bewildered that so much activity could occur underground.

Lee Anne kept repeating herself to the clerk, more slowly and enunciated each time. "Park. Street. We. Need. To. Get. Back. From. Park. Street." Finally she hung up, frustrated. "That lady could barely understand my accent, and I could barely understand hers," she said. Only by sheer luck did we get on the right train and make it back to our hotel.

We stayed only two days. It wasn't enough time for me to form an impression of the city. By the time I was home, the shape of Boston had condensed in my mind to an amorphous gray heap of skyscrapers, cars, and concrete. All I could say for sure about it was that it was a drastic change from Tazewell. Which was all that really mattered.

Something shifted after that trip. Tazewell felt smaller, more confining. More depressing. In high school, a new student from New Jersey had described Tazewell in those exact words, and I'd rankled at them. An insult to the place was an attack on its people.

Now I understood what he meant. The only way I got through

my long, drudging workdays was by envisioning my new life. There would be cute little cafés and big cozy libraries and cavernous lecture halls with brilliant professors. Trains and taxis and roommates and parties and *freedom*.

I couldn't wait to leave again.

Except for the one thing I was afraid to leave behind.

After my parents, Jeremy was the first person I'd told when I got into Harvard. "Hell yeah," he'd said. "Get the hell out of here. Go do something big." But we both knew that would probably mean the end of our friendship, and the hope that we would someday regain the wild, carefree magic of the previous summer. Things were heavier now that I was leaving. Now that my time in Tazewell had an expiration date.

That was the unspoken difference between us: I got to make an escape, and Jeremy didn't. He was going in the opposite direction, falling deeper and deeper down the hole.

At the end of July, Jeremy got fired. I walked into work one evening expecting him to be there. Stacey was behind the register instead.

"Angie let him go last night," Stacey said. I could tell she'd been crying. "He got in a fight in the parking lot. With Shayla's boyfriend. On the clock."

Our coworker Shayla had a boyfriend whom none of us liked. He called every hour to "check in" on her, paid her surprise visits to make sure she wasn't flirting with male customers, and came to collect her paycheck every Friday, talking in low, threatening whispers when she tried to resist. A couple nights earlier, he'd called during the dinner rush. Shayla and I were working together. I'd answered in a hurry—our line was to the door—and told him that Shayla couldn't come to the phone. Right away, her cell phone, which was lying on the prep table, lit up. *That fucking bitch Emilee won't let me talk to you. Call me back NOW.*

I told Jeremy about the text later that night.

"Next time I see him, I'm gonna beat his ass," Jeremy replied in a nonchalant way that made me think he wasn't serious.

He was, though. Stacey showed me the blood in the parking lot, which was dark as an oil stain.

"Jeremy got him good," she said, trying to sound more proud than sad.

I tried not to cry. It was my fault he was gone.

For weeks I didn't see Jeremy anywhere. There was no way to get ahold of him: He didn't have a cell phone, and he'd been hopping couches, living out of the Baby Car. I didn't have much free time between my jobs, but I circled the roads near the lake every early morning and late night, waiting, hoping, that I'd see him one last time before I left for school.

In early August, I learned Jeremy was in the county jail.

I'd never visited anyone in jail. I didn't even know where the jail entrance was, and I walked into the courthouse next door before a security guard pointed me in the right direction. When I finally made it to the right place, a voice demanded identification from behind a mirrored glass panel. I slid my driver's license through a slot. My own eyes stared back at me.

The visitation room looked as I'd expected. There were three metal chairs, three black phone receivers, and three boxy computer monitors. I sat down in the third chair, which the voice behind the glass had assigned me to, and put the phone to my ear, unsure of what to do next.

Without my prompting, the black screen in front of me came to life. A very grainy Jeremy appeared. He stared into the screen, so still that I thought it was frozen, before blinking a few times and grabbing the phone on his end.

"I'll be goddamned." His voice crackled in the receiver. He broke into a big grin. "What the hell are you doing here?"

"What are *you* doing here? I've been looking for you everywhere."

He rattled off the list of his most recent charges: improper exhaust; no insurance; driving with a revoked license, again. "I would've bailed myself out," he said, "but I'm broke as all hell."

Jeremy's jumpsuit was blue. It was large on him, made for someone his height but not his weight. His nautical star tattoos peeked out of the V-neck below his collarbones.

"We miss you at Subway," I told him. "It's not the same without you."

Jeremy's replacement was a high schooler who never ever spoke, who was too shy to even answer the phone. She told me she didn't like music and turned mine down so low you could barely hear it.

Everyone else was less fun without Jeremy, too. There were no jokes or games, no goofing off or cutting up. In spite of the distance that had grown between us, Subway wasn't Subway without Jeremy. I was looking forward to my last day.

"When do you leave for school?" Jeremy asked.

"The twenty-first," I said. He nodded and said nothing. I had nothing to say either. The silence acknowledged the chasm between us.

It was ironic, I thought. Jeremy, my silly, wild, first taste of freedom, was locked behind bars, talking to me behind a thick concrete wall and a computer screen.

"I wish I could see you before then," I said finally. "In person."

"I'm working on it," Jeremy said. He glanced over his shoulder at the blue-suited inmates milling around behind him. "I won five bucks at poker last night."

In the corner of the screen, the countdown timer began to flash red, a one-minute warning.

"Come see me," I said.

"I'll try," he said. He put his hand up to the screen, and I put mine up to touch his. The timer ran out, and the screen went black.

A couple weeks later, the day before I left for Harvard, my doorbell rang.

I was home alone, packing my suitcases to a cranked-up radio. I hadn't heard the Baby Car coming. It was parked in my driveway, and Jeremy was standing on my porch.

"Surprise!" he yelled when I opened the door.

He pulled me outside and swooped me up in a hug. When he let me down, he bounced excitedly on his toes. He said he had somewhere to take me.

Jeremy didn't tell me how he'd paid his bail. We tore down my road doing eighty, grinning and laughing as if there had never been any silent strain between us at all. The devil-may-care energy of last summer buzzed between us, electric and achingly wonderful, even though—or maybe because—it was my last day in Tazewell.

Fifteen minutes down the highway, then a hairpin turn onto a gravel road. It descended steeply down a hill before another sharp turn. We crossed a set of train tracks. There was no road on the other side, only flattened grass where tires had been. Jeremy followed the tracks for a while before forging his own path.

He cut the engine at the edge of the field. Beyond the tree line was the bank of the Clinch River.

"Come on," Jeremy said, rolling his pant legs up. "We're getting in."

I took off my shoes, cuffed my pants, and followed him into the water.

The river rocks grated my tender feet. Jeremy walked along as if he didn't even feel them. He waded against the current, keeping close to the bank where the water was only knee-deep. I clumsily stumbled behind.

As we splashed along, the sun sparkled on the slow, clear water, which rose from my knees to my thighs to my hips to my stomach. Jeremy promised there was a swimming hole up ahead. I knew we'd made it when I could barely skim the rocks underfoot with my tiptoes.

I'd stumbled and tripped so many times that I was already soaked anyway, so I swam along fully clothed. Jeremy tossed his shirt on the bank and followed me. We floated and splashed and laughed and shouted, all alone in the middle of the river in the middle of the woods, until our arms and legs were wobbly and we climbed up on the bank to dry. The sun moved in a hot, lazy arc across the sky.

"I wish you didn't have to go," Jeremy said. He put his arms behind his head, tattoos on full display. I rolled over and drank him in.

In that magic moment, I wondered how I could trade something like this for the unknowns of city life. I wondered if Jeremy would be okay when I was gone. My heart pulsed with tenderness and worry while he stretched out in the sun, with closed eyes and a dimpled smile. It was the first time in months he hadn't smelled like weed or liquor. But he was broke, homeless, and now jobless to boot. It suddenly felt wrong, disloyal, to leave him, and everything else, behind.

In my Appalachia, loyalty is synonymous with respect. You are raised to revere the mountains and their people. *Your* people. The sense of community is so strong because the world beyond, you hear, is strange and cold and unforgiving, and you know this must be true because that's where the politicians are, the coal barons, the rich and powerful who look down on Appalachia and care about it only as far as they can take advantage of it.

There are many reasons people don't leave Appalachia, but this narrative of trepidation is a major one. When you belong to such a rooted and close-knit community, leaving it for something far away and unknown almost makes you a traitor. Like saying *you're not good enough for me* to the people and places that raised you.

That sentiment was part of the reason I'd stuck with Sam so long. And with my churches, and with God. Why until recently I'd never considered leaving. Why I felt as if I owed it to Jeremy to stay. Loyalty makes for committed, unbreakable bonds.

It can also foster fear and discourage change.

And I couldn't stay just for Jeremy's sake, or for tradition's sake, or because staying was the easiest thing to do. Before, I'd feared a life beyond the familiar. Now I feared never knowing anything else.

Later, when the sun was almost touching the hill behind my house, Jeremy and I held each other in a long hug on my front porch.

"I'll come visit," he promised, pulling my head to his chest.

"You better," I said into his damp T-shirt, even though I knew he wouldn't and I didn't want him to besides. Old life and new: In my mind, the two did not—*could* not—mix.

Goodbye was goodbye, and Jeremy was my last one. The rest of my loose ends were already tied up. I'd quit both my jobs, cashed my last paychecks, and packed most of my belongings, except for the gifts my Subway coworkers had given me on my last day of work. They'd thrown me a surprise party with a Food Lion deli cake and a cash-stuffed card and all kinds of goodies from Dollar

General next door, including half a dozen scratch-offs I didn't win a dime on.

I didn't know yet if it was right to leave everything I knew. I didn't know if I could escape what I was running from, and I didn't know exactly what I was running toward either. I *did* know, with a conviction I hadn't felt since my most devout days, that it was time to go.

Part THREE

32.

Well," Mom said, sizing up my room from the doorway, "it's a little . . . small."

Dad squeezed by her with a tote box. I flattened myself against the closet door as he passed. To fit between the dresser and the wall, he hoisted the box above his head, then dropped it at last onto the bare twin mattress.

My dorm room, Cabot E210A, was a narrow eighty-five square feet. The three of us could barely fit inside. The furniture was packed so tight it couldn't be rearranged.

Still, I thought it was great. So what if I was living in a closet? I was living in a closet *at Harvard*.

The previous morning, I was the first one in the car, more than ready to go. The drive was marked by a solar eclipse. A good omen, I thought. We pulled over and watched its passing shadow through borrowed glasses at a Pennsylvania rest stop. In New York, when we took a series of wrong exits and turns that landed us in creeping bumper-to-bumper Manhattan traffic, I took pictures of skyscrapers whose top floors I couldn't even see and texted my Subway friends, *I'm so excited I can't breathe.* At a Texas Roadhouse outside Boston, the waitress asked me to repeat my order twice, then brought out the wrong food anyway.

It was all so wonderful. I was having so much fun.

After a night in a hotel room overlooking the Charles River, Mom and Dad helped me move into my dorm. None of us trusted the birdcage elevator, so we heaved all my belongings up two stuffy flights of stairs to my room, which lacked an air conditioner and held heat like a greenhouse even with the window open.

"I thought it was supposed to be cold up north," Dad said. Sweat dripped off his nose and onto the splintered wooden floor.

I hadn't expected the heat either. I hadn't known what to expect. For months my brain had swirled with vague idealistic notions of how thrilling it would be to live in a place so totally opposite from the one I was leaving behind. Whatever Harvard threw at me, whatever my *new life* entailed, I was ready. I was going to conquer. I was going to make something of myself, and be somebody, and be healed, and be happy.

My parents offered to let me stay the night in their hotel room, but I declined. I sat at my dorm room desk, which was wedged in the corner between the bookshelf and the bed, and stared out the tiny window. Below was the bright, patchless Quad lawn. It was bordered with freshly pruned maples cast in a rosy sunset glow. There were clusters of white Adirondack chairs and a patchwork of picnic blankets and lounging students. A snow-white Pyrenees barked playfully at its owner, who was readying to toss a Frisbee. The scene was straight out of a movie. Act 1, scene 1: the opening to the rest of my life.

Though my window was angled away from direct sunlight, I felt aglow, too, warm to the bones with happiness. A phrase came to mind: "a land of opportunity." That's what this place was. I had only a window-frame snapshot to judge my new world by, but it was enough. I could see myself falling in love.

"Get out of the bike lane, bitch!"

A cyclist zoomed by me so fast that he had already passed by the time I turned to look at him. I froze where I was standing and looked down.

Bike lane?

I stepped back onto the sidewalk, confused. The blue arrow on my Google Maps app was stuck, spinning aimlessly no matter which direction I turned. Back home, I'd oriented myself by the mountains. Here, I was confused by the tall buildings, grid-like streets, and clogs of traffic. It was an assault of sight and sound.

Eventually, after a two-mile walk that should have been only a mile and a half, I made it to Dunster House for dinner with the other transfer students. It was eighty-five degrees outside. I was embarrassed to meet people in a sweat-soaked shirt, and even more embarrassed that they didn't look nearly as flustered as me. "Thank God for the shuttle," I heard someone say.

Shuttle?

We were a group of twelve, small enough to fit around a single long dining table. I took a chair in the center. As I scooted in, I noticed the diversity of accents and skin tones. I had never sat at a table with so many people who were so unlike me.

We went around and introduced ourselves: name, hometown, which college we'd attended before Harvard. There was a boy from South Africa. A girl from Washington state. Another girl from New York City. They'd all come from four-year universities, even other Ivies. I felt very small announcing that I'd come from a community college, and even smaller saying the word "Tazewell," knowing no one there had ever heard of it.

"How interesting," someone said. I blushed because I knew it wasn't. I picked at my dinner plate, suddenly intimidated beyond words. What was I doing here?

I nervously tried to make conversation. I brought up the vintage elevator in my dorm, how my parents and I had opted for the stairs instead. A girl across the table stopped me mid-sentence and asked me to repeat myself.

"*Stairs*," she said. "Say it again!"

I did.

Her mouth was agape. "I *love* that!" she exclaimed. "I've never heard anyone pronounce 'stairs' with two syllables."

I laughed nervously and didn't finish my story.

The next day, I joined the transfers on a tour of the city. We took the subway from Harvard Square to Park Street, which I recognized from my family's misadventure a month earlier. We wandered aboveground and around Boston Common, then followed the Freedom Trail past the Granary Burying Ground, the Old State House, and the stately Faneuil Hall. Next we turned toward the harbor, stopping for ice cream along the way.

I could already see friendships forming. I watched my peers gravitate toward each other, converse easily, naturally. One was talking about her summer on Martha's Vineyard. Another was talking about his brother who'd just graduated from Harvard that previous spring, and how he'd once run into Mark Zuckerberg on the street. Another was saying that she'd met a Kennedy in the student center that very morning.

These were all proper nouns with a weight and valence that terrified me. Who was I to be in the presence of such wealthy, connected people? I dropped back quietly, thinking how all of my conversation topics—working at Subway, for example—would be laughable among this crowd.

After trailing for a few minutes, I followed the group to a patch of grass near the water's edge. A chattering circle formed. I sat on the fringe, wordlessly eating my mint chocolate chip ice cream, making tiny spoonfuls and taking long, slow bites. As long as my hands were busy and my mouth was full, I could excuse my anxious silence.

After a minute, I noticed someone else doing the same. The sandy-haired boy was a few feet to my left, also sitting apart from the group, also eating his ice cream quietly, with exaggerated slowness. His soft, dark eyes seemed a little nervous. I couldn't remember his name.

"I'm Emilee," I said, taking a chance.

"Patrick." He reached over and shook my hand. It was awkward, and we both giggled.

"So what do you think of Boston?" I asked.

"I grew up just outside New York City," Patrick said. "So I like the slower pace."

"Slower pace!" I laughed. "I'm from southwest Virginia. *That's* a slower pace."

Like me, Patrick was a sophomore. He'd transferred from a public university in New Jersey. "I applied to Harvard last minute," he told me. "I never thought I'd get in."

"Me too," I replied, warmed by the similarity.

At his old college, Patrick had majored in communications, edited the school newspaper. Here, he was toying with the idea of concentrating in anthropology.

I told him that I was switching my major, too. On my application, I'd declared "human developmental and regenerative biology" as my intended concentration. It was completely impulsive. I had no clue what I would do with such a degree, or even what earning the degree entailed. I just liked its wordiness, the way it sounded intelligent. The way it would make *me* sound intelligent. More than anything else, it was a projection of insecurity, the feeling that my being here was a fluke in the admissions process.

Still, I was sure I could do it. Or pretty sure, at least. I'd gotten into *Harvard*, after all, either by luck or by merit or by an unknowable combination of the two. At this point, it didn't matter. The very fact of my being here meant that nothing was impossible.

Stoichiometry. Chemical bonding. Intermolecular forces. On the first day of class, a bearded professor blazed through twenty-seven slides in fifty-three minutes. I didn't understand half of what he said, but I scribbled nonstop.

I looked over the notes at lunch. Not a word made sense. I'd been so focused on copying down the professor's words that I hadn't absorbed their meaning. An adviser had assured me that this was the easiest science class at Harvard. *Surely not*, I thought as I tried to decipher the frantic scribbles.

After lunch, I walked across campus to my biology class. I'd earned an easy A in my community college biology class, so I confidently took a seat in the front row of the dim lecture hall.

Totipotency. Somatic cell nuclear transfer. Oocyte enucleation. More words I'd never heard and didn't understand. Thirty-five slides and six pages of notes later, I walked out of the class feeling as if I'd been spinning on a swivel chair. My right hand was exhausted, and so was the rest of me. I went back to my dorm and slept through dinner.

When I woke, it was dark. Ten o'clock, to be exact: my usual bedtime. I got out of bed groggily and shuffled to the dining hall for a bowl of cereal. When I returned, I sat at my desk, unsure of what to do with myself. My notebook lay open in front of me. I turned to it and stared, wondering if my notes made any more sense now.

Nope. Nope. Nope. My brain protested as the letters and numbers distorted into shapeless smears. I blinked once, twice, to get them to return to their correct forms, but my eyes watered and my head buzzed and my body slumped back to my bed.

At eight thirty the next morning, my alarm shocked me out of a fitful sleep. My dreams had been punctuated by car horns and accelerating engines, voices in the hallway, and the laugh track from a sitcom my neighbor had watched all night.

I got dressed and brushed my teeth in the bathroom across the hall, then headed toward the shuttle stop. A handful of students were gathered there. I joined them in waiting.

Five minutes passed. Six. Seven. Eight.

"Running late," someone near me said.

I nervously watched the time. My expository writing class started at nine. It was in a building I'd never been to, a mile away.

At eight fifty, someone else sighed. "Guess we'll have to walk," a boy said to his friend, and the pair started down the sidewalk together.

How long did it take to walk a mile? I wondered. I pulled the route up on Google Maps.

I was going to be several minutes late.

A mad dash down Garden Street; frantic power walking across Harvard Yard. Distracted by panic, I passed the building I was looking for. I realized my mistake, then darted back and sprinted through the double doors.

After a minute of wandering, I stumbled upon the classroom in the dark corner of a basement. There were two entrances. I slipped into the nearest one.

Suddenly I was standing beside the professor at the front of the room.

She cut her eyes at me, then went back to reading from the syllabus. Everyone else stared. I mumbled an apology and took an empty seat, shrinking into it as far as I could.

The class was a seminar for freshmen. It was similar, as far as I could tell from the syllabus, to a college composition class I'd taken back home. Easy peasy, I thought. The only matter of concern was the strict attendance policy, which was written in bold: ***Class begins promptly on the hour.***

Forty-five minutes later, after the professor's dismissal, I scurried out the back entrance in lingering shame. When I was outside again, I pulled out my phone and looked at my schedule. My next class—Scottish Gaelic, which I'd chosen to fulfill a language requirement—was in Warren 201.

I typed *Warren Hall* into Google Maps.

No results found, it said.

Warren Building, I tried.

No results found.

Perplexed, I started walking in no particular direction. Class started in less than ten minutes, and apparently the building didn't exist.

I tried different variations—*Warren Library*, *Warren Office*—until something I typed finally gave me an address. I jogged that way, ending up at an old yellow house with four chimneys.

Surely I wouldn't have a class in someone's *house*, I thought, then walked around the block looking for buildings or signs that said WARREN. There were only dorms, apartments, and other houses—nothing that seemed to be what I was looking for.

I glanced at my phone. Class had started. I was late again.

I darted back to the yellow house and walked up to its door.

Holding my breath, I slipped inside. At the top of an ornate staircase, in a large, oak-paneled office turned classroom, was a professor giving a slideshow on the history of Scotland.

I tiptoed in, relieved to have found the class but embarrassed by my repeat tardiness. I sat through the PowerPoint holding back tears. That day, on top of the previous one, had been violently frustrating. I was lost in the classroom and lost in the city, constantly disoriented. When would I catch a break?

Not that night when I once again slept through dinner. Not the next morning when I got off at the wrong shuttle stop and was late to chemistry. Not the next day or the next day or the next, each of which was an endless sprint between classes, meals, dorm meetings, advising fairs, and rare, blissful moments of bone-weary sleep.

On Friday night, I tallied up my homework. Somehow, after only a week of class, half a dozen assignments demanded my attention.

No break on the weekend either.

I considered leaving it all for Saturday. There was a throbbing ache behind my eyes, and even though it was barely nine o'clock, my pillow looked awfully inviting. I stacked my books on my desk so they would be the first thing I saw when I woke up.

At that moment, my phone chimed. There was a message in the transfer group chat. *Study session in Adams House?*

Yes! I replied without hesitation, stuffing my books back into my backpack. The last thing I wanted to do was look over a dozen pages of hieroglyphics, but the prospect of company was too enticing. I had barely spoken to anyone all week.

For all its noise and movement, the campus was an unexpectedly lonely place. I was too shy and too hurried to introduce myself to my classmates, and few people introduced themselves to me. It was strange to pass dozens of people on the sidewalk and be ignored by every single one: no smiles, no hellos, no *how-are-you-doing-todays*. Back home, this would be the height of rudeness. Here it was the norm. A small part of me liked that feeling of anonymity, knowing that no one knew me, but the larger part of me resented it. I was invisible. My presence was inconsequential.

Guided once more by Google Maps, I headed toward Adams. Garden Street was just as busy at night as it was during the day. So was Massachusetts Avenue, which was alive with horns and shouts and the electric red glow of bumper-to-bumper traffic. I darted across the road, wary even when the sign told me to cross, then paused at the edge of the sidewalk and watched a torrent of cars speed by. How strange was this world of Priuses and Teslas. I thought of the Baby Car, how monstrously, wonderfully out of place it would be.

Every now and then, Jeremy wandered into my mind. I'd get a glimpse of him in the unruly hair of strangers. I'd see him smoking a joint on a park bench or lurking by the subway after dark. I wondered what he was really doing at that moment, whether he was staying out of the bottle and out of jail. There was no way to talk to him. No way to find out.

I'd been in Cambridge only two weeks, but my Subway friends were fading fast. They couldn't relate to the oddities of city life—street performers, twenty-four-hour restaurants, and, of course, the bike lane—and quickly lost interest in hearing about them. Nanny and my parents, who called every few days, couldn't understand the utter strangeness of my new life either. The other transfers seemed far less shell-shocked by Cambridge than I was.

And less overwhelmed by their work, too. I turned down the narrow sidewalk on Plympton Street and wandered into the cavernous Adams dining hall. I was briefly stunned by its skylights and floor-to-ceiling windows. After a moment of searching, I saw familiar faces near the back of the room. Patrick and a couple of other transfers were sitting at a book-strewn table. They were already deep into studying, scrolling through walls of text on their laptops and combing through thick stacks of printed lecture slides, starring and underlining terms and definitions.

For a moment I just watched, amazed by their focus and foresight. It hadn't occurred to me to print lecture slides. I didn't know you *could* print a PowerPoint, or how to go about it, or even where the printers were. Instead, I sat down and pulled out my chicken-scratch notes and a highlighter. I stared blankly at the first page.

I had never done this before. Never learned how. I'd breezed through high school, then taken the easiest community college classes possible to *avoid* having to learn. For too long I had approached my education lazily, with the attitude of someone who'd never cared to challenge herself. "Book learning" had only been really important to me when that book was the Bible.

Now I was at Harvard and had no clue how to study.

33.

I worked late into the night Friday, then got up early Saturday and started again. Most of my assignments were readings. They were either long and incomprehensibly difficult—one was on stem cells, one on balancing chemical equations—or tear-jerkingly boring: how to synthesize arguments in a persuasive essay; how to make adjectives agree in Gaelic. My focus would slip every few minutes, and my eyes would drift to the Quad below.

Around sunset, I noticed big groups of students walking eagerly toward my dorm. Somewhere on the first floor, music started playing. My floor throbbed with the thumping bass.

That was the end of my feeble concentration. I watched the commotion below. Music and chatter blasted every time the door beneath my window opened. Groups of friends filed in and out with red cups in their hands.

I looked on jealously, wondering what it would be like to have friends to go to a party with. I had never even been to a party. Weed was one thing, but alcohol—that was a different beast. Once I'd considered it a sin almost as evil as fornication and avoided it with the same fear and disgust. As I watched the students below, an impulsive bolt of bravery hit. Why not try it? Why not go make friends?

Downstairs, someone stumbled out the door as I went in. The smell of beer and sweat hit immediately. There was a stickiness to the heavy, bitter air, which was heated by too many bodies crammed into a too-tight room. I squeezed my way to the self-serve bar and grabbed a red cup.

There were too many bottles to choose from. Gin. Rum. Vodka. Tequila. If there was a difference, I didn't know it, although I didn't want to let on, even to this crowd of strangers. With false confidence, I picked a bottle with a picture of a goose and poured my cup halfway full.

"Fuck yeah!" said a boy in a tank top behind me. Embarrassed, I replaced the bottle and escaped into the crowd.

I took a big gulp of the clear liquid. I choked as it went down. Surely this couldn't be what all the fuss was about, I thought. All around me, people were dancing and laughing and shouting to each other with careless ease. If this was what it took to make friends, I had to do it.

My resolve lasted only a few more gulps. I stomached the drink until I couldn't anymore, then waited for the courage to kick in.

And then, I was sinking, blurring, fading at the edges. The hard lines that separated me from the crowd melted away. Soon I was one of them, swaying and shouting in the pulsing darkness.

For a moment, at least. I tried talking to a boy in a flamingo-print shirt, but my loudest voice was still soft and the music was too loud and he kept repeating that he couldn't hear me, he couldn't hear me, and then somebody bumped him from behind and his beer sloshed down my leg, pooling in the sole of my sandal. "I'll get a paper towel," he yelled over the song. He disappeared into the crowd. I didn't see him again.

The smell of beer was starting to get to me. My cheeks were flushed, then on fire. I pushed my way to the door and burst into the relief of the night air. Beneath my window, a girl was vomiting into the mulch. I rushed past so I wouldn't, too.

The next morning, I woke up to a roaring headache and roiling stomach. My room smelled faintly of beer. Last night's clothes were thrown carelessly in the corner. I dragged myself out of bed to take them to the basement laundry.

So much for that, I thought on the way down. I berated myself for my shyness and insecurity. I hated that even alcohol wasn't enough to remedy it.

How *did* one make friends on this campus? I thought of my old friends back home, how our relationships had formed naturally, easily. Was it through the fact of our upbringing, a built-in kinship formed by the mountains? It seemed so, especially since our ties were frayed now that I'd become "citified."

When I was growing up, that was a word I'd heard spoken with more scorn than jest. It was bestowed on anyone who left their small, rural town for somewhere even moderately urban, who spurned their country roots in favor of a self-important, progressive city culture. It was an insult. A designation of unbelonging.

As hard as I was trying to embrace Cambridge, it seemed insistent on not having me. No one back home saw me stumbling, bumbling my way into the bike lane, down crowded sidewalks, across busy intersections, or to wild, sweaty parties where I didn't know a soul. They didn't see me getting questioned for my accent or struggling to even say hi to my peers. If they had seen, if they had known, they would have realized the word "citified" didn't describe me at all.

A couple hours later, I went to retrieve my laundry.

A boy was humming energetically at a washer by the door. "Hi!" he chirped. My headache was still very present, and I gave a weak smile. His eyes dropped to my shirt.

"Are you from Virginia?" He looked at the outline of my home state, which was silk-screened in white across my chest. I said yes.

"What do you know! Another southerner." He reached out to shake my hand. "Not too many of us in these parts."

I perked up at the colloquialism and took his hand. "Where are you from?" I asked.

"Tennessee," he said. "I know I don't sound like it. I've been here for two years. I guess I lost my accent along the way."

"Hopefully I'll lose mine," I said.

"No, don't!" he exclaimed. "I think it's beautiful."

I like this guy, I thought.

His name was Harrison. He was a junior, a history major, and lived a floor above me. We stood there talking for twenty minutes, trading comparisons of how life in Boston was so terribly different from our small, rural hometowns. Everything moved slower down south, we agreed. Everyone was friendlier. The weather was nicer. The landscape was prettier. And good Lord, the *food*. It seemed nothing in the dining hall was cooked with butter or salt.

"That reminds me," he said. "This club I belong to, it's having a little get-together by the river Friday evening. They'll have fried chicken and sweet tea. My idea." He gave me a smile. "You want to come?"

I smiled back. "I'll be there."

Even with my heavy heap of laundry, I floated back to my room. It seemed as if I'd finally made a friend.

With something to look forward to, I thought the week would fly by. And it did. But only because I was busier than ever.

When I slid into my seat at nine o'clock on Monday morning, my chemistry professor had just pulled up a fifty-slide PowerPoint titled "Intermolecular Forces" on the screen behind him. "We're moving into more challenging material this week," he said.

Great. I wilted in my seat.

Meanwhile, backs straightened across the room. The professor clicked to the first slide and asked if anyone could recite the first law of thermodynamics. A hundred hands shot up.

He called on a red-haired girl a few seats down from me. "The law of conservation of energy states that energy can be neither created nor destroyed."

I copied down her words exactly, wondering what thermodynamics was.

The professor asked for the second law. The red-haired girl's arm flew into the air again, but he called on one of the many others waving across the auditorium.

"The entropy of an isolated system is always increasing," called out a baby-faced freshman near the wall.

"Entropy." Entropy? I drew a circle around the word. That was another I'd have to look up later.

I stared out over the room, watching dozens of eager arms pop up every time the professor asked a question. There was something *different* about the students here, I realized. It was a composure, a confidence, that eluded me.

In every class, I was surrounded by students who asserted their presence and knowledge. There was a boy in biology who asked questions so complex that I didn't even understand what he was asking. There was a girl in my writing seminar who always volunteered to read aloud. There was a PhD student in my Scottish Gaelic class who was perfectly fluent in both Welsh and Irish. She took to the new language intuitively, soaking up the strange spelling and grammar rules with ease.

Meanwhile, I floundered. My overwhelmed brain sealed itself off, rejecting even the simplest of concepts. *No more learning*, it seemed to say. *That's it. I'm done.*

And it was only the second week of class.

"Everyone is crazy smart here," I complained to Mom on a phone call one night. I knew Harvard was many steps up from community college, but I hadn't expected *this*. I'd never struggled in school before. "It makes me feel so dumb."

"You'll catch up," she told me. "Just give yourself time to adjust." I was momentarily calmed by the assurance: Once this awful period of adjustment was over, my classwork would get easier, and I'd fit right in with my peers.

When I got off the phone and Mom's soothing voice faded to the clamor of traffic and people outside, the reality of my situation came back into focus. My homework assignments were piling up faster than I could complete them. My notebook was full of terms I didn't understand. I could barely keep up with my professors, who flew through PowerPoints with lightning speed and little explanation. The more they talked, the less I understood.

I wanted to be optimistic, wanted to tell myself that I knew more than I felt I did. But with every class, my confusion snowballed until even words and concepts I *did* understand lost meaning. *Molecule? What's a molecule?*

On Friday afternoon, after my last class of the week, I met with my adviser for a check-in.

"How's everything going so far?" she asked brightly.

"Fine," I lied, forcing myself to return her smile. The day before, I had barely scraped out a C on a mini-quiz in chemistry. It was nothing more than a review, a matching of terms and definitions. Still, it was like reading another language. I had strategically taken a seat next to the red-haired girl and copied some of her answers. The answers I didn't copy, I got wrong.

I didn't want to admit that I was struggling. Not to my adviser, not to myself. I conceded that my science classes were a *little* bit challenging, but nothing I couldn't handle.

"Great!" she said.

I was grateful she didn't ask about my expository writing class, and I was careful not to mention it. When the professor had returned my first essay, it was so marked up I could barely sift through the comments and edits. I didn't know how to analyze a text or structure an argument. I broke all kinds of grammar rules that I didn't know existed. After my second essay, which was just as abysmal as the first, the professor had sat me down in her office and tried to explain, one-on-one, the concepts I just wasn't getting.

Progression of thought. Integrated quotes. Reflective conclusion. I heard every word she said, I understood their individual meanings. Still, her sentences passed through my brain without comprehension, in one ear and out the other.

It was like that in every class, every conversation. Words were little more than meaningless sounds. I listened and spoke without processing, feeling as if I'd lost my ability to comprehend English.

What was it, this strange and sudden unraveling of language? Every lecture, every assignment, and every conversation left me feeling outpaced, off-kilter, as if I were broadcasting at a slightly different frequency from everyone else. Academia was on another wavelength, a dialect unto itself. I didn't know how to tune my eyes and ears.

Summer was waning, but Friday evening was still warm enough for shorts. I walked across the Quad as others headed toward the dining hall, imagining a big plate of fried chicken and, even better, sitting with Harrison by the river.

The thought put me in a grand mood. So did the promise of the weekend, a short respite from the busyness of classes. I had more homework than I knew what to do with, but I chose to put it and the other challenges of the past two weeks out of mind, at least for the evening. Suddenly I felt an odd rush of affection toward the quaint old houses on Garden Street, the bright spread of grass on Cambridge Common, and even the people crowding the sidewalk, smiling and strolling with Friday leisure. As I passed, I absorbed their joy. Tonight was going to be a good night.

I crossed the street near an intersection, then waited at a curb to cross again. That was yet another oddity of city life. Back home, there was no need for crosswalks. Here, walking was stop-and-go, stop-and-go, just like the heavy flow of traffic. Usually I found it frustrating. This evening, though, I was unbothered. For the first time in weeks, I wasn't in a hurry to be somewhere.

I stood at the curb and soaked in the city, taking in everything I'd failed to notice in my constant rush. Behind me was a great stone church. I shielded my eyes against the low-hanging sun and stared up at the church's bell tower. After a moment, I looked down to its tiny fenced lawn. The grass was dotted with hundreds of little flags, some red and some white, like a field of spring flowers.

Off to the side was a bleak black sign. EACH FLAG REPRESENTS A VICTIM OF GUN VIOLENCE IN MASSACHUSETTS, it read. Beneath that line, another: WHITE INDICATES INJURY. RED INDICATES DEATH.

I lingered on the memorial longer than I should have, barely making it through the crosswalk in time. The visual stayed with me as I walked away, jabbing lightly at my pleasant mood.

There were so many little flags. So many *red* flags. Back home, the phrase "gun violence" was pejorative, spoken about only in terms of liberal sensationalism: It was a misunderstanding, an exaggeration, of gun-involved crime, words of propaganda by people who wanted to revoke the Second Amendment. *Guns don't kill people; people kill people.* How many times had I heard that? How many times had I heard that in church, where congregants carried holstered pistols on their hips? Pastor Ron had praised those men, lauded their courage. *The best defense against a bad guy with a gun is a good guy with a gun.* Those red and white flags would have never made an appearance on Deliverance's front lawn.

Neither would the rainbow flag, which flew over the steps of the Unitarian church in the Square, or the Black Lives Matter sign at the gate of the Baptist church a few blocks down. Here, churches proudly supported issues of conservative contention. To me, that was even more evidence of an upside-down world.

But the evening was light, and those thoughts were heavy. I shook them off as the river came into sight. On the other side of Memorial Drive, a couple dozen students were gathered on the grassy bank. Some were lined up at a folding table. Others were circled up in the grass, listening to a boy read from a book.

My eyes landed on waving arms. Harrison was standing near the table.

"I'm so glad you made it!" he said. We headed to the back of the line together. The greasy smell of fried chicken was heavenly.

As we inched forward, making small talk about classes and the weather, my eyes drifted over Harrison's shoulder to the circle of students. They were listening closely to the boy with the book. He had a commanding, emphatic voice—a voice that, for some reason, sounded familiar to me. I turned my attention to it.

"Do not be conformed," he read, "to the ways of this world."

I was jolted by my recognition. The verse completed itself in my brain without any conscious effort. *But be transformed by the renewing of your mind, so that you may prove what is the good, acceptable, and perfect will of God.*

I looked back at Harrison. Had he invited me to a *Bible study*?

"What is this club?" I asked.

"We call ourselves Faith and Action," Harrison replied. "We're the largest Christian organization on campus."

I nodded slowly. *Oh.*

Harrison went on, explaining the club's mission and principles. We moved forward in line. I stepped up to the chicken guiltily, not wanting to take food from a club I was most definitely not going to join, and dropped a single thigh onto my plate.

Harrison followed me as I moved away from the table. "I think it's important to surround yourself with like-minded Christians. Don't you?"

I said nothing, confused by the assumption he had apparently made about me. Did he think I was a Christian just because I was from rural Appalachia? I nibbled uncomfortably on my chicken thigh. "Honestly, religion isn't really my thing," I finally replied.

Harrison seemed surprised, and tried to push back. "You should come to our next meeting. See what we're all about."

I started to decline, but a girl in glasses walked up and interrupted our conversation. Harrison introduced her as the club vice president. She smiled and reached for my hand.

"This is Emilee," Harrison said to her. "She's thinking about joining the club."

What? I looked at Harrison and started to protest, but the vice president spoke first. "We'd love to have you!"

"We're studying Romans the next few weeks," Harrison said, looking toward the circle.

I realized it was finally my turn to speak, but I didn't know what to say.

Harrison kept smiling, though I could tell he could tell he was losing me. "Stick around awhile," he urged.

I thought about staying just to avoid the discomfort of saying no again, but the thought of sitting through a Bible study was unbearable. Harrison hadn't invited me here to be my friend. Or maybe he had, but only on the condition of my joining his club.

"Join us next week?" he asked.

There was an all-too-familiar expectation in his smile. It reminded me, suddenly, of a time long ago: of a dark room and watchful faces; of people who I thought were friends, but weren't.

I spotted a trash can nearby and tossed my plate in. "I've got to go," I said. With a few feet between me and Harrison, it was easier to refuse his pull. I told him I'd see him around, hoping I actually wouldn't, and started the mile back to my dorm alone.

34.

Four weeks into the semester, my biology professor announced an upcoming midterm. He would be holding extra office hours to help students prepare and strongly encouraged everyone to come. I didn't know what office hours were, but I figured that if the professor himself suggested going, I should probably go.

I was growing somewhat used to the hectic pace of each lecture, but the material was as impenetrable as ever. A week earlier, the teaching assistants had arranged a collaborative homework help session. I'd eavesdropped on other students' questions, too embarrassed to ask my own, and copied off their homework sheets when they weren't looking. That strategy had earned me a B minus. Not terrible, I thought. But not great either, especially since none of the work was my own.

Early one morning, I followed Google Maps to my biology professor's office. I had no idea what to expect: how many people would be there, if I should come with specific questions, or whether I was dressed appropriately. I'd thrown on a pair of khakis for good measure. Office hours did not sound like a casual event.

The building was on Divinity Avenue. I walked up to the fourth floor and wandered until I found my professor's office. The door was closed. A boy from my class, the one who always asked complicated questions, was standing nearby. I joined him in waiting. After a minute or so, our professor came around the corner.

"Come in." He unlocked the door.

We all sat at a round table. Right away, my classmate launched into a question about the previous day's lecture. "So you were talking about the development of transcriptional networks in early blastocysts," he started.

That was enough to flip the off switch in my brain. I didn't hear anything that followed.

After a lengthy question and the professor's even lengthier explanation, the boy stood, said thank you, and left.

Suddenly, terrifyingly, I was all alone with my professor. I couldn't think of anything to say.

He spoke for me, though. "Do you also have a question?"

"Uh . . . no. I'm sorry." I wished desperately that I had prepared one.

The professor sat back in his chair and looked at me with quizzical eyes. For a moment, he was silent.

"Your accent," he finally said. His words were sharply enunciated, but they came out exaggeratedly slow, as if he thought I wouldn't understand him. "Where are you from?"

"Southwest Virginia," I told him.

He raised his eyebrows. "Coal country?" he asked.

Surprised, I said yes.

"Bituminous coal, right?" he asked.

I had no idea, but I didn't want to look stupid, so I said yes again.

He crossed his legs, folded his hands, and gave me an examining stare through glasses with round frames that were barely bigger than his eyes. For several seconds he didn't speak.

I squirmed uncomfortably in my seat.

"So how's the economy there?" he finally asked, voice polite but pointed. He was smirking now too. I didn't know why.

"Well . . ." I started nervously. What did this have to do with class? I scrambled for something to say, and remembered a couple mines had reopened in the months before I'd moved. I told my professor as much. "A couple mines reopened this year."

That was the wrong thing to say, though. The professor smiled wider, cocked his head slightly.

"The world is going the way of renewable energy. Do you think coal mining can be sustained?"

There was clearly only one right answer, but I chose not to say it or anything else.

I left his office soon afterward, confused about more than just the test material. My accent had marked me from the beginning; now my insecurity was realized. It wasn't just my professor. Every time I opened my mouth, someone asked where I was from. If they were too polite to ask, they'd knit their eyebrows and tilt their ear toward my voice, as if enough concentration would reveal my unknown origins. It happened almost every day.

"You don't sound like you're from Virginia." This was the reply I usually got. It was true: I didn't sound like the metropolitan Virginians most people here knew. Sometimes I'd explain further, although that was dangerous. "Southwest Virginia." "Appalachia." "Coal country." The words would put a spark of recognition in their eyes, and a slight unease would wrinkle their forehead. Most said nothing, though a few said what I knew everyone else thought: "Have you ever shot a gun?" "Are you a Republican?" "Did you vote for Trump?" The questions were presumptuous, accusatory, condescending. *So how's the economy there?* My professor's smirk infuriated me every time I thought about it.

There. I was from *there.* I was from an abhorrent black hole of rural southern conservatism, which was all anyone heard every time I opened my mouth, every time I revealed my background. The questions, stereotypes, strange looks, and assumptions, from Harrison and my biology professor and everyone else, were beyond embarrassing. I felt like a zoo animal, a specimen. Whether I wanted it or not—and I did not—my very presence on that campus invited constant probing and analysis.

Over the next few days, my insecurity ballooned until it took up all the space in my mind. All I could think about were the differences between me and my classmates: their intelligence and my ignorance; their confidence and my timidity; their eloquence and my quiet, nervous bumbling. By comparison to the clear, polished voices that surrounded me, my own was slanted and shaky and graceless, trudging up a mountain one syllable and tumbling down headfirst in the next. It began to sound stupid even to my own ears.

Maybe this was my punishment for leaving the mountains, I thought. Maybe there was truth to all the warnings I'd heard. Beyond Appalachia, the world was hostile, unkind. How naive I was to think I could conquer it. I couldn't even pretend I *belonged* in it.

For a week, I studied—or did what I called studying—nonstop. I stared at notes, PowerPoints, and practice quizzes for hours a day until, bleary-eyed and half delusional, I had every word, image, and graph memorized.

At office hours, my professor had given me exactly one piece of advice about the midterm: "application over memorization." I didn't understand what that meant until a teaching assistant laid the test down in front of me. It was a double-sided stack of papers with complex essay questions that required paragraphs of detailed explanation.

Illustrate the Cre-Lox system.

Explain how endogenous retroviruses may be favorable for fetal development.

Differentiate between the trophoblast, epiblast, and hypoblast in an early mammalian embryo.

I had never seen a test like it. It was the hardest test I'd ever taken.

I regurgitated the few terms I remembered, explaining concepts I didn't understand as best I knew how. An hour later, I nervously flipped through the test one last time before turning it in, realizing there was a *lot* of blank space.

If I struggled, surely others did, too. This was the only comfort I could give myself.

But a few days later, I got an email.

> *Hi Emilee,*
>
> *I wanted to reach out to you before I hand back the midterm exams and let you know that you scored 46.5 points out of 100, which means your score was more than three standard deviations below the course average.*
>
> *I would suggest stopping by after lecture to talk to me about your options regarding the course.**

---

*This email has been slightly condensed for clarity.

I stared blankly at the screen. "Three standard deviations" meant nothing to me.

What it meant, I learned that afternoon, was that most of the class had done quite well. When I walked into class, a slideshow of test statistics waited on the projector screen.

"We had a wide range of scores," the professor began, clicking to the first slide. A bell curve popped up. He circled its height with a laser pointer. "The average grade was a B."

I was floored.

"The highest grade was 100. In fact, there were several of those." He pointed to the far right of the curve, then paused. "The lowest score," he said, flicking the pointer to the opposite end of the screen, "was a 46.5."

A nervous murmur passed over the room. Someone in the row behind me whispered, "Oh, shit."

Don't worry, I thought. *It's me, not you.* I felt my face get hot, ashamed of my failure, even though nobody else knew.

The professor launched into a lecture that I paid absolutely no attention to. Instead I pulled out my syllabus and tried to crunch numbers, hoping I could somehow recover from the F that was 30 percent of my grade, but each assignment was weighted differently and I had no idea how to do the math.

I stared down at the syllabus. I stared up at the professor. I stared at the slide projected on the wall, and when I saw the title—"Anterior-Posterior Patterning of the Neural Tube"—I knew my fate was sealed. I opened my laptop and dropped the very class I was sitting in.

It was stupid, I thought with a flush of anger, to have ever believed I would belong at Harvard. I was from the wrong place. The wrong background. I wasn't prepared. I hadn't even known *how* to prepare. If I'd ever had a fighting chance here, I'd already lost.

A teaching assistant handed back the tests after class. When I walked up to him, he gave me a sympathetic half smile.

"Have you talked to Professor—?" he asked gently, but I interrupted.

"I already dropped." I took my test. The grade glared at me from the front page. I tried polite-smiling back, but suddenly my face was cracking, tears coming on fast. I turned just before they spilled out.

I pulled up my hood to conceal my wet face, then fast-walked out of the windowless basement of that lecture hall, desperate to get back to my dorm as quickly and unnoticed as possible. I felt as if my failure were written in bold across my body.

Why are you so stupid? I kept my head down as I passed people on the sidewalk. *Stupid. Stupid. Stupid.* As I scurried down the street, my thinking began to shift. I couldn't blame my background for my unpreparedness. I couldn't blame Harvard for its intensity and rigor. It was my *own* fault, my *own* weakness, my *own* stupidity for failing to acclimate. By being so recklessly ambitious, I'd set myself up for failure.

The only way I could see forward was by dropping out.

I stopped then suddenly. I'd been walking in what I thought was the direction of my dorm, but with my mind on my future dropout status I had gone too far, either taken a wrong turn or not turned at the right street. The campus was still as embarrassingly foreign to me as it had been on day one, so I'd have to retrace my footsteps to reorient myself.

I turned back toward the right direction, still crying, and went about getting unlost.

35.

The wall beside my bed was flat white, painted with the cheap kind of paint that shows every mark and flakes off in brittle chips. Slowly, very slowly, I traced old scratches and dents with my nail. Who were the people who left them behind? Where were they now, and what were their lives like? I pictured them clinking glasses at fancy dinner parties, sitting in penthouse office suites, and sunbathing on the sleek white decks of mega yachts. They were lawyers. Bankers. CEOs. In my mind, their success was as exaggerated as my failure.

In the days that followed the midterm, I tucked myself away in the solitude of my little room, watching *King of the Hill* on my laptop and eating bowls of overboiled spaghetti from the dining hall downstairs. I skipped most of my classes. I ignored emails, homework, and the transfer student group chat. I spoke only to Patrick, who noticed my withdrawal. He texted me every day. Once I told him I was thinking about dropping out.

"Go talk to your adviser," he urged. "Don't give up yet."

I waited a couple days, then scheduled an adviser meeting when the thought of dropping out began to seem scarier than staying.

What kinds of looks and behind-my-back whispers would I get back home if people heard I'd flunked out after a *month*?

My adviser replaced my science classes with a single easy elective I had no interest in. Sometimes I went to lecture; sometimes I didn't. Most of the time I stayed in my room and stared at the wall or my phone screen, crippled by sorrow that felt like shards of glass in my heart, aching for something I didn't know how to name.

What I longed for, desperately, was connection. Failing the test was one blow. Failing while everyone else passed was another. But solitude—my perpetual disconnect with all my peers and professors—was a constant, infinite battering, a wrenching and inescapable reminder of how out of place, how inferior, I was on that campus.

I suppose my idea was born of desperation. It came to me late one night in the darkness of my dorm room. My window was closed and the shade was pulled, but bright, merry voices still streamed in from the Quad below. The pang for a voice to respond to my own was shattering.

I opened up my phone and downloaded the only solution I could think of.

Dating apps were entirely foreign to me. I had never used one. Not that I had any real interest in dating. At that moment, I had no interest in anything, really, except distracting myself from my own shame. After my breakup with Sam, I had escaped that feeling by turning to other men. Now, at Harvard, I would do the same.

Every day, a dull, endless stream of strangers popped up in my inbox. I didn't care if they were dull. I didn't care about them one way or another. They didn't care about me either. Some wanted to take me to dinner. Most just wanted me to come straight to their apartments.

Often, I declined.

Sometimes, I didn't.

Sometimes, I took the distraction as far as it could go.

It was the last thing I needed to be doing, but it was as if I were severed from all consciousness, my body acting of its own accord. There were several nights I floated from my dorm to the subway station, propelled by pain, disengaged from both brain and legs. I stared at my reflection in the train window and felt it belonged to someone else. Often my gaze would slip past myself and into the distant black water of the river.

There was no telling where I'd end up. Downtown Crossing. Boston Common. Apartments of absolute strangers whose names were forgotten as soon as I learned them. I barely remember walking into those rooms or leaving a few hours later. What happened in between is more vivid to me: the almost-tender moments with hungry-eyed men; the sense of being wanted and seen. The paradoxical pleasure in my anonymity. When I was lying in bed with someone who knew nothing about me, fully disconnected from every aspect of my daytime identity, I was a different, more infinite self, one with no past or present, no flaws or insecurities.

It was a relief to be nobody at all.

One night, a man with dark eyes picked me up in a Jeep, drove to a park, and asked me to join him in the back seat. After, he handed me a hundred-dollar bill.

"Is this enough?" he asked.

This had never happened before. I hesitated, searching his face, then played along with whatever assumption he was operating under. "Yes." I took the money.

Later, in my dorm, I pulled the bill out of my pocket and smoothed it out on my desk. A hundred dollars was a lot of money. A lot of money for something so mindless that I'd already forgotten the face of the man himself.

I was so low, so numb, that the fact of what I'd just done didn't sink in right away. An hour later, as I lay in bed replaying that night's events, the realization came on slowly, fully, in a wave that hollowed out my chest. It pierced through my ribs. Scooped out my lungs.

For the past couple weeks, I'd numbed myself until not even my depression registered anymore. *This* took my breath away. The feeling wasn't of guilt or regret but of shock: that something I'd once and perhaps still subconsciously considered the most immoral thing a person could ever do was so *easy* to do; and that it had been so easy for *me* to do it.

The rest of the night, I barely slept. Dark turned to dawn. The morning rolled into another long day of ignoring emails and staring at my bedroom wall. The hundred-dollar bill glared at me from my desk. I put it in the drawer, then took it back out.

As the sun sank and night returned, another feeling peeked at me from behind my faded shock.

What would it be like to walk the knife's edge again?

My brain, twisted by its own sickness, lit up with a dark, delicious thrill at the thought of doing something so dangerous again. I searched around online and found out there was a dating app specifically for "transactional" relationships. I downloaded the app, created a profile, and was swarmed almost instantly with dozens of men.

Some offered a hundred dollars just to meet me. For anything more, I bargained myself like a piece of furniture at a flea market. Two hundred. Three hundred. Four. Five. I didn't know or care if what I demanded was fair. The money wasn't the point. The challenge of discovering what I was worth, was.

One morning, the man I'd spent the night with pulled the thin gold chain off his neck and insisted I take it.

"I can't," I said. Cash was one thing, but this seemed sentimental, and I would never see the man again. Like the rest, I'd block his number as soon as I was out the door.

He grabbed my arm and pulled me close. He ran his other hand through my hair, lacing his fingers into the roots, and yanked my head back to meet his eyes.

"Take it," he said.

The little clasp clicked like a lock as he secured the chain around my neck.

I left in a hurry, following the sidewalk along the river, and took the chain off as soon as the man's apartment building was out of sight. I held it in my palm, a silky ball of warmth, and thought of hurling it into the water.

After a moment of consideration, I stuck it in my pocket instead. It was gold, after all. Probably worth a lot of money.

At that thought, a certain heaviness came over me. It wasn't the feeling of guilt, exactly. Instead, it was the awareness that I *should* feel guilty: one, for thinking of selling a necklace that was not mine; and two, for taking it—albeit unwillingly—from a man who expected to see me again, which was certainly not going to happen.

And then another thought came to me. Why was I weighing the immorality of selling this stranger's necklace when I hadn't made the same considerations about my own body?

All those nights and all those strange men, and I'd never once felt guilty. I realized that I *should*—I was worse than any whore in the Bible, worse than the evil Jezebel herself—but the feeling had never come. It was as if I'd maxed out my lifetime allowance of guilt, spent it up on things like how many times a day I'd prayed or whether my shirt had covered enough skin. Now I was having sex for money, one of the most grievous sins I could have ever imagined, and I couldn't force a single ounce of shame.

So I didn't stop. I didn't know how. I was addicted to the sweet and terrible callousness with which I used and was used by others. My brain buzzed like TV static and I watched myself from across every room, disembodied, a stranger to my own life. I couldn't reconcile her with the good church girl I'd been just a year and a half earlier. I couldn't *fathom* her, knowing who I was now, or trace the blazing path between us. How quickly I'd become my own antithesis.

How inevitable, I think, that becoming was.

Because it wasn't enough to merely run from God. It wasn't enough to run from my old pious self. The dissolution of her required *this*—an eruption, a burning down. Metamorphosis by the hottest fire.

One night, I got a frantic text from a girl in my dorm.

> *Some guy's pounding on your door.*

I read the message in a stranger's kitchen. Down the hall, a red-bearded man called to me from his bedroom.

Another text came through.

> *He says you have something of his and he's not leaving until he talks to you.*

Three days had passed since I'd seen the man who'd given me the gold chain. It was lying in the top drawer of my dresser.

> *I'm going to call the cops.*

The third message appeared while I was still staring at the first and second. I stood frozen, panicked. How had the man discovered where I lived? Gotten through security? Found my room?

I caught one of the last trains back to Harvard Square. When it pulled into the station, I dashed across the platform, up both sets of stairs, and onto the street. As I was coming out of the station, my phone dinged with one more update: The man had finally, forcefully, been escorted out by police. It was a loud, raucous scene that the whole dorm now knew about. My email inbox chimed with a new message. A dean was already asking where I was and whether I was okay.

I was sinking. I was crashing. I was swallowed up in the noise and the crowd and the cheerful mocking brightness of the busy square. My face was warm and the warmth was wet and I was sobbing, sobbing, and the hollow of my chest was alive again with electric shame. I cried in gasping, aching breaths as I walked Massachusetts Avenue.

It was all the same, wasn't it? Endless and inescapable. I'd traded one wrong, one extreme, for another. Whatever I was searching for couldn't be found.

Headlights and taillights. Honks and flashes. My feet stumbled along, and the darkest despair I'd ever known shot like lightning through my arms and fingertips.

I wondered how it would feel to step in front of a speeding car.

36.

Patrick held the door open, waiting in the unlit entranceway. Even in the dark, I saw worry all over his face.

It was past midnight. Still, he'd answered my text as soon as I sent it. I don't remember what I said. I don't remember him inviting me to his room or even walking there, or what we talked about when I arrived. Inside, Patrick offered me his bed to lie down.

I didn't move.

"You don't have to stay," he said. "But I'll be on the floor." He tossed his duvet to the ground.

Slowly I crawled onto his mattress, tucking myself tight under the bare sheet. The window beside the bed looked over a dark, silent courtyard: a small square of calm in the middle of the city.

Patrick's voice floated up from the floor. "I don't know what's going on," he said, "but everything's going to be okay."

The words were so soft that I started crying. I rolled away from the window and toward Patrick's voice. "You don't *want* to know."

"You can tell me if you'd like," he said.

Though we barely knew each other, there was a tender sincerity about Patrick that made me burst. I told him all of it. Not just about the necklace, not just about the sleeping around, but about Sam and my church and the way my whole life before Harvard disqualified me from being here, and how I would rather die than stay in school or go back home.

When I finished, I lay in silence, spent. Patrick was silent, too. He didn't seem like the type to condemn me, but I half expected it—even wanted it—anyway. *Someone* needed to tell me how evil and terrible I was.

He said nothing at all.

My arm was dangling over the side of the bed. Patrick reached up from the floor. His fingertips found mine. Our hands wrapped around each other.

It was a gentle hold, more healing than words. For the first time since coming to Harvard, I felt seen.

Minutes later, I was asleep.

After that night, Patrick and I were together every moment. It started with breakfast, then carried over to lunch. We got dinner and dessert and had a study session after, then stayed up late talking. Patrick admitted his own loneliness, his struggle to keep up with classwork. The sense that he, too, was an impostor on this campus.

I fell asleep in his room once more.

First we were friends and then, almost immediately, more than friends. I deleted all my dating apps right away, long before we decided to be exclusive a couple weeks later. I latched on to his empathy, the softness in his eyes and his hands, and clung to him wildly, desperate to be saved. His companionship—meaning the absence of my loneliness—motivated me to stop skipping class and work on bringing up my grades.

Night after night, we holed up in steamy little coffee shops and old, cavernous libraries. Patrick worked on his homework while I slogged through a backlog of my own. After a few weeks, I managed to pull my grades above failing. Once I was in the clear, Patrick and I set aside occasional nights just to ourselves. We'd grab pizza, watch a movie, or walk in the dark by the river.

One late night we walked across the river to the business school. There, on a lawn that was surprisingly green for autumn, was a large sculpture of a woman's head. At a distance, nothing about it was unusual. As I got closer, though, the head flattened, distorted. It was an optical illusion. I circled around. With each step I took, the woman's face shifted, changing in increments with my changing perspective.

Patrick was just what I needed. Or what I *thought* I needed. When I think back to those nights, I first recall the sweetness of Patrick's company: the warmth in his smile, the assurance of his arm around my waist. It was an overwhelming comfort to look up from my work and rest my eyes on his face, or my hand on his.

Less easy to explain is the disembodied hollowness that lingered even in my happiest moments with him. Sometimes it was little more than a twinge, that nebulous sense of isolation that defies the presence of others. Sometimes its force was so strong that I couldn't leave my room. Patrick would come all the way to Cabot House to see me because I was too sad to catch the shuttle or walk the mile to Adams. I couldn't identify that deep dark void, where it came from or why it lingered.

I wondered why Patrick wasn't enough to make me happy.

At Patrick's relentless, worried insistence, I booked an appointment at the university mental health clinic. I went hesitantly, almost angrily, frustrated that I apparently couldn't resolve my own unhappiness.

The psychiatrist assigned to me was a white-haired man with a tiny gray office. "Tell me what brought you here today," he said as we settled into our chairs.

I wouldn't budge. "My boyfriend wanted me to come."

The psychiatrist blinked behind big square glasses. He asked me about my background, then what I thought about Harvard. I answered as vaguely as I could: I came from a small town, the city was too big, the schoolwork was too hard.

He nodded again, saying that many students from rural backgrounds felt similarly, and typed some notes into his laptop. Then he asked whether I was depressed or suicidal.

Even though it defeated the purpose of the appointment, I lied and said no. The last time I'd been asked that question, I'd answered honestly, and I was still seared by the embarrassment of being denied help. Of course I wasn't going to be honest now. I trusted this man far less than I trusted anyone from back home.

The psychiatrist nodded and typed. He asked more questions, which I answered as benignly as possible, except for his last. "Do you hear voices or see things that aren't there?"

I laughed a little at that one. "Used to."

He raised his eyebrows, and I immediately regretted my words. "You used to hear voices and see things?"

"A long time ago!" I scrambled. It wasn't actually *that* long ago, I realized, but didn't say so. I tried to explain that I'd once been very religious, that my church believed in literally seeing and hearing God.

The psychiatrist's eyes got wider. I wasn't helping my case.

In my memory, I staunchly insisted I was fine, that I was there only to appease my unnecessarily worried boyfriend, but I must have revealed enough for the psychiatrist to see I was struggling, badly. I walked out of that office with a prescription for an antidepressant in one hand and, in the other, a referral to the neurology department for a brain scan. "Just to make sure nothing funny's going on up there," he'd said, tapping his forehead with a pen.

The prescription I reluctantly filled. The referral I trashed.

It would have been laughable if I'd been in the mood to laugh. A practice of my ex-religion was so foreign, so outlandish, that an actual doctor suspected it might be tumor induced. Apparently it was not normal to audibly hear God call your name, or to be transported out of your body to another time, another place.

How *could* I explain what I'd seen and heard? Until that afternoon, I had never considered the strangeness of what I had experienced in church. I hadn't realized that it *would* be considered strange, what to me had once been so normal.

On a cold day in November, I nervously tallied up my grades. Somehow, to my astonishment, I was holding a B average.

Considering how poorly I had started the semester, it was nothing short of a miracle. I was especially surprised about Scottish Gaelic: After I dropped chemistry and biology, it had become my hardest class. The tests had gotten a little easier over time, though I sensed that had more to do with my professor taking pity on me and less on my improved understanding.

Expository writing was a different story. I'd put hard work into bringing up my grade. It was embarrassing to google basic grammar rules even when no one was watching, but I had to learn to not write the way I talked. I studied essays to model my own after, and once I finished a draft, I asked Patrick to check for mistakes. Each essay was a days-long slog that was prolonged even further by having to write about the most boring topics I could imagine. Over time my grade climbed, and my essays were returned to me with fewer corrections. "Better," my professor scrawled in the margin of one. That lone word made me intensely proud.

I was proud, too, of a particular essay. It was the only one for which I got to choose the topic, which came to me while browsing old *Life* magazines for another assignment. I was flipping through a January 1964 issue in the basement of Lamont Library when I landed on a page with an unexpectedly familiar image. It was a black-and-white of an Appalachian holler: of snow-topped ridges, a tiny tin-roofed house, and a swinging footbridge over an ice-crusted creek. I would know that landscape anywhere. The caption cited Letcher County, in eastern Kentucky.

Looking at that picture, I felt the stillness in the air, the snowy hush of every sound. I heard the gurgle of frigid water and smelled the blue woodsmoke hanging in the bare treetops. There was a dog barking, maybe, and the ringing echo of someone chopping firewood. I stared at the image for longer than I meant to, suddenly and intensely homesick.

The accompanying article was titled "The Valley of Poverty." To my disappointment, it was a grim, patronizing exposé of a supposedly hopeless otherworld. There were photos of tall, ugly coal tipples; newspapered walls; weary women; dirty children; a man who'd lost fingers in the mines. The captions and text spoke of "desolation" and "depression," of "pollution" and "disease." Every image, every word, compounded on Appalachian stereotypes of poverty, ignorance, and helplessness.

I angrily decided my next essay was going to be about that article.

My professor didn't like the idea. Or rather, she didn't like my thesis. I wanted to argue that the photographs exaggerated stereotypes about Appalachian culture: that they showed the worst of poverty but presented it as the norm. My professor said this would be difficult to prove, that it was hard to quantify perception.

"Don't you think there's a certain truth to what these portray?" she asked me, looking down at copies I'd made of the photo spread.

On the other side of her desk, I frowned. "It's an extreme version of the truth."

"How can you prove that?" she asked.

Unsure, I frowned deeper.

"Maybe you should compare these photos to more recent ones," my professor said. "Look at other sources. See if Appalachia is presented differently—more accurately—now. If so, explore why. If not . . . explore why."

I went back to the library. There I found a book of Appalachian photography from 2006, titled *Coal Hollow*. I hoped and figured it would be a more conscientious representation of Appalachia. But its images were in black and white, too, and showed the same depictions of misery and squalor. Toothless men. Tired-eyed women. Dilapidated trailers with trash strewn around the yard.

I couldn't decide which I hated more, the book or the article. No wonder the world had such a negative perception of Appalachia. Why had the authors focused on the extremes of poverty and struggle? Was this how readers *wanted* to see us?

I'd spent months in silent frustration at the stereotypes that seemed to define Appalachia and, by extension, me. My paper ended up being a heated protest of both sources. I argued that their photos portrayed the region's economic and sociocultural struggles in an exaggerated and one-sided way. I angrily wrote that the authors were detached from the complex realities of Appalachian life—that poverty rates had been decreasing for decades while literacy rates, unemployment rates, and health outcomes had improved. I said all the furious things that I'd wanted to say to everyone who'd snidely asked me about the coal market or whether I'd voted for Trump, or raised their eyebrows when they learned the origin of my accent. Emotion spilled all over the page.

Ultimately, no one saw that paper but me and my professor. It was probably for the better. There were weaknesses in my argument, holes in my logic, and grammar mistakes I still hadn't learned to identify—which, as always, she noted. But I'd written an entire ten-page defense of my home when so far I hadn't been able to defend against it at all, only take criticism in silence and shame. Now I had a rebuttal. A voice. It was only on paper, but still, it was my own.

"Emilee! Could you wait a second?"

I was walking out of a small basement auditorium when I heard the voice behind me. A teaching assistant was heading my way.

"You're not in trouble," she said, meeting me in the doorway. Her eyes were kind. "I noticed you don't participate in discussions. I know the semester is over in a few weeks, but I'd love to hear you speak up sometime."

I didn't talk in any of my classes—no more than politeness called for, anyway—but no one had ever called me out on it. "I don't have anything to say," I replied, embarrassed.

"I'm sure you do." She smiled gently. "Don't be afraid to share."

Growing red, I forced a smile back. I walked out of the room, resolving to pay more attention. For the next class, at least.

It was pure irony that my adviser had swapped my ill-fated biology and chemistry lectures for an elective called "World Religions in Multicultural America." No other professor would let me enroll so late in the semester, so it became my third and final class. I knew I should be grateful, but it was hard to feign interest in a topic that repelled me so strongly: I didn't want to think about religion in any context ever again. I'd skipped most of the readings and sat silently through discussions, paying as much attention to whoever was speaking as I did to the drone of the air conditioner. The only reason I was passing was that the grade was heavily based on attendance. Now, even though the semester was more than halfway over, I barely understood the premise of the class: *how faith and freedom are negotiated in a complex society.**

The night before the next lecture, I pulled up the assigned reading on my laptop. I sighed at the page count and forced myself to dive in, skimming until my eye caught on a familiar word: "evangelicals." I stopped and scrolled back to the beginning of the text. It was a case study on a group of evangelical parents who'd sued their children's school system for teaching yoga in PE class. The group believed that yoga, which was rooted in Hinduism, negatively influenced their children's Christian faith.

There was no more skimming. I pored over each page. When I finished, I shoved my laptop at Patrick, scandalized. "Read this!"

The parents' logic was absurd to me now. Once, though, had I known anything about yoga, I would have believed the same. I'd believed that any spiritual practice originating outside the Christian tradition was sinful, an open door to satanic corruption.

I thought about this the next day as I listened—really, actually listened—to my professor and classmates discuss the lawsuit. For the first time in that lecture hall, my concentration was not forced.

It was strange to learn about religions so different from the only one I'd ever known. Even more strange was the courtesy and candor, the way opposing beliefs were talked about without criticism

*This quotation has been paraphrased from the syllabus.

or dismissal. Until that day, class discussions had sounded like a drone to me not because they were boring but because they were *calm.* As an evangelical, I'd only ever heard religion discussed in one mode: Either you were a born-again believer in Jesus Christ, or you were a sinner headed straight for hell. There was only one Truth, and it was as black and white as the page it was printed on. Most of that I'd learned through shouting and wailing, the fever pitch of a riled pastor.

This was oddly, wonderfully different.

There were only a few weeks of class left, but I held on to every word. I learned about world religions from the people who practiced them. Islam, Judaism, Buddhism, Hinduism, Sikhism, and even Catholicism took a new, more benevolent shape in my mind. I began to realize there was no one Truth. There was rebirth and afterlife, karma and salvation. There were sacrifices, offerings, rituals, and rites. There were many gods. One god. No gods at all.

There was also a universal quest for morality and, opposite of what I'd once believed, many paths to achieve it. There was a greater emphasis on kindness and compassion than I'd known in my own religion.

What was it like to believe in the goodness of others? I wondered. What was it like to believe in your own goodness?

On the last day of the semester, the teaching assistant moved the desks into a circle and handed an index card to each student. "Write your name, then pass your card to the right," she told us. "When you get your neighbor's card, write down where you see them in five years, then pass again. Keep going until your card gets back to you."

I expected my note card to return to me blank. I had barely spoken a word the entire semester, even after the teaching assistant's prodding, and only *really* paid attention for a few weeks. Besides, I had no sense of my future. My classmates certainly wouldn't.

To my surprise, my card was so full that the writing spilled over to the back.

Always learning and trying to understand others.

Open to lots of opinions.

Bringing religious, political, and social understanding back home.

Author about religion.

I was taken aback. Though I felt more educated for having taken the class, I didn't feel nearly as observant or receptive as my classmates perceived. The last answer was especially unexpected. Religion was something I was only beginning to understand. The last thing I could see myself writing about.

37.

December came fast, and so did the deadlines for my final assignments. After a three-hour Gaelic exam and twenty-five pages of essays, I finished the semester with an astonishing A minus in every class.

"See, you're doing great!" Mom told me on a phone call.

I agreed. I didn't want to worry her. I'd never told her or Dad about the psychiatrist or the antidepressants or all those strange men. As far as they knew, my only struggles were biology and loneliness. Even those I'd minimized into oblivion. They didn't know I'd pleaded with half a dozen administrators to move out of Cabot House and into Adams House where Patrick lived. That way, we would never be far apart.

Fresh snow was falling on top of old, crusted slush the morning I went home for break. *Winter* break, I had to keep correcting myself, not *Christmas* break. Until now, that was what I had always known it as. Patrick rode with me to the airport. I had never been inside one, and the thought of navigating it alone was terrifying. He waved me off as I struggled to stuff my backpack into a plastic bin. A couple hours later, I sent him a text from the Charlotte tarmac: *Miss you already.*

But oh, how I'd missed the mountains. The ache for them did not compare. My uncle Danny picked me up and we started the three-hour drive back to Tazewell. The flat interstate slowly started to curve, then climb. Soon we were at the crest of a ridge that looked over a miles-long valley of rolling hills, which were blue-purple with the winter cold. It was a shock to my eyes, the openness of the land. I stared as though I'd never seen it before.

"Happy to be home?" Danny asked.

Happy was an understatement. There was no word strong enough for what I felt.

We crossed into Virginia, then briefly into West Virginia. In Bluefield, as we got off the interstate and headed back south, the world became familiar to me again. There were faded billboards advertising lawyers, strip clubs, churches, bars. Yellowed plastic letters spelling WE BUY GOLD dangling on a pawnshop sign by the highway. A chewed-up guardrail still waited to be replaced.

A few months earlier, I'd been smothered by the smallness and sameness of this place. All I'd seen was what I wanted to escape. Now my city-weary eyes looked on with appreciation. This was home. *Home.* The word was far sweeter than when I'd left.

It was late afternoon by the time we pulled in to my driveway. Danny cut the engine, and I opened my door to a complete, almost ringing silence. My ears strained for any sound at all, but not even a whisper of wind blew in the trees. How strange, that arresting stillness. Earlier that morning, I'd been in five frantic lanes of rush-hour traffic. Here there was no movement except for the occasional passing truck or coal train, no noise except for the echoing bawl of dogs down the valley.

That kind of thinking framed the rest of my winter break. Really, it had framed my whole semester. My conception of Cambridge had been formed through the lens of Tazewell, a constant comparison between the two worlds. Now the city was my reference point. Two landscapes, two experiences, rallying against each other. *Here* versus *there. This* versus *that.*

And compared with the utter misery of the past few months, home was utopia. I couldn't imagine leaving again.

The days were short and punctuated by snow squalls that dappled the mountains in white. I watched the flakes fall from the living room couch, alternating between watching Netflix and catching up on all the sleep I'd missed over the past four months. Dad said he'd never seen me act so lazy. Mom wondered if I was sick. I insisted I was fine, just tired, although that was the understatement of the year. The constant busyness of the semester had finally caught up to me.

In mid-January, after we'd both had time to recharge, Patrick came to visit. My family oohed and aahed over my "Yankee boyfriend," assaulting him with questions about New York City and what it was like to be from "up there." He handled it gracefully—"as polite as any southerner," Nanny remarked—but I apologized to him later. I knew what it felt like to stick out in an unfamiliar place.

For the next week, I drove Patrick all over Tazewell County, showing off the mountains as if I'd created them myself. Patrick had never been south of Washington, D.C., let alone anywhere as rural as central Appalachia. I was a very eager tour guide.

"That's a coal camp," I told him, cruising past a shabby row of old houses. "And there's a miners' cemetery." I passed a hillside pocked with sunken graves. I laughed when Patrick startled at a train whistle, then rattled off the history of the railroad that ran in front of my house. Patrick nodded and listened with saintly patience. I was having much more fun than he was.

On the last day of the visit, I took Patrick to Grundy. It was the first time I'd been since Nanny had moved away a year and a half earlier. Nothing had changed much, but to me the coal-dusted town had a fresh charm that defied its appearance. I pointed out the coal miner statue and the Levisa River and the three-story Walmart, then drove on. Half an hour later, we ended up at an overlook on the Kentucky state line. Blue ridges spread across the sky, cut through by a thousand-foot gorge.

Patrick snapped picture after picture. I was pleased by his enthusiasm. "This is incredible," he said from behind his camera.

I couldn't have agreed more. I'd been to this overlook a dozen times, but I felt as if I were seeing it with new eyes.

For the first time in my life, I felt an odd sense of pride in the wildness of Appalachia—in its shameless, even willful, lack of refinement. I didn't avoid passing the roadside junkyards. I didn't try to justify the fading Trump signs or rebel flags. I just drove and drove and drove, flaunting my home in all its gritty glory.

Not that Patrick showed the slightest prejudice or disdain. I liked that he didn't have a preconceived notion of Appalachia, didn't pass judgment even after visiting. Still, I felt a need to defend even the parts I didn't like, to prove that my part of the world wasn't as terrible as it was made out to be. Especially since I now knew what people on the outside seemed to think about us.

Patrick packed his suitcase while I packed mine. We had train tickets to Washington, D.C., and bus tickets to New York. It was my turn to meet Patrick's family, and he wanted to introduce me to the city. Afterward, we'd catch a bus to Boston. The spring semester started in a week.

It was cold the morning Dad drove us to the Amtrak station. Patrick and I settled into a near-empty train and watched the mountains fade behind us. Soon we were winding through the hills of central Virginia, then the flats of the coast. Green turned to gray as the city closed in. A weight started pounding in my chest.

I choked it down until that night, when Patrick gave me my first-ever tour of the capital. As we topped the steps of the Lincoln Memorial, my eyes grew wet and hot.

"I can't go back to school," I said in a voice I barely recognized. The high of the past month was gone, replaced by a visceral, consuming panic that made me unsteady on my own feet. The building was shaking, shifting, growing smaller and darker and colder.

Suddenly Patrick's arms were around me and I was pressing into him, sobbing into the warm brown coat that smelled like his dorm room.

"Hey, it's okay," he said.

His voice sounded strange, too. I looked up.

The worry on his face scalded me with shame. Here I was, once more at the height of emotion; here was Patrick, once more talking me down. It was the enduring dynamic of our relationship. This sudden recognition made me recognize something I didn't like about myself. Was I so weak that I couldn't function without Patrick? Was I so weak that I'd bow to a little homesickness?

Another whiplash of emotion. I sucked up my tears and violently shook off Patrick's arms. I announced too brightly that I was fine, I was fine, that we were going to New York City and then back up to Harvard. This semester was going to be better than the last. Everything was going to be just fine.

Patrick looked baffled, but he surrendered his arms and cautiously played along.

"It'll be just fine," he echoed weakly.

38.

What's going on?" I held Patrick's coat with both hands.

"I think," he said, looking out over a sea of pink hats, "it's the Women's March."

I grasped tighter. I'd seen photos of last year's marches, but I hadn't known there'd be more this year, or that I'd accidentally end up in the thick of one. Patrick and I were trying to get to Central Park. It was only a couple blocks over, he promised, but on the other side of the protest.

"There's no way around. We're going to have to march to get to the other side," he said, stepping toward the crowd.

"Wait!" Still holding his coat, I lurched forward with him. "Let's just find something else to do."

"You're in New York City. You *have* to see Central Park." He stepped off the sidewalk and into the street. I had no choice but to follow.

There was something dystopian about so many people in the streets. It seemed to me as if they were marching toward the end of the world. I expected to immediately get trampled or, at the very least, whisked away from Patrick and lost in a sea of strangers. But the protesters adjusted just enough to make a bubble of space for us.

Suddenly we were two faces in a hundred thousand, walking slowly and purposefully and free from the chaos that, from the outside, I had feared.

After a minute, I started to feel silly for being scared. I let go of Patrick's coat. He pulled out his camera and took pictures of me walking slightly ahead, surrounded by pink-hatted men and women with signs that said things like WOMEN'S RIGHTS ARE HUMAN RIGHTS and DON'T HATE, EDUCATE! Someone behind us started chanting, and the words spread in a wave across the crowd. Soon every voice, including Patrick's, was shouting in unison:

Hey hey! Ho ho! Donald Trump has got to go!

"Is that what we're protesting against?" I asked Patrick above the noise.

"Of course," he said, then joined back in.

Even in the divisive year since Trump's inauguration, I hadn't paid much attention to politics. What I *had* noticed was how strongly people felt about the president, how differently they saw the same man. Here and in Cambridge, his name was practically a slur. In southwest Virginia, he was a hero, a deity. I'd never admitted to anyone except Patrick that I hadn't voted for Trump. I worried it would make me look like a traitor. As if I'd voted against my own people.

I tried to explain this to Patrick.

"But Trump is a *horrible* person," he'd countered. This was early in our relationship, and the first of the same conversation we'd have a dozen times. He didn't understand how so many people could support someone like Trump. I didn't understand why he *couldn't* understand. Of course Trump wasn't the saint a lot of people liked to think he was. But even though I hadn't voted for him, I still felt a strange urge to defend those who had—those whose motivations were, by and large, fear. Fear of losing their jobs, of their families going hungry. Fear of their towns drying up. Their livelihoods. When you're starved for hope, you want—*need*—to believe whoever promises they can save you. Most people I knew had voted for *that*, not Trump's vulgar persona.

But if that was something even Patrick struggled to understand, then what did all those protesters think?

I took the aim of that march personally, interpreting a protest against the president as a criticism of his supporters. It was an immediate and angry reaction, one of blind defensiveness. I was always on high alert for perceived judgments against Appalachia and its people.

I took that attitude back to Harvard with me a few days later. One of the classes I enrolled in was about the lingering influence of the Civil War. It was in the large basement auditorium of an art museum, and almost all of its three hundred seats were full. A professor in a sharp-shouldered suit launched into a lecture about reconceptualizing the war through the lens of modern racial justice issues. He talked about recent acts of racial violence, particularly in the American South, and the Trump administration's seeming apathy. This turned into a tangent about the president himself. I bristled.

Then the professor told a joke.

"Many southerners say they voted for Trump because he's 'relatable.'" The professor smiled wide, hands in his pockets, and readied for the punch line. "And I completely understand. Trump has a vocabulary of about six hundred words."

Laughter erupted across the auditorium.

My annoyance turned to fury. I pulled out my laptop and began to email my adviser about dropping the class.

Then, suddenly, I changed my mind. I stopped, erased the draft, and started writing something else instead. A rebuttal.

It wasn't just the content of the joke that upset me, or even the fact that most of the room laughed. It was the joke's total irrelevance to the lecture, the class, everything. What did my professor hope to gain from it? Why insult the intelligence of people whose culture you weren't part of and whose concerns you didn't understand? I penned a long, frustrated opinion column rebuffing all the southern stereotypes I'd heard since coming to Harvard. Then I sent it to the school newspaper.

In that article, I came close to saying there was absolutely no truth in any of those stereotypes—which, of course, was no more accurate than the negative stereotypes I was trying to combat. But I was insecure about my place at Harvard and fiercely defensive against the idea that my home, family, or identity was inferior to anyone or anything else, so I indignantly defended it all, even the social, political, and religious aspects of my culture I disagreed with, because I was so tired of the belittling by people who knew nothing of the South—especially Appalachia—beyond its stereotypes. *I* could criticize where I came from. Not outsiders.

The semester had only just started, but I was already sinking. It was a quick, steady spiral that my antidepressants didn't touch. Despite spending every second outside class with Patrick, I felt more and more alone.

Once again, I considered dropping out.

Patrick talked me off the ledge every time I mentioned it. He tried to think of distractions, new places to eat and fun events to attend. He went with me to parties and helped with my homework. He encouraged me to start reading and running and drawing again, old hobbies I'd almost completely dropped.

Sometimes I appreciated his efforts. Sometimes I resented them. I felt that I owed him happiness—or at the very least stability—and hated myself for being so volatile. I tried to be okay. I wanted to be okay. I wanted Patrick to look at me without concern, without plotting another way to temporarily cheer me up. One day I walked to an art supply store, bought a poster-sized sheet of drawing paper, and taped it to the wall beside my desk. I sketched a hasty portrait of a young girl.

Patrick gave a big smile when he saw it. "That looks great," he said.

I didn't think so. The hair was limp. The smile was awkward. The eyes were too small and spaced too far apart. Later, I erased them both and resketched. This time they were too big. I erased some more. Too small again.

My eraser had worn two pale moons in the creamy paper. I lifted my pencil and restarted a fourth time. The lines were warbled and thick, my worst rendering yet.

Suddenly I couldn't stand the sight of that eyeless girl. I scribbled wildly across the face with a force that broke the graphite and snapped the pencil. I tore the drawing off the wall.

Later, when Patrick returned, his gaze lingered on where the drawing had been. Now there were only four pieces of translucent tape with ripped corners of paper trapped beneath. In the trash can by my bookshelf, the drawing had been reduced to confetti, and the broken pencil lay in splintered halves on the floor.

I said nothing, just curled up in my sheets. Patrick watched me silently, worry seared into his eyes.

"I've got to say, Emilee." The psychiatrist tapped his pen against his laptop, staring. "You don't seem like you're doing very well."

I drummed my fingers on the arm of my chair and glared at the rug below. I was angry that Patrick had urged me to come back here. I was angry at all the words my psychiatrist had thrown at me over the past fifteen minutes—"bipolar" and "mania" and "mood stabilizer"—that I didn't fully understand and didn't want to care about. I was angry at myself for blurting out the truth when he'd asked whether I was depressed or suicidal. I was so angry that I don't remember exactly what I told him, whether I finally admitted just how angry and lonely and up and down I was.

Whatever I said, the psychiatrist went quiet for a while. He stared at me with searching eyes, a demoralizing look of pity and concern.

That made me angriest of all.

"I'm worried you're a danger to yourself," he continued. There was a calculated calm in his voice, the tone of someone who's getting ready to deliver bad news. "In these situations, I usually recommend inpatient psychiatric care. I think you would really benefit—"

"I'm not going to the hospital," I cut in.

"It would give you a break from the pressures of school. A chance to rest. Like a reset button—"

"No." I shook my head. I imagined all the classwork that would pile up, and being alone in a strange place, far from Patrick.

What I really needed, or what I *thought* I needed, was to go home. In my mind, it had become the only solution to my depression. I fixated on it even though it made no sense. At home, I'd been just as turbulent. But I didn't realize that then, and I needed something, anything, to blame my misery on, to prove there wasn't something wrong with *me*.

The psychiatrist pressed his lips together, then crossed and uncrossed his arms. Finally, he sighed. "We'll give the mood stabilizers a chance to work. If I don't see some improvement soon, you'll have to get inpatient treatment." His face told me I had no say.

At the height of winter, the days felt endless. The sun set before five and the darkness made late afternoon feel like midnight, and the brief daytime hours dragged on infinitely, blue and breathtakingly cold. Appalachian winters were tropical by comparison.

I figured that the slowed-down feeling had to do with my medication. It made me feel heavy and distorted, as if I were walking underwater with half-closed eyes. I slogged through my classes. One was intermediate Gaelic. One was an impenetrable philosophy seminar called "The Meaning of Life." One was my Civil War class. Every week, the professor found openings for snide, denigrating jokes and comments about southerners and Trump supporters. I wondered if he'd seen my article in the school paper. Either way, he wasn't deterred.

I liked only one class, a journalism workshop that Patrick had encouraged me to sign up for. It was taught by Jill Abramson, a name Patrick said with reverence but I'd never heard of. "The former editor of *The New York Times*," he'd told me excitedly, as if that were supposed to ring a bell. As if I'd ever read something so irrelevant to me. "One of *Forbes*'s Most Powerful Women!" I had never heard of such a list.

On the very first day of class, Professor Abramson had worn high-top sneakers and propped her feet up on the table. After a moment she kicked them down again and reached for her bag on the floor. "Snacks!" she announced, digging out a bag of potato chips and a box of cookies. My classmates passed them around the conference table. I was astonished that such an accomplished person could be so casual. So *normal*. Based on everything Patrick had told me, I'd expected her to act even more aloof and self-important than the other professors I knew.

In some ways, Professor Abramson *was* unusual. She was no-nonsense to the core. She spoke slowly, almost in a growl, and with absolute, unapologetic bluntness. My class was always at attention, knowing that at any second she might lash the room with some sharp-tongued criticism or abrasive, over-your-head wit. Her gaze was even more intimidating than her voice. When making eye contact, she turned her nose down slightly. The effect was almost threatening, as if you'd *better* have something important to say. It wasn't an unkind look, but it certainly wasn't gentle. Neither was her presence. She owned her spot at the table with a confidence that I couldn't imagine.

I was terrified of her.

I had rarely known women who didn't soften their edges, who believed in their own power. It seemed unnatural. Aggressive. It occurred to me that Professor Abramson was not unlike my male professors—opinionated, self-assured, and certain of their place at the front of an Ivy League classroom.

I wondered what it would feel like to be someone who used her voice and asserted her belonging. Who didn't shrink herself to invisibility.

I flew home for spring break in early March, then returned to Cambridge six days later. My molasses brain barely processed that I was home before I had to return to school. Back on campus, in the quiet loneliness of my room, I expected tears, but emotions didn't come as strongly anymore. Crying was more effort than I could muster.

Even though I felt as stagnant as swamp water, my psychiatrist was pleased. "Much improved," he said at my next appointment, after I told him that my moods had smoothed into a dull, flat line.

"Am I supposed to feel this *blank*, though?" I asked.

"Give yourself time to adjust," he said, waving me off. It was beyond my ability to ask further questions. I stood and left, annoyed by *that* word. Since coming to Harvard, I'd been in a perpetual state of adjustment. It never seemed to end.

A couple weeks later, I met with Professor Abramson in her office. She was interested in my background and wanted me to write about the politics of coal country for my next essay.

"So what exactly has Trump done for the coal industry?" she asked. In class, the president was her favorite topic of discussion. She talked a lot about how he negatively influenced public perception of the media, but she talked more often, and with more enthusiasm, about the possibility that he'd committed some act illegal enough to warrant impeachment.

"A couple mines have reopened," I answered. I realized this was the exact phrase I'd spoken to my former biology professor, and hoped the conversation wouldn't go in the same direction.

"Was that *Trump's* doing?" Professor Abramson asked, raising her eyebrows.

"Well . . . he made a lot of promises to bring back coal," I said.

"A promise is one thing. Delivery is another." Her stare was hard, but not demeaning. I didn't feel stupid for not knowing the answer—only challenged, and expected, to learn what it was. *Had* Trump revived coal? Or were Appalachians, including me, giving him unjust credit?

That night, I dove into my research. It started with a history of Appalachian coal: its fast, frantic rise and long, agonizing fall.

The towns it built, and the towns left to crumble. The people it drew, the people it forced away, and the people like my family who stayed in spite of it all. I wrote about the "feeling of being forgotten." Appalachians largely felt ignored—*deplored*—by the rest of the country, which was why so many were swayed by Trump's special interest. Finally, someone with the power to bring about change was listening.

Supposedly.

Almost any conservative candidate would have done, though, after eight years of Obama. The former president's environmental legislation had placed stricter restrictions on mines and pressured power plants to move away from coal. It was a "war on coal," I'd grown up hearing. There was a palpable air of bitterness at President Obama, Democrats, and liberals at large. Trump's opponent, Hillary Clinton, had sealed her fate with a comment that her energy plan would "put a lot of coal miners and coal companies out of business." In coal country, around 80 percent of votes were for Trump.

As far as I could tell, Trump didn't appear to have business dealings or property investments in coal country, no direct ties to coal at all. So why was he so interested in it? Was a New York City billionaire truly concerned about the plight of a few hundred thousand Appalachians?

I started looking for evidence. I looked for Trump's platform on improving Appalachian health care, education, and infrastructure. I looked for his plans to combat poverty and the opioid epidemic. But all my late-night video watching, transcript reading, and Google searching yielded almost nothing—no plan for coal; no plan for anything, really—just Trump's superficial recitations of all the things Appalachians had wanted to hear.

So what was Trump's preoccupation with coal country, then? I turned to Trump's campaign donation records. They showed that coal companies and executives had thrown hundreds of thousands of dollars at Trump's fundraising committee and super PACs. One man—the CEO of one of the largest coal companies in America—gave particularly generous donations both before and after Trump's election. With that money came a wish list, which was for Trump to reverse Obama-era legislation that hindered the CEO's company's performance.

And ultimately, Trump did. His environmental rollbacks included a repeal of the Stream Protection Rule, which aimed to reduce water pollution by regulating mine runoff, and a pledge to repeal Obama's Clean Power Plan, which placed restrictions on coal-fired power plants. These repeals made it easier to open and maintain coal mines.

Over the past year, the coal industry *had* been in an upswing, but that had less to do with Trump's repeals and more to do with decreased production overseas. A recent cyclone had flooded Australian mines, and China's mines had been crippled by environmental restrictions. American coal exports had increased 70 percent to compensate. Which was something Trump couldn't take credit for.

Back home, though, Trump was still seen as the patron saint of coal. The mere fact of rolling coal trains and reopened mines was evidence that Trump had followed through on his promise to revitalize Appalachia.

Really, in the year since his inauguration, Trump had barely involved himself in Appalachian affairs. Once he'd proposed a total defunding of the Appalachian Regional Commission, an agency focused on bringing "self-sustaining economic development" through means like increased internet access, workforce training, and higher education programs—including a new cybersecurity program at the community college I'd attended. Then he'd halted a health study of people who lived near mountaintop removal coal mines. The study was a follow-up to an Obama-era study linking coal dust to lung cancer, which led to environmental rules aimed at limiting coal dust exposure. Trump signed a bill reversing those rules—just as his CEO friend had asked—ending research that would have given insight on rising cases of coal-related disease.

I read all this with a sinking feeling. Just two years earlier, Trump had paid special attention to Appalachia. I'd watched him with my own eyes claim to be its best friend and savior. Now he was actively working against the region with quiet proposals and policies that hurt, not helped. Trump wasn't pro-Appalachian. He wasn't even really pro-coal. He was pro-money, a greedy billionaire politician bankrolled by other greedy billionaires.

It made me furious. Not just at myself for believing Trump's lies, and not just because he'd preyed on coal country's hardship. I was angry that my dear Appalachia was still so vulnerable to outside exploitation. It's the curse of generations: Outsiders come in, make promises they never intend to keep, and use us for their own gain. Of course we don't trust them.

Except, wrongly, for Trump.

How terrible it is to be blinded by hope and desperation. To hear only what you want to hear. To believe everything you're told. That had been me once, sitting in a pew. Now it was me again, trying to defend my already-shaky faith in an indefensible politician. It's a painful thing to learn you've been deceived. But that essay was my admission: You can't trust everything you believe.

A few nights before the end of the semester, I walked with Patrick to the business school.

The statue on the lawn, I'd discovered, had a name: *Inés*. I had come back to visit her several times, always after dark. I was drawn to her by something I couldn't name. There was mystery in her calm, contemplative expression, her closed eyes and neutral lips. Her face was always slightly different from the last time I'd seen it, changed in subtle ways I couldn't discern.

We stood on the quiet lawn, Patrick and I, and admired the statue. It was one or two in the morning. Dark, magical hours. I went forward. Up close, the features were obscured, lost in the slant of the smooth gray stone.

After a moment, I stood back again. I could never see the face at just the right angle. It seemed as if I were always on the verge, as if the smallest shift would turn the flattened face into a proper portrait. No matter where I looked from, though, *Inés* was a *little* off, skewed toward somewhere that was slightly beyond reality.

As I stared, Patrick faded from my periphery. *Inés* and I were alone on the lawn. In the silence, something passed between us. There was a recognition, an awareness. The sense of a sharpened eye.

39.

"Have a good day, sugar pie."

The words were directed at me, but at first I didn't realize. I looked up from the hand dryer and saw the bathroom attendant smiling.

"You too!" I replied, beaming. When was the last time a stranger had smiled at me? I was definitely home, or close enough. The Charlotte airport was a three-hour drive from Tazewell, but at least the two were on the same planet. Cambridge was a world unto itself.

It was mid-May. Appalachia was in full bloom. The pink-budded trees swayed with the wind. Lake Norman sparkled brighter and bluer than I'd ever seen, and the rolling Carolina fields were so green I had to squint to look at them. As Dad drove toward Virginia, I started to thaw, too. Despite my struggles that semester, I'd somehow finished up with another streak of A minuses, and now I would be home for a full three months. The thought felt like sunshine, melting away the last of the New England chill.

The late spring days were warm and slow, and summer came in hot. Strangely, I felt a new energy. My mind came back into focus.

I processed the world in real time again. Maybe my medication was starting to work, or maybe I could think more clearly without the constant distraction of noise, people, and school. Maybe I'd been right: All I'd needed was to go home, back where I belonged.

In June, I started an internship at a local news station. Patrick had encouraged me to apply after proofreading my Trump essay, insisting I'd make a good journalist. I didn't know about that, but I *did* know that the internship paid $8.75 an hour. That was more money than I'd ever made.

The news station was tiny. It covered twelve counties in Virginia and West Virginia but only employed a handful of reporters. My boss was eager for the extra help even though I had no experience. On my second day, he put a professional video camera in my hands and turned me loose.

"I don't know how to use this," I told him. I cradled the heavy camera like a baby, unsure of how to even hold it, intimidated by its dozens of buttons with symbols that meant nothing to me.

"You go to Harvard," he said, laughing me off. "You'll figure it out."

I went on my way irritably, knowing full well I wouldn't.

I was discovering that the fact of my education made people think strange things about me. Earlier that week, I'd gone for a dental cleaning. My dentist had asked how school was going, then cut me off mid-sentence, surprised I hadn't lost my accent.

"Surely you don't talk like *that* up in Boston, do you?"

"I've always talked like this," I said. He knew that, too—I'd been seeing him twice a year since childhood—but he only raised his eyebrows behind his face shield.

"When in Rome . . ." He trailed off.

I didn't reply. My dentist was obviously educated, more so than me, and there was still a slant to his words. Why was someone with an accent like mine judging me for the way *I* spoke? Did he expect me to present myself differently according to where I was? Did *he*?

I knew too well what people thought when they heard Appalachian-speak, and I understood the temptation to hide it—or, better yet, not speak at all. The accent overshadowed any semblance of intelligence or education. People heard our background, not our words.

Still, why should I have to shed that background to be taken seriously?

A few weeks later, I went to the salon for a trim. My stylist draped a plastic cape over me and asked what Harvard was like.

"I feel bad for you." The interruption came from a sweet-faced old lady in the next chair. "Being up there with all those *socialists*." She eyed me suspiciously over her magazine, searching for signs of corruption: If I wasn't already a liberal, my education was likely to turn me into one.

For the past year at Harvard, my background had rendered me a constant target of judgment and assumption. Now, back home, my education brought even *more* judgment and assumption. In Cambridge, my Appalachian roots meant I was ignorant and conservative. In Tazewell, my Harvard education meant I was the opposite.

I listened to the voices too readily. I could almost ignore the opinions of strangers in Cambridge, but these were mountain people. *My* people. I was one of them.

Wasn't I?

The weeks passed quickly, a nine-to-five, Monday-through-Friday rush between news tips. I never quite got the hang of my own camera, so I tagged along with other reporters to interviews and investigations. The job was depressing. I spent a week helping cover an attempted double murder, then another week on an underground mine fire that was igniting homes from beneath. We covered boil-water advisories, budget cuts, and drug busts. We covered an animal abuse case involving a guy I'd graduated from high school with.

Every day after work, I opened up my phone to a text from Patrick. *Hope you've had a good day,* it would say. *I've been thinking about you.*

Sometimes I replied. Sometimes, and with increasing frequency, I didn't. A queue of unanswered messages was growing in my inbox, from Patrick and the few friendly acquaintances I'd made in Cambridge. I justified my silence with work stress and exhaustion. It wasn't entirely untrue. But the root of the matter was a subconscious distancing from all things Harvard.

One hot weekend morning, I drove to town. I parked in front of Subway and watched the dusty OPEN sign flicker in the window. It was strange to think of all that had happened since I'd last stepped inside. The places I'd been, the things I'd seen—how odd to go from here to there, then all the way back again.

I couldn't sit in that parking lot without thinking of Jeremy. I wondered how he'd spent the past year. Maybe we could go out to the lake and catch up. I hoped one of our old coworkers could tell me how to find him.

The new manager, a woman I'd once trained, burst out laughing.

"Who the hell knows!" she said. "Last I heard, he stole a car and headed out west."

I stared. "He *stole a car*?"

"Wrecked his old one." She looked past me, remembering. "Wasn't long after you left for school, actually."

On the way home, I drove slowly past the tow yard. There it was, way up on the hill, with weeds growing around the tires. The roof of the Baby Car was crumpled and flattened into its body. Somehow Jeremy had walked away.

I drove on, emptier than I'd been in months. I wanted to be glad that Jeremy had gotten out of Tazewell, but really I was gutted. Now that he was gone, I suspected I would never see him again.

It's a scary thing to feel you've lost your identity. To sense a growing rift between you and your roots, the one thread of continuity in your life unraveling. The upheaval makes you grasp wildly at whatever remains.

I called up old friends and friends of friends, people who had rarely been beyond the mountains, and started spending every weekend with them. We went four-wheeling and off-roading, had bonfires and drank cheap beer. We loaded rifles and used empty beer cans for target practice. It was a fun but artificial means of asserting my Appalachianness, of trying to prove the city hadn't obliterated my rural roots.

At the end of those long, long days, I'd head home in middle-of-nowhere darkness, the kind where you can't see an inch beyond your headlights, with my windows rolled down so I could hear the frogs peeping in the creek beside the road. It took twenty minutes before I drove back into cell service. My phone would light up in the passenger seat. *Are you alright? Is everything okay?*

On those days I barely talked to Patrick. I'd "forget" to tell him my plans, apologize guiltily, then lie about where I'd been and what I'd been doing. I didn't know how to explain that I was trying to recapture the person I'd been before meeting him.

One Saturday night in July, Patrick wanted to talk on the phone and I didn't. I typed out a cold text in frustration. *You remind me too much of Harvard. It's never going to work out.*

The breakup text was impulsive, but what fueled it had been building for weeks. My identity was so suddenly in crisis that the mere fact of Patrick's presence in my life, even though he was hundreds of miles away, felt like an infiltration of the city life I was desperately trying to escape.

That, and I didn't need him anymore. For months I'd used Patrick as a crutch, the way I'd used every man since Sam: sucked out every ounce of attention and validation he could offer, then discarded him in the space of two sentences. Once there was nothing left for me to take, I was done.

To this day, I'm ashamed of my cruelty. I justified the breakup by telling myself that Patrick surely understood that he belonged to one world and I belonged to another—that there was no reconciling the two, and therefore no future for us together. I told myself this to stifle my guilt, knowing how undeserving Patrick was of the hurt I'd heaped on him, especially in such a sudden, impersonal way. I told myself that my future was a small, slow, simple life in the mountains. Something Patrick would never want or understand.

But the life I lived that summer *wasn't* my life, not really. I had never purposefully surrounded myself with trucks, guns, beer, and people who planned their weekends around those things. It was forced and false. A caricature of the very stereotypes I had spent the past year denying.

40.

My new dorm room was in Westmorly Court, a stately old building at the corner of Bow Street and Arrow Street. The hallways were dark with ornate paneling. Long red rugs spanned the glossy black-and-white-tiled floors. I arrived at my door and opened up to the smell of old, warm wood. Sunbeams fell in long, golden panels on the floor. Panes of dust sparkled in the air.

I dropped my suitcases near the windows. Here I was in the heart of Harvard Square. My view was of dull brick buildings and long lines of traffic, far less picturesque than my view from Cabot House. Still, something about it—the newness of the scenery, perhaps, or the glow of the sunset—reminded me of when I'd moved into Harvard a year earlier. Not the image itself, but the feeling it ignited—some teensy bud of optimism, anticipation, hope. It felt like a promise, steady and light in my chest.

I signed up for five classes even though my adviser recommended no more than four. I couldn't explain my newfound motivation to her, especially since the previous semesters had been a sleepless, slaving drudge to keep up my grades. I spent the first few weeks of class proving to both of us that I could manage.

Occasionally I worried that my strange high would soon pass and the subsequent crash would be even more devastating than before. But the weeks ticked by, and there was no sign of imminent catastrophe. This was unexpected, especially without Patrick's support. Somehow, understanding came more easily to me now. I could read quickly, and with concentration; finish an assignment in hours, not days. It was as if I'd started out with my head above water instead of kicking endlessly toward the surface.

Part of that shift was in finally knowing how to write, listen, and study like a college student. A *Harvard* student. Being able to anticipate what was expected of me made the work more manageable. The nature of my classwork had shifted, too. I'd signed up for as many literature and writing courses as my adviser would allow, then declared an English concentration so I could take even more.

Before we broke up, Patrick had urged me to consider another writing workshop. I had often talked of writing essays about home, but I'd never really tried because I didn't know how or where to start. To put the majesty of the mountains onto paper, to distill Appalachia into mere words—it seemed naive and trite and very nearly impossible. A tale too big to tell, especially for me.

Patrick had browsed the course catalog and suggested a workshop called "The I's Have It: Reading and Writing the Personal Essay." The professor was Michael Pollan, another name Patrick was surprised I didn't know. I kept the class in mind all summer, then applied to take it as soon as I was back on campus. A few weeks later, I was selected to enroll.

I wanted to tell Patrick, but couldn't. I felt too guilty to approach him, even to say sorry. A simple apology seemed completely inadequate for what I'd done.

If I hadn't blown up our relationship, I would have told him why I felt so comfortable in Michael Pollan's class. Most of my professors so far had emanated a certain bravado, a cool, unapproachable edge. Michael—he insisted students call him by his first name—was the opposite. He had a gentle presence that radiated humility and warmth. He looked at my class thoughtfully, perceptively, as if his goal were to learn from *us* instead of the other way around. The atmosphere of the classroom was one of openness and safety.

Under any other circumstances, I couldn't have written honestly. A personal essay, as it turned out, was about more than the people and places I knew. It was about how those people and places affected me: how I saw them, how I interpreted them, how I understood them in my greater understanding of the world.

So far, my life before Harvard was something I spoke of as little and as vaguely as possible. I thought its telling had no place in Cambridge. The mines, the mountains, Subway, Sam, the extremes of my former religion—I feared they would make me even more of an outcast than I already was. Once at a party, I'd drunkenly told someone about almost getting married as a teenager. A circle of people around me went quiet. The curious looks they gave were enough to sober me up instantly, and the embarrassment chased me all the way back to my dorm.

Luckily, Michael didn't demand our deepest, darkest secrets. His approach was soft, a gentle unraveling of ourselves. The very first assignment was to write about a food of personal and cultural significance. It was supposed to be fun. Light.

Instead, it stumped me for days.

Night after night, long after I should have gone to bed, I pulled up a blank Word document and stared. It was a challenge to have to consider not just the *what* but the *why*. What food was significant to Appalachians? To me? What made a food *significant*? I thought about it maybe a little too hard, then finally decided what to write on: tomatoes.

Every Appalachian garden had tomatoes. They were a staple. You could fry them, can them, or slice and salt them for sandwiches. You could even eat them straight from the vine, their earthy spice lingering on your fingertips. There was a more personal story in them, too. One of Dad staking tomato plants with roof bolts he brought home from the mine. The length of our deck railing lined with tomatoes, gifts from our neighbors' gardens, in return for what Dad gave from ours.

Once I started writing, I didn't stop. I wrote and rewrote and wrote some more, wandering off again and again to the memory of home.

That innocuous little essay untangled some aching knot inside me. It was liberating to put my memories to paper, to see them exist outside my head, and to let down the wall between my present life in Cambridge and my past life in Tazewell. Writing that essay was a bridge between incongruities. Or the start of one, at least.

It was the first time I spoke about my Appalachian background without the shame I was supposed to feel.

One moment it was September. The next, October. One day I realized the handful of trees outside my window were yellow. A few days later, I noticed they were bare.

My days began at six o'clock. I walked three blocks to my job at a donut shop in the dark, before the traffic got heavy and the city got loud. I got off around noon, headed to class, went to another class after that, and, depending on the day of the week, went to a third class. It was dark by the time I got dinner. Afterward, I would procrastinate on homework by talking to my roommate or her friends, a group of girls who kindly adopted me into their circle. Later, I'd head up to my room and call a boy back home.

His name was Eli. We'd gone to high school together. I'd started hanging out with him and his friends that summer and fallen for him at the same time I was pulling away from Patrick, largely because he was so similar, but Appalachian. Eli was gentle and steady and the embodiment of everything I'd spent the summer chasing. He worked dawn to dusk on his family farm and had a country accent that made the city outside my window melt away. *You feel like home*, I often told him. I told him how badly I wished I was there.

And it was true. A part of me was always craving the mountains. But another part was growing strangely content for reasons I didn't understand. Every day, it was a little easier to be away.

All my classes were going well, but Michael's was my favorite. Words came easier to me by hand than mouth, and writing was my outlet for everything that shyness kept me from saying aloud. Michael was nothing but encouraging. I grew bolder with each essay.

One was about Jeremy. I reminisced about his car, his tattoos, and the lazy days we smoked away by the lake. A few weeks later, I wrote a longer essay about Sam, about his fury when I pretended to cut my hair and the cold, terrible silence that followed. Then, a few weeks later, I wrote pages and pages about Winter Ramp, speaking in tongues, and the young girl at church who'd collapsed under the weight of the Holy Spirit. I wrote how I'd wiped away her blood with paper towels. How after, I was too sickened to pray.

Once recalled, the memory of these things shocked me. How was my life now so different from that one? As the semester went on, I began to question myself. Were these *really* my experiences? Had this *really* been my life? Being so far removed from those people, places, and beliefs made me wonder whether I'd constructed them all in my mind.

I didn't tell Michael that I was struggling with my own reality, but he could tell I wasn't making sense of what I wrote about. Once, at office hours, he mentioned my essay on Sam.

"You give the facts," he told me, "but you don't offer interpretation."

"What do you mean?" I asked.

"Most readers are going to be unfamiliar with your culture. So give them some insight. Show them the mindset. Ask yourself what it means to be from Appalachia—a *part* of Appalachia—to help them understand."

I stared. I didn't get it.

"For example." Michael spoke gently. "In what world is it okay for an eighteen-year-old to date a fourteen-year-old?"

I remember these words exactly because they were compassionate, not critical. Most people who took an interest in what little they knew about my life were voyeuristic, condescending. Michael knew more of my story than anyone else, and only sought to help me understand it myself.

In what world? Those words swirled in my mind for days. I had never questioned the norms that had shaped my life in Appalachia. Until Michael asked, I hadn't realized the age gap between me and Sam was something to question. My parents were the only ones who'd seemed concerned.

What else had I not realized?

Since coming to Harvard, I had grown aware that many of the things I accepted as normal were *not*. Yet I had never investigated why. Instead, I'd stubbornly defended those norms without examining their origins or endurance. I'd justified them with dismissive explanations like *that's just the way it is. That's just the way we are.*

But without challenging the ways of the world I'd grown up in, I could never have a complete understanding of the choices I'd made, or the girl I'd once been. The woman I had become.

Funny, I thought, how my distance from home made me see it more clearly.

41.

The view from the balcony was of pastures and fields, of golden-gray hills pocked with sheep, cattle, and the pale, dry stubble of cornstalks. The land had been in the family for generations. So had the house. Entire lives had been lived in that valley. Eli often spoke as if his would be, too.

I spent much of my winter break on the back of Eli's four-wheeler, roaming the mountains that shadowed the farm. I wrapped my arms around his middle to tuck my hands into his front coat pockets, and when I pulled them out, they smelled like woodsmoke and dust. I melted into it, and into his ruggedness, and into the smile he almost always wore, ultra-white against his year-round tan.

I wanted to be with Eli as much as I could to make up for the months we'd been apart, even though I'd called him from my dorm room every night. He'd talked about his farmwork, driving fence posts and deworming cattle. I'd talked about the obscure translations that constituted my Advanced Gaelic homework and all the plays I had to read for my Shakespeare class. Sometimes the vast difference between the lives we lived when we were apart weighed on me, especially when one of us would say something the other had no response to. When we were together, though, it was easy enough to pretend there was no difference. Or at the very least that the difference didn't matter.

In January, I flew back to Boston. Once again I signed up for five classes. Most of them were in literature and writing. One was an off-the-wall environmental studies course I'd heard Patrick mention long ago. It had something to do with the rapid change of landscape and culture in postindustrial America. Patrick had taken a different seminar under the same professor, John Stilgoe, and raved about his intelligence and eccentricity.

On the first day of class, I walked in half an hour early. The room was empty except for Professor Stilgoe. He was sitting in the front row. He turned and watched as I entered from the back of the room.

"You can tell a lot about a person by the way they dress," he said.

"Sorry?" I took a seat near his.

The professor's eyes were on my coat, a faded Carhartt with holes around the cuffs. Sam had given it to me for my fifteenth birthday. "Where are you from?"

I was taken aback. It was one thing to be judged on my accent, but even worse to be judged before I opened my mouth. How many times would I have this conversation? I braced myself and told him that I was from southwest Virginia.

Professor Stilgoe met my gaze now. "I've driven through there. All over the coalfields, actually. Just beautiful, those mountains."

I was taken aback again. Minus Patrick, I didn't know anyone at Harvard who had been to my part of the world.

Before I could respond, Professor Stilgoe continued.

"Now that. *That's* a coat. Practical. Warm. Not one of those flimsy little things that some of these kids here wear. And those." He pointed at my knee-high Muck boots, which I wore when the sidewalks were slushy. "You've got sense to dress for the weather.

Some of these kids would wear sandals in a snowstorm." He rolled his eyes. "My father was a New England boatbuilder, and *he* knew how to dress for the weather, believe you me. Now tell me. What do *your* parents do?"

I stammered out my answer, surprised by Professor Stilgoe's interest. He listened intently, then asked more questions about my family and home. We talked until it was time for class to start. I returned early before the next lecture, and then the next. Every time, Professor Stilgoe wanted to know more.

I loved his class even though I didn't understand its purpose. For weeks it was hard for me to articulate what I was learning, and it was impossible to predict what Professor Stilgoe would teach from day to day. One lesson was on the history of urban planning. Another was on mid-century automobile advertisements. In one lecture, we studied an image of an old farmhouse kitchen. In another, we studied a photo of a topless woman lounging by a condominium pool.

"Look," Professor Stilgoe urged the class. "Then look *closer*." We stared at the photo stretched across the screen, waiting for its hidden meaning to reveal itself.

Professor Stilgoe fired off questions to make us think about what we were looking at. He pointed out a row of hedges behind the topless woman. Why were they there? he asked. Were they planted around the pool for privacy, or were they meant to convey a false air of modesty? Why did the woman angle her body toward her neighbors rather than away? What was the significance of her flat smile and vacant eyes? Of holding a magazine? Crossing her legs?

Professor Stilgoe told us to think, then think again. What gender roles did the woman conform—and not conform—to? What was this image trying to tell us? Sell us? How did the woman's body and behavior quietly influence other women to think about themselves?

There were no right answers. No wrong answers either. Each question led to another one. To a more complete understanding of what we were looking at and, more importantly, how we were thinking about it.

Over time, I began to understand what the class was about. Professor Stilgoe taught about many seemingly insignificant things to make us realize one important thing: We were not paying attention. There was so much to see when we looked past the obvious and defamiliarized what we knew, or what we thought we knew. When we broke through the glass domes of our own minds.

Even in the lingering cold of late spring, the Lamont Library basement was summer warm. Earlier that day, Professor Stilgoe had announced the end-of-semester assignment. His instructions were to "write on the theme of modernization" through the lens of old magazine advertisements. I wasn't sure what that meant, but I pulled a small mountain of Depression-era *Life* magazines from the shelves and started flipping, hoping a topic would eventually jump out at me.

I pored over the ads, especially the ones with photographs. I tried to look at them with the trained eyes I'd acquired in class. I noticed ads for clothes and makeup pictured young, smiling women in short skirts and high heels. Ads for household appliances and food brands, on the other hand, pictured wives with their husbands, or mothers with their children. Those women were more clothed and more serious, with muted smiles and solemn eyes and dresses that fell well below the knee. The quiet expectation behind that juxtaposition was my essay: A woman grows up and belongs less to herself, and more to her responsibility for others.

Decades later, I wrote, *I would grow up with the same belief.* I'd believed that the two phases of a woman's life were youth and freedom, and marriage and motherhood. There was no nuance in my understanding. None in those ninety-year-old magazine advertisements either. What did that say about modernization? I asked.

The week after I turned that essay in, I went to class early as always. Professor Stilgoe was waiting in the front row. I sat down near him. He turned to face me and gave me a hard look.

"Are you going to marry him?"

I blinked. Professor Stilgoe's questions always caught me off guard. "You mean Eli?" I asked.

"The farmhand. Yes."

Sometimes I pictured spending the rest of my life in Eli's valley. Sometimes the thought of all that big, empty space was suffocating.

Professor Stilgoe raised another question. "What will you do after you graduate next year?"

"I don't know," I said slowly. "I guess I'll go back home."

Professor Stilgoe nodded. He was quiet for a moment, concentrating on some unspoken thought.

"You know, farming is honorable work. *Hard* work, but good. And marriage can be good, too. Sometimes." He paused again. "Have you considered graduate school? More education?"

"Not really," I said.

"You should. That would be good for you, too." He looked at me earnestly. "I'll write letters, recommendations, help you out however I can. Anytime. Anything you need."

Other students had started to trickle in. Professor Stilgoe stood. "Think about it," he said.

42.

In February, I'd drafted a proposal for my senior thesis. I envisioned a collection of personal essays, a continuation of the work I'd done in Michael's class. "The longer I'm at Harvard," I'd written, "the more questions I have about the culture I grew up in."

The project was approved. Michael would be my thesis adviser.

When the semester ended, my friends scattered to cities across the country for internships and senior thesis research. I went home to write and work. I applied to the same places I had in high school—Dollar General, Pizza Hut, Food Lion, Sonic—with about the same luck. One day I ran into Angie, my former boss from Subway, who offered my job back. I came desperately close to accepting.

At long last I landed an interview at a coffee shop. It was the only one in Tazewell County, a little mom-and-pop place with one barista on duty at a time. There were Bible verses on the walls and Bible tracts on the bar. The owners were a friendly, upbeat couple who told me the mission of their shop was to spread the love of Jesus. They asked whether I would support that mission, too.

I shifted in my seat, then said yes. I'd come too far from Subway to go back.

For the first few weeks, I enjoyed the slow, steady rhythm of my new job. The sink leaked. The espresso machine hissed. There were long minutes and hours between customers. I learned their names and orders, and I could predict almost to the minute what time they'd stop in each day. But soon I came to dread the monotony and spent each week looking forward to Sunday, when the coffee shop was closed so my bosses and coworkers could go to church. My Sundays, I spent with Eli.

I enjoyed that, too, until something shifted. It came on slowly in the mountaintop pastures, where we'd share a six-pack and look out over all the world, breathing in the hazy stillness as silently and comfortably as if the other were not there. It seemed to me that Eli always had something on his mind, but he never said what. My asking annoyed him. I stopped asking.

My growing sense was that he and I weren't right for each other, but I tried to ignore it. Tried to prove it wrong. In the same way, I tried to deny my sense of unbelonging, both on the farm and in Appalachia at large. That summer, unlike the last, it was not pointed out to me as often as I felt it myself. I felt like an impostor drinking beer and shooting guns. I felt like an impostor at my job, surrounded by people who incorporated Jesus into casual conversations. I felt like an impostor at Food Lion when I watched a man pay for a gallon of milk with dimes and nickels, knowing I'd soon return to Adams House, where the foyer wall paint was flecked with real gold.

I never mentioned my impostor feeling to Eli, but he noticed. The evening before I headed back to school, we went shooting on the mountain behind his farm. After a couple hours, tipsy and tired of the heat, we leaned against the four-wheeler, backs to the retreating sun.

"You don't really like this, do you?" Eli asked.

I turned to look at him. Neither of us had spoken in a while.

He returned my gaze, then spoke again. His tone was observational, not accusatory. "You only pretend for my sake."

"I'm having fun," I said. "Really."

"Not just *this*." He looked at the rifle, the pocked and shredded beer cans littering the hill. Then he waved over the pastures in the valley below. "*This*. Here. Everything."

I then understood what he meant: the life I had lived before Harvard, and the life I would live if I returned.

Even though I wasn't certain, I protested that I *did* like it. That after graduation, I wanted to come home for good.

Eli shook his head. "You won't stay."

I disagreed emphatically: I *would* stay. I would come home and dig my feet into the mountains until I wasn't a stranger to them anymore. Never mind that I had no plans, career or otherwise, for after my return. That was far less frightening than the thought of not returning.

43.

I began my senior year at Harvard thinking about my senior year of high school. How skeptical I'd been of college. How my whole future had revolved around marriage and church. Now, at the end of the school year, I'd be free to follow any interest, any opportunity. My seventeen-year-old self could have never fathomed.

And yet I thought only of returning to the place she had almost not escaped.

I didn't talk about my after-graduation plans with my friends. There wasn't much to say. One friend was applying to PhD programs. Another was studying for the MCAT. Another was flying to New York City for an interview at a major consulting firm. The starting salary, which she mentioned casually over dinner one night, was eighty-five thousand dollars.

I didn't envy my friends, exactly, but I was jealous of how clearly Harvard had paved their paths, and how certain they were of what they wanted their lives to look like. All the things that excited them—moving to other cities, starting their careers, spending more time in school—paralyzed me. I knew I was capable of changing and challenging and stretching myself, and I knew I should *want* to do so, but diving into the unknown again so soon felt impossible. In theory, I appreciated the countless possibilities for the future. In reality, I was too scared to choose any of them. All I wanted was to go back to Appalachia. To prove that home really was still home.

I kept myself busy with my thesis and a new job at a campus coffee shop. I also signed up for a graduate-level seminar at the divinity school. It was made up almost entirely of doctoral students, and the weekly readings were some of the most dense historical texts I'd ever laid eyes on. In the past, I had avoided far less demanding classes. This one I couldn't pass up.

"It's called Evangelicalism in America," I told Eli over the phone one night. "It's about the origins of the evangelical movement."

Eli sighed. Our calls were growing fewer and further between, and our patience with each other was dwindling, too. "Haven't you had enough of that fundie nonsense for a lifetime?"

"*Learning* about it is different from *practicing* it," I said pointedly.

Evangelicalism, at least as far as I had ever heard it discussed, was deeply controversial: You knew either nothing or everything about it, and if you *did* know, you probably had very strong opinions. It was a novel opportunity to understand the beliefs of my former denomination from an academic, analytical perspective, rather than a personal and emotional one.

So I went to every class and pored over every reading, fascinated by how the Pentecostal church had come to be. Sometimes the professor played reels of long-ago revivals and church services. I was startled by their familiarity, how they were as noisy and chaotic as the services I'd known. The congregants wept and waved and called out to Jesus, strangled with emotion. If not for the grainy black-and-white footage and outdated hairstyles, I would've wondered whether *I* had been part of those hysterical crowds.

At the end of each video, my classmates were quiet. I didn't need to look at their faces to know what they were thinking. Sitting in that room, far removed from my old beliefs, I wondered how I had ever considered something so bizarre *normal.*

Later that semester, I found myself having dinner with a friend of a friend. Our conversation somehow turned toward religion, and I told her I'd grown up Pentecostal. I tried to explain what it was like to belong to a church where you had visions and spoke in tongues.

"It was the craziest thing," I told her. That was often the word I used to describe it: "crazy."

This time, it tugged at me as it left my mouth.

For years, I hadn't been able to recall any aspect of my former churches without bitterness: The scars of control and deceit occupied my entire field of memory. But over weeks of watching those reels, those worshippers' faces, I'd come to remember the sensation of rising from the altar at peace. I remembered the forgotten catharsis of shouting in tongues with all the breath and power in my lungs, and the heady high of supernatural love. I remembered the members of my churches, people stricken with illness and grief and every manner of silent suffering. I remembered my own mother's quiet, mysterious tears.

So many beliefs and practices of my former faith were unquestionably harmful. They'd turned me inside myself, made me small and scared. Yet my faith had given me, if only briefly, a powerful hope in something beyond the world I knew, where hope was not always easy to find. And the *worship*, the natural expression of that hope, the crying and shouting and freedom to *release*—well, that was the most healing part of what I'd once believed.

I sat on my judgment until I decided it was the wrong thing to feel.

But there was nothing wrong, I knew now, with finding other ways of healing.

Every day I tapped away at my thesis, organizing my life into neat little chapters. Still, no amount of writing helped me explain why I wanted to return home after all that had happened there. After I'd been so eager and determined to leave.

Desperate to understand, I turned to Michael. We sat in his office one evening and tried to make sense of my inexplicable call back to the mountains. He rested his chin on his fist, thinking. "Your roots are deep . . . maybe too deep to flee," he finally said. "Maybe that rootedness defies explanation."

I nodded. That insight was good enough for me.

Michael straightened up and went on. "My sense is that you won't stay in Tazewell, though. Not forever." He trailed off, then smiled kindly. "Maybe that's the end of *this* story. But not the end of *your* story."

I returned the smile, but left his office annoyed. It was as if he and Eli both knew something I didn't. I hated feeling ignorant of my own life, my own future.

Later that evening, I wrote about that rootedness and some other, more defiant assertions that would eventually become the conclusion of my thesis. I remember a squeeze of doubt in my chest as the words appeared on my laptop screen: "Very simply, Appalachia is where I belong. I just *know* it, instinctually."

It wasn't instinct. It was insistence. I was trying to convince myself.

44.

The deer was half hidden behind a tree, only visible against the underbrush by its white speck of a tail. Dad spotted it first. Fifty yards upslope, we straightened, watchful. I could never bring myself to kill. Slowly, silently, Dad readied and aimed his gun.

The blast tore through the forest. The deer leaped in the air and bolted, disappearing down the mountain before the gun's echo had died. It was a miss. Dad and I stood and followed the path of the bullet. It had come to rest in the trunk of a sugar maple, in a fresh hole of splintered wood.

It was a weekday morning in late December. Dad had been furloughed from his job at the rock quarry until sometime after the New Year, although he admitted to me that morning that he wasn't sure if he, or anyone else, would be called back.

"Aren't you worried?" I asked. "What if you lose your job?"

"I'll cross that bridge when I come to it," he said, staring into the forest and away from me. I couldn't determine whether his tone was one of calm or resignation.

That winter break was a busy one. There were hunting trips and family visits. I picked up a few hours wrapping presents at the gift shop where I'd once worked. I spent a couple snowy afternoons on Eli's farm, too, holding on to him even in the winter of our relationship.

In between, I finished a full first draft of my thesis. I scrolled through, beginning to end, beginning to end, amazed. At 115 pages, I thought it was a monster of a thing.

Still, something seemed to be missing.

Christmas dinner was at my parents' house. Everyone spoke at the same time, asking me questions about school as if I hadn't been in contact all semester. Classes were good, I nodded. My grades were great. I carried multiple conversations at once and didn't mind repeating myself. This was the rowdy, rambling way my family had always talked. It was more natural and sincere to me than the calm, articulate, linear conversations I'd become used to at school. My ears welcomed the assault of sound.

"Well, one more semester," my uncle Danny said to me from across the living room. "What are you going to do after you graduate?"

"Come home," I said.

Danny's mouth flattened slightly. "And do what?" he asked. "Where will you work?"

"I don't know," I replied. "I'll find something."

Now Danny frowned outright. I hadn't expected that. Mom and Dad and everyone else in the family seemed happy I was returning.

"There's nothing for you here," Danny said. "Look around. Look at the economy." He adjusted himself on the couch. There was something anxious in his posture, the way he crossed his legs. "I mean, I sold mining equipment for years . . ."

I paused on the past tense. "What do you mean, *sold*?"

Danny raised his eyebrows as if I should have known. "I got laid off last week."

I knew southwest Virginia's economy was struggling. It had for all my life. But was it getting worse? Or did it just seem that way because my family was suddenly and directly affected?

That same month, a *New York Times* article made its way to my email inbox. It was about Buchanan County's dying coal industry. I clicked on the link and was greeted by the familiar sight of dirty coke ovens standing against a backdrop of foggy, colorless mountains. Below were other images I didn't need captions to recognize. One pictured a retired miner gazing through the window of the local Dairy Queen. One was of a man I recognized from Vacation Bible School at Nanny's old church. Another was taken in the cafeteria of the high school my parents had graduated from. The principal—a woman my parents had gone to school with—stared out the window. Deep, anxious lines creased her forehead.

Most of these photographs were underexposed, captured in the blue light of winter dusk. They brought to mind "The Valley of Poverty," the photo essay I had analyzed for my expository writing class two years earlier.

How ominous, that title.

The focus of the *Times* article was predictably economic. It highlighted Buchanan County's "inexorable decline": an aging, dwindling population, few job opportunities, and a median income that was far below the national average. What, if anything, could revive Grundy? There were ideas for drawing the eyes of tourists and manufacturers, or any industry that wasn't coal. But every hope was doubly tempered by worry and frustration—a "new sense of alarm" felt by citizens and leaders alike. Embedded in the article was a quotation by Larry Summers—a former Harvard president, ironically—explaining how economic challenges in rural areas like Grundy often create a sense of being forgotten and ignored.

Summers wasn't wrong. Buchanan County, and Appalachia at

large, needed help. Hope. What could be done, though? It seemed as if everyone trying to solve the problem was only turning in circles.

"There's nothing to come back to," read one of the closing lines.

I meditated on the article long after it left my screen. The hard and terrible numbers were real, quantitative proof of job loss, population loss, and income loss, an arresting testament to the quiet fear in the eyes and voices of everyone around me. Not that I doubted the fact of decline. I just didn't want to believe it was as serious as it seemed.

Dad got called back to work in January. It was the one bright spot in the weeks I was home that winter. Otherwise, bad news kept coming, one thing after another. I couldn't tell if I was more attuned to the negative, or if southwest Virginia was experiencing a particular streak of misfortune.

It seemed as if every time I drove to town, another business had put up a sign announcing reduced hours or temporary closing. A couple even shut down permanently, leaving dark, solemn storefronts that were ghostly even in the daylight.

Then, a few days after the New Year, the local newspaper printed a startling front-page headline: Tazewell County now had one of the highest opioid overdose rates in Virginia. Surrounding counties had similarly abysmal rates, making southwest Virginia one of the most opioid-affected regions in the country.

Most jarring to me were all the familiar faces in the county jail's mug shots. Each Wednesday, the newspaper devoted an entire page to the photos and charges. I always recognized at least one or two names. Over the course of my winter break, three former Subway coworkers turned up. All were booked for a batch of charges relating to drug possession. One day I opened up to a photo of my old manager Crystal. Her long hair was stringy. Her already-slim face was gaunt, angular. I hadn't seen her since her dramatic exit from Subway years earlier. She looked like an entirely different person from the one I remembered.

Overwhelmed, I pulled up a blank document on my laptop and began writing: "I'm worried that things—not just the economy—might actually be getting worse."

I expected some small relief from acknowledging, even if only to myself, that the state of my hometown was beginning to frighten me. Writing it only worked me into a greater panic. "Do bad things happen more frequently and intensely in Appalachia, or do they only seem worse because our world is smaller, more insular, and everything is felt more immediately and acutely?"

I played with that document for weeks, anxiously detailing the layoffs and shutdowns, the newspaper articles and mug shots. It occurred to me to tack those pages onto my thesis as an epilogue.

After listing all I'd seen of Appalachia's supposed decline, would it still make sense to want to return? Would readers understand my logic?

Definitely not, I decided, then deleted the entire addition.

All the bad news was like an omen. Was it a warning to not come back? A foreshadowing of what would happen if I did? Before that winter, I had insisted on returning home from the fugue of being far removed from it: The "negatives" of Appalachian life were easily forgotten when I didn't have to think about them year-round.

In that way, I had idealized Appalachia from afar. The best parts of mountain life had become brightest in my mind, especially when I was homesick and overwhelmed by the city. The worst parts stayed tucked away in a corner that I had downplayed and excused:

That's just the way it is. That's just the way we are. In my mind, Appalachia was the antithesis of the elite and inhospitable world of Harvard. These exaggerated and one-dimensional narratives had taken root in my first days on campus, and in two and a half years they had changed very little.

But I had changed very much. Enough to almost see beyond the black and white of the stories of belonging and unbelonging I'd told myself, or the insecurities that kept me from adapting to Harvard and feeling worthy of the opportunities it offered. I had almost changed enough to stop echoing the sentiments of a culture that lay claim to my past, present, and future. To live up to the rules I made for myself.

Almost.

Even though it didn't seem quite right, my thesis was tied up neatly and definitively. It had a narrative arc that I was proud of, if not for accuracy, then for execution: a story of coming full circle *from Appalachia to Harvard and back.* Without the epilogue, the end was optimistic and certain. The opposite of how I really felt.

45.

On the morning of March 10, three days after I submitted my thesis, a succession of emails popped up in my inbox.

Classes will begin transitioning to virtual instruction.

Students are asked not to return to campus after Spring Recess.

Students will be required to move out as soon as possible.

Dad was the first person I called. “Well ain’t you lucky,” he said brightly.

“What?” I asked.

“You get to come home early!”

“Right,” I said, then hung up the phone and cried.

I didn’t know where the tears came from, but I didn’t have time to think about it. I spent that day and the next frantically packing my room, suddenly alarmed by the word “coronavirus” when I’d thought nothing of it before. It drifted in and out of my nervous conversations with friends. We gathered as much as possible in our remaining hours together, dazed by the abrupt ending to our time at Harvard.

The two days between being ordered out and leaving were a blur. I was in my dorm room, I was in the post office, I was on Weeks Bridge watching a periwinkle dawn break over the icy Charles, I was drinking beer with my friends for breakfast.

And then I was in a tiny underground café with Patrick. We'd rarely spoken since our breakup, but had crossed paths in the dining hall and decided to talk one last time.

The café was dim and cool. It stirred up the memory of a night early in our relationship more than two years earlier, in the murky in-between of autumn and winter, one of the first truly cold days. We were studying late in the Cabot House common room. Beyond the glow of the wall sconces, the edges of the vast room were shapelessly dark. Portraits of long-dead deans lined the walls.

Sometime past two in the morning, Patrick looked up from his laptop. "Feels like a graveyard in here," he said. His soft voice was enormous in the silence.

I looked up, too. The faces on the walls were watchful. "Maybe this place is haunted."

Patrick smirked. "What kind of ghost haunts a dorm?"

At that very moment, the walls came to life. The old pipes and radiators popped, clanged, and banged in a clamoring roar that made the two of us jump and grab for each other. It was just the heat kicking on, metal expanding against metal, but the timing of the cacophony was like a voice from beyond: a wail of confirmation we were not alone.

The little café was crowded. Patrick and I sipped from small stained mugs and tried to think of things to say.

"So I guess you're going back to New York," I said.

"For now. Until the virus passes," he said. "I guess you're going home, too?"

"For now," I echoed.

Listening to ghosts. That was what we were doing, having that forced and pointless conversation. Weren't we all ghosts on this campus, in the world, now, aimless and unresolved?

Patrick and I said goodbye on the street. I did not see him again.

That evening, I double- and triple-checked the South Station departure schedule. My train left at nine. Knowing that, and knowing that I had to navigate the subway to get to the train station, I went to a last-minute party and drank too much champagne anyway. And then, after dozens and dozens of watery, drunk goodbyes, I turned from my friends and walked out.

The hallway was empty. I didn't feel ready to leave. I turned toward the stairs that led to the underground steam tunnels, where the walls were a collage of color. Decades of murals had been left behind by long-graduated Adams House seniors.

The art, like me and everyone else, would soon be gone. Adams House was slated for total renovation that summer, and architects had determined there was no way to preserve most of the crumbling plaster.

Wasn't it strange, the impermanence of things? In the coming years, the whole of Adams House would be stripped to its frame and rebuilt from the inside out.

My heart grew heavy at the thought. How painful is the loss of the familiar, the comfort of what you know and love. But to render a new creation on top of old bones is a necessary, life-giving resurrection. Otherwise, buildings will splinter and crumble; people will shrivel into their own small selves.

Change, I think, is the opposite of decay.

But rootedness defies explanation, and it was well past time for me to head to the train station. I climbed a spiral staircase and opened a door into the cold. Massachusetts Avenue was pulsing with electric life, people who were laughing and drinking to ward off the strange turn of the world. The sound followed me to my dorm room, where I heaved my suitcases to the door and flipped the lights off. In the dark, the square of the window came into focus: the webby treetops beneath the ledge, and beyond, the staccato of brake lights, red halos cruising into the distance.

I stood. I lingered. My lips parted in reverence, and off my tongue rolled a thick, clumsy "thank you."

I didn't know where the words came from, or even what I was thanking. Still, they seemed ripe. Proper.

But even drunk I felt absurd talking to no one, so I turned with my suitcases and let the door fall shut behind me.

Part FOUR

46.

The air conditioner on the wall was a relentless droning hum. So was the refrigerator, the ice maker, and the broken coffee brewer, which hissed and steamed and spewed hot water at unpredictable intervals. I leaned into my laptop, full volume, next to the cash register. On the screen, the speaker's mouth lagged behind his voice.

There were many forces working against me witnessing my graduation, and most of them were succeeding. The front door squealed. A customer walked in. I stood and muted my laptop.

Most of my customers were regulars. I recognized the man behind his mask, knew his order before he said it. We made small talk as I steamed his latte. When I handed it across the counter, he asked what I was watching.

"My college commencement." I spun my laptop around and pressed unmute.

He watched for a moment, then raised his eyebrows.

"You went to Harvard and now you're working in a coffee shop?"

"Yes," I replied.

The man studied me as he sipped his latte. "Well. What's next?"

I dreaded this question. I got it almost every day. Now that I was back in the mountains, most people who knew I'd gone to Harvard were too polite to say exactly what they thought. I heard it in the tilt of their voices, in their questions of *What are your next steps?* and *Where are you going to go?* and *What are you going to do with an English degree? Teach?*

I'd reply with *I don't know, I don't know yet*, and they'd watch me make their coffee with eyes that seemed to say, *Well, you should be doing something better than* this.

In the months since I'd come home, time had passed strangely. I kept track of the days only by my work schedule. I'd taken my old coffee shop job back as soon as my bosses offered it to me, desperate for any employment, for distraction of any kind. The uncertainty of the pandemic was exhausting, even though southwest Virginia was virtually untouched by COVID, and would remain so for months.

That had always been the best part of coming home: its dogged familiarity; its stubborn resistance to change. Tazewell was deeply insulated from the rest of the world, and I was glad for that now more than ever, as far as COVID went. But there was something heavy about *this* return. It sat in my chest all the time, stifled and restless, its slender roots and straining buds creeping into every empty space.

Tazewell wasn't the easiest place to find a job in normal circumstances. The pandemic, of course, didn't help. Neither did my English degree. I checked online job boards every day. I asked my customers if they knew anywhere hiring. One man, a lawyer, offered me a receptionist position at his office. I almost took it until I learned it paid less than what I already made.

Erik, meanwhile, was working at a plant that manufactured rebar and mining roof bolts. It was the first job he'd been able to get after community college. He'd studied criminal justice, and found his degree to be as useless as mine. At night he came home coated in a silky skin of ultrafine metal dust. He reminded me of Poppaw that way—black and gritty from hair to boots, his eyes as white as a pair of moons. He quit that job as soon as he found another, loading trucks at a UPS facility in West Virginia. His shifts started at four in the morning. To get there in time, he had to wake up at three.

Spring rolled into summer. At the coffee shop, business was barely a trickle. Most days I tucked myself beneath the shade of the front-porch patio umbrella and watched traffic crawl by. One afternoon I saw Sam's car approaching. He slowed as if he were thinking about stopping in. For the first time in more than four years, we met each other's eyes. He accelerated then, disappearing around the bend of the road.

It was strange to watch the past and the present converge. The coffee shop's Christian branding attracted worship teams and youth groups, pastors and preachers—people I'd once run in the same circles with but hadn't seen or spoken to in years. When we recognized each other, there was always a beat of awkwardness, then an uncomfortable attempt at polite conversation. It was always a relief when we ran out of things to say.

Late in the summer, one of my coworkers quit. The position was filled by the first person who applied for it: Lindsey, Pastor Alan's wife.

"I felt like God was calling me to work outside the home," she told me, soft-spoken as ever, on her first day. We made small talk as I trained her on the register. I told her I'd just graduated from college. She told me she'd just had another baby. Neither of us ever alluded to the fact that I'd once gone to her husband's church, or the fact that Sam had never stopped. We operated on the silent pretense that there was no history between us, that our lives and beliefs had never intersected.

I was grateful for that. It was hard to wrap my mind around leading such different lives over the past four years, only to end up in the same place.

One morning, I took my car for an oil change. I gave my keys to the receptionist and went to the waiting area.

After a moment, I realized I was sitting across from my former youth pastor.

Pastor Will straightened up when he saw me. "Emilee!" he said. When he spoke again, his voice was uncertain. "It's been so long."

The last time we'd talked was the night Jared had urged me to go back to Sam. I remembered Pastor Will watching, silent in assent. The years had only slightly softened the sting of that memory. Pastor Will leaned forward in his chair, extending a hand. I was stunned enough to forget we were in the middle of a pandemic, and shook it in an awkward truce.

We were the only people in the room. We talked above the noise of the Dr. Phil rerun on the wall TV. I asked if Pastor Will was still the youth pastor at Deliverance. He said he was. He asked if I'd really gone to Harvard, as he'd heard. I said I had.

"I'm proud of you, girl," he said. "For rising above."

That made me pause. I asked what he meant.

Pastor Will hesitated. He shifted in his chair, and I saw conflict in his eyes, a realization that he'd started something he didn't want to finish. He leaned forward again, slower this time, and dropped his voice even though no one was around to hear.

"Just so you know," he said, "I never trusted Sam as far as I could throw him."

Later, I would wonder why Pastor Will admitted this to me. I would wonder why, if his distrust had been true, Pastor Will had allowed Sam to volunteer with the youth group. Why instead of warning me about Sam, he'd encouraged me to *marry* him.

But in the moment, all I could think about was the *fact* of the statement. It was the first time I'd heard Sam's name spoken by a member of Deliverance leadership since the night of Sam's arrest—the first time I'd heard his involvement in that church acknowledged. It wasn't much, this small breaking of taboo, but it almost felt like a concession: that years ago in that small dark room, I had not failed God, or chosen to leave church in sinful defiance. That the *church* had failed *me* instead.

In July, another lawyer offered me another receptionist position. He sipped his double espresso while I felt my heart rise: The job paid one dollar per hour more than what I was making at the coffee shop. Then he told me it was only a temporary position to cover the current receptionist's maternity leave.

After my shift, I slumped into my car and sat and sat in the parking lot, not wanting to go home or anywhere else. It was a familiar restlessness, always wanting to be somewhere I wasn't. I started my engine and headed in no particular direction.

This aimless driving became my after-work routine. Some evenings I'd make a quick loop through town. Some evenings I'd drive to the county line. I wandered along, following whichever road seemed right in the moment, reliving memories as I passed the places that held them: the foggy back side of the lake; a grassy clearing near the river. I blasted Pearl Jam and Eminem and all the other artists Jeremy and I once listened to. On those drives, I kept company with ghosts.

One blue twilight, I found myself on a narrow, curvy stretch of road. I slowed in the growing dark, and topped a hill near a church.

As I was coming down, there was movement ahead. I slowed again. A man was standing beside the road in the driveway of a trailer park, almost invisible in head-to-toe black. I braked as I passed, trying to get a glimpse of his face. It was almost too dark to see.

But it looked a lot like Jeremy.

He watched me drive by. In my rearview mirror, I watched him watching me. I swerved into the next parking lot, spinning gravel, but by the time I turned, he was already gone.

It couldn't have been him, I reminded myself. He'd stolen a car and gone out west. Why would he ever come back?

Then again, why had I?

Even though I'd been home for months, Eli and I had rarely made an effort to see each other, using the pandemic as an excuse to let the remains of our relationship fizzle. Neither of us was willing to explicitly end it—the world felt too unstable to fully let each other go—so we drifted, faded, spoke just enough to maintain a thin connection, until one day, without realizing it, we spoke for the last time, and fell out of each other's lives for good.

I'd seen the end coming for a while. I sensed Eli had, too. Our relationship had always been surface level, based on little more than the fact we'd grown up in the same town. Much like with Patrick, I'd used Eli as a crutch, though not so much for emotional support as to affirm my Appalachian identity. Although ultimately our relationship did the opposite, only emphasizing my disconnect from home.

My relationship with my parents, on the other hand, was filling out, taking a new shape. For years we'd been strained by figurative and literal distance: my deep dive into church, the wild year after I left it, and the back-and-forth between college and home. Living with them again forced a reconnection. A tender noticing of things I hadn't before. The silver peeking through Mom's hair dye. Dad's crow's-feet when he smiled, the way the wrinkles curved down toward his stubbled cheeks. I was startled by how much he reminded me of Poppy. I'd only ever seen my parents through the eyes of a child, ageless and invincible. Now that I was grown, I felt the fragility of our time together.

But the smallness of our house was stifling, and sometimes the only way I could breathe was to get away. One rainy evening, a rare Saturday I was off work, the house was quiet except for the drone of whatever Dad was watching on TV. I'd been growing more and more frustrated all day without anything to blame it on. I wasn't in the mood for reading or TV or even driving, but I finally exchanged my pajamas for real clothes and grabbed my keys.

I drove fast down the valley and slowly through the curves of the holler, turning onto the highway at the train trestle. After a few miles of cruising, I swerved last second down an exit toward town, drawn by something I couldn't name.

There was no traffic on Riverside Drive. The river was swollen, almost spilling into the road, and the rain was shifting from a drizzle to a downpour. I passed the post office, then a row of gray houses. Someone was walking in front of the elementary school ahead.

It wasn't a hallucination, a ghost, or a mailbox. It was Jeremy in the flesh, strolling down the sidewalk in the pouring rain.

I cruised right past, too shocked to brake. Jeremy stopped and watched me go by. I pulled in to the next driveway and turned around. He was still watching as I stopped in the middle of the road.

I rolled down my window. "Want a ride?"

"*Shit!*" Jeremy yelled. He darted across the road. "It *is* you!"

I unlocked the passenger door. Jeremy jumped into the seat. Suddenly we were ten inches from each other, together again after almost three years apart.

We stared as if neither could believe the other was real. A heartbeat later, and the years melted away as if they had never come between us at all. I laughed and Jeremy laughed and we yelled instead of talked because we couldn't convey our emotions at a normal volume.

"Where the hell you been?" Jeremy shouted.

"Harvard!" I shouted back, and we howled at the absurdity of it. I told him about coming home early and graduating virtually. Then I asked where *he'd* been. He told me about his cross-country road trip, the national parks and the dusty deserts and how the Pacific Ocean was as blue as the sky, and that he made his way back east for a construction job in North Carolina before finally coming home.

"I never thought I was going to see you again," I said.

"Serendipity." His dimples flexed with his smile.

I drove to the nearby Dollar General. With the car still idling, we jumped out and hugged each other in the parking lot. Jeremy picked me up and spun me around, squeezing so hard I thought I might break in half.

I buried my face in his sweatshirt, which was rain damp and smelled like wet dog. When he let me loose, I looked him up and down. He'd let his hair grow to his shoulder blades and gotten a star tattooed under one eye. There was a ragged hole in his pajama bottoms, and one of his thigh tattoos peeked through.

"So how've you been?" I asked.

Jeremy deflated a little. We climbed back in the car to get out of the rain.

"Ah, shit," he said, as if he didn't know where to start. "Got messed up with some bad people. That's why I'm back here, you know, trying to get away."

I asked him what happened. He pulled the right leg of his pajamas up. On his calf was the dark, round scar of a gunshot wound.

"It was bad. Really bad." A shadow crossed his face. He showed me another scar on his stomach. This one was a shiny, crooked seam.

"And I don't even remember getting this," he went on, pointing to the tattoo under his eye, "because of *this*." He rolled his sleeves up. There were healing track marks in the crooks of both elbows.

I sucked in my breath. The scars hurt to look at.

Jeremy pulled his sleeves down. He spoke in a strange voice. "Three weeks detoxing in the hospital."

"Three *weeks*?"

"I died and they brought me back."

Jeremy never once said the word "overdose." It was too powerful, too loaded: It meant that you were a certain kind of person, had a certain kind of problem.

He'd changed. It was deeper than the hair, the tattoo, the scars. There was a distinct hardness to him, to his voice and the way he held his shoulders, that I had never seen. His eyes were flatter. Sadder.

"What was it like?" I asked. "When you died?"

Jeremy spoke incredulously, as if he didn't believe his own truth. The first thing he remembered, he told me, was a flood of light. He stood alone in a blindingly white room. There was someone standing around the corner—he couldn't see the corner or even the person, but knew they were there—and he knew, too, that the person was about to call his name.

The pause before his name was tense. He could sense the word about to ring out. He waited. Waited. "It felt like a million years," he said. The first consonant sounded; the breath left his lungs. Suddenly he woke up in a hospital bed, revived.

I'd never heard fear in Jeremy's voice. My Jeremy, who'd once dangled his feet over a cliff and told me he had nothing to lose, had never feared death until he tasted it—or, rather, until his name was on the tip of Death's tongue. He'd lived recklessly, carelessly, full speed ahead, until nothing became everything and he almost lost it all.

Maybe I was confusing his hardness for caution, I realized. Maybe he was on defense, resisting that light, that call, with a terror I did not understand.

I *had* felt that terror, but mine did not come from experience. Mine came from sermons and dreams and vague imaginings of fire and flames; screams and caves and creatures with sharp little horns. Which was somehow a lot less frightening than emptiness.

"Do you remember that one night at the lake?" he said. "When I asked you about God?"

I nodded.

"I still don't know what's out there." He paused, thinking. "I don't know what would've happened if I'd heard my whole name. Maybe I would've gone somewhere. Maybe it would've all just gone black."

"I don't know either," I said. The afterlife wasn't something I thought about much anymore.

Jeremy shook his head as if he were trying to force the thought out. This was the most serious conversation we'd ever had, and it was starting to wear on us both. To lighten the mood, he showed me the new tattoos I'd never seen: his last name across his back; little stars and suns to fill in his sleeve.

I pulled the back collar of my shirt down and showed him my own tattoo, a mountain range between my shoulder blades. I'd gotten it in Boston on a day I was particularly homesick. It was my own drawing, inspired by my favorite mountains in Tazewell—

gentle blue ridges half tucked behind other mountains. They were barely visible as you were driving into town. You could see them clearly only on your way out.

We talked about that, too. Out. Where we wanted our lives to go. Jeremy didn't have a plan any more than I did. He spent all day playing his guitar and lying low, although the past was creeping up on him, too, and he didn't know how much longer he could last.

"I got pulled over in town last month. First time in years," he told me. "And the cop remembered my name."

Jeremy had lost his license a long time ago, so he was taken to jail. His car—I didn't ask whether it was the stolen one, or how he'd avoided a larceny charge—was impounded, and he couldn't afford to get it back. Now he just wandered the streets, trying to fill the meaningless days.

"You ought to get out of here again," I told him. "Go stay out of trouble somewhere else."

Jeremy laughed a little. "Where?"

I didn't have an answer. We had both returned to Tazewell because we didn't know where else to go.

Twilight was falling by then. The rain had tapered into a fine mist on my windshield. "I should probably head home soon," I told Jeremy, but couldn't bear the thought of goodbye. We talked for another hour until the Dollar General closed.

After the employees left, when my car was the last in the parking lot, I slowly started my engine. I asked Jeremy where he wanted me to take him.

He chewed his lip, thinking. He was couch hopping between his sister's trailer and a friend's apartment. At last he decided to stay with the friend and directed me to an apartment complex across town.

There were no empty spots in the parking lot, so I stopped and idled in the road. We turned to each other. Jeremy leaned over and hugged me.

"You get the hell out of here, too," he said.

It was my turn to laugh. I echoed his reply. "Where?"

"Anywhere." He pulled his arms away and smiled. "Let's run away together."

I smiled, too, at the fantasy of fleeing. Of taking only the good memories with us. Of leaving the bad, and the world that came with them, behind.

Jeremy opened his door and stepped out, then ducked back in for a second. With the streetlight at his back, I could barely make out his features. The shadow erased the dark under his eyes, the strain in his smile.

"Be careful," he said. I'd never heard him say those words before.

"You too," I said.

He stepped back and shut the door.

47.

Summer gave way to a warm, dry fall. The mountains turned briefly golden, dappled with muted crimson and rust, before the leaves dropped and the ridges turned the purple of a bruise and the bare trees looked like bones.

Just before winter, I applied to graduate school.

Professor Stilgoe had planted the idea in my mind more than a year earlier, and Michael made it grow. *Have you thought about a creative writing MFA?* he'd asked in an email over the summer. I hadn't, but I loved the concept of a master's degree focused wholly on writing. I sent applications to the programs that offered the most generous stipends.

Each application required a statement of purpose explaining why I wanted to attend a creative writing program. I answered that I wanted to become a better writer, maybe make writing a career. Which was true. Also true was that I couldn't find a job, and the pandemic was suffocating, and I felt like a weird warp of my high school and Harvard selves, suspended in time while living the same aimless day on repeat.

Over the past months, living in my parents' house and working at a coffee shop for a quarter above minimum wage, I often felt that Harvard had been a strange hallucinatory interlude between parts of my *real* life—a life where time passed, and I got older, and the sun rose and set behind the mountains, and everything beyond was little more than a mirage. But in early spring, when I got an acceptance letter from Vanderbilt University, when I started browsing course catalogs and searching for apartments, the fact of my Harvard education began to crystallize into something real and valuable and propulsive. My year in Tazewell, I realized, was the interlude. Not Harvard.

Spring bloomed into summer. I packed up my bedroom and thrifted furniture. The evening before I moved to Nashville, Dad and I walked up the hill to his backyard garden with a fistful of Food Lion bags. He wanted to send me off with enough vegetables to fill my fridge. "So you can save on groceries," he said.

What he really meant was, *I'm proud*.

We picked quietly, lulled to silence by the spell of crickets chirping in the corn. My mind slowly turned from everything except what was in front of me: the chunky dry dirt, the prickly vines, the papery leaves brushing my bare shins. The satisfying heft of a round, ripe tomato. When my back couldn't take another second of bending over, I stood and gazed at the road stretching down the valley, at the long ridge funneling into the head of the holler.

This was what I loved most about Appalachia: how easy it was to savor, to lose yourself in its bounty and beauty. For a while I'd neglected to look. A year had passed, and all I'd seen were the things I wanted to flee.

It was a perspective shift I'd never understood, as many times as it had happened. Sometimes I was infatuated with the mountains, comforted by their constancy. Sometimes that constancy was stifling. Sometimes I was heartened by the hardiness of mountain people. Sometimes I hated that there was so much adversity to persist against. My relationship with home was a pendulum of adoration and criticism that was difficult to balance, even knowing that good and bad could exist in the same space. That the existence of one did not negate the other.

For most of my life, my view of the world had been black and white, as extreme as the beliefs that had shaped it. It was a confusion I'd wrestled with over and over: reconciling a person's sins with their enduring kindness; or the abuses of religion with its many comforts; or the strangeness and loneliness of Harvard with its transforming powers, the way my mind expanded when I was forced out of the familiar. The juxtapositions were challenging, and competed for dominance in my brain. Which would be the victor?

It was the wrong question to ask. I was learning that there is space for the whole of a thing, its spectrum of contradictions and complexities.

And yet, as I stood in that hilltop garden, old narratives resurfaced. I remembered my churches. My engagement ring. I remembered a decorative sign that hung in my house for most of my childhood. BLOOM WHERE YOU'RE PLANTED, it said in a cheerful font with a border of smiling bumblebees and flowers. Writing had given me purpose and direction before, and I wanted to trust it would again, yet I couldn't help but doubt my ambition and feel guilty for having it. Who was I to think I could be a writer? Why did I have to go to school in a city so far from home to develop my talent? Did I even *have* talent, or was I just going to waste time writing words nobody cared about?

The crickets were quieting now. I looked toward the western

ridge where the cooling sun hung low, and my heart clenched with something like guilt. Leaving Appalachia, especially for the second time, felt like a judgment, a declaration: *This is not enough for me.*

I loved Appalachia. I did.

But right now, I couldn't stay.

Epilogue

In November, four months after I moved to Nashville, Dad had a heart attack in his sleep.

I'd woken before the construction workers, when the city was quiet except for men hosing beer and trash off the sidewalks. I'd stumbled my way into my running shoes, bleary in the predawn dark, and went jogging toward the Cumberland River, where the sky was just beginning to pale behind the illuminated arch of the great bridge. That morning, the arch glowed magenta, and the dawn warmed to a soft primrose. The pink-on-pink contrast was as stunning as a mountain sunrise.

From my spot on the river, Nashville seemed stretched to its seams. Cranes dotted the brightening skyline. Soon the streets would be jammed with cars, and the sidewalks would fill with rowdy barhoppers in western boots and cowboy hats. My apartment window looked out over the concrete foundation of what would eventually become another high-rise. I was gazing out that window, shedding my clothes for a shower, when my phone rang.

It was Erik.

Erik never called me.

I expected the call to be about Nanny. My parents had moved her to a nursing home two weeks earlier. She'd been in and out of the hospital in the months before, strangely confused and paranoid, and thin from forgetting to eat.

She was only half herself now, Mom reported—frail and vacant-eyed. Her hair and voice were thin. When she talked, she talked of her childhood, her father, and the early days of her marriage. Sometimes, when the nurses came with pills, Nanny would say how *she'd* wanted to be a nurse, and reminisce about that lost dream, all that never came to be. She'd tell the story of moving from Grundy to Lexington and back. Her world grown big, then very small.

The next morning, I made the seven-hour drive to Roanoke, where Dad was in the ICU. His room had floor-to-ceiling windows that faced a long wall of a mountain. The trees were at the peak of their autumn color. The beauty ripped at the ragged crater in my chest.

"He'll have a great view when he wakes up," I remember telling a nurse.

She looked down at her clipboard and said nothing.

Dad looked strong and healthy, even under all the tubes and wires. But it was his heart, the invisible thing, that was in crisis. There were doctors and nurses and specialists who tried to explain how it had gone wrong, but I couldn't understand. When I watched Dad's belly rise in shallow, jagged breaths, or watched Mom, so grief-stricken she could speak only in a whisper, watching Dad wither under thin sheets and strange medical apparatuses, my own heart broke at the cruel irony of Dad's life, how he'd spent it trying to avoid the backbreaking work of the mines, how he'd feared getting old before his time, only to be dying in a hospital bed at the age of fifty-three.

Erik took the curves slowly. I was in the passenger's seat, and Mom in the back. The hearse led the way, winding through mountains that were quilted with dying kudzu that covered even the dormant trees. Every few miles was a cluster of houses falling in on themselves, and billboards that said things like COULD FENTANYL BE IN YOUR DRUGS? and THIS IS A SIGN THAT YOU SHOULDN'T DRIVE HIGH.

The cemetery was on the far end of Home Creek. My grandparents were buried here. Generations of my family were buried here. Their headstones were scattered among rainbow bouquets of polyester flowers, under the eyes of an open-armed Jesus, whose pale stone skin was veiled with mold.

At the crest of the mountain, you could see the cradle of the holler where Dad had grown up. We knew he would want that, to spend eternity in the mountains that raised him. Like all those generations before. It seemed very weary to me then, that holler of hollers and its hill full of bodies, groaning with the burden of ancient wisdom and mystery and heartbreak that I had felt in my earliest memories, and called magic.

And it *was* magic. It was the forever gaze of the bronze coal miner. It was the ache and fullness in my mountain bones. It was the tidal force of my mountain blood, the push and pull of contentment and restlessness, that would carry me back to Nashville, and later back home, and to many other places in and beyond Appalachia, in the years to come.

It was rootedness that did not defy explanation.

I couldn't see that future then, those seasons of coming and going, although surely I must have sensed their imminence: I could never stay gone from the mountains for long. My dear Appalachia, so painful and holy. I loved it despite needing something it couldn't give me, something I couldn't even name. I loved its grit, its richness, its culture and people. I was *proud* to be one of those people, to be from a place so certain of itself—a place undefinable, so worn and wild, that had been stripped and scavenged and shaken and robbed, yet never conceded to the forces that tried to hold it down.

Appalachia endured, always.

And I would, too.

I would.

Acknowledgments

When I was young, writing and illustrating my little stories on notebook paper, I never imagined I would *actually* publish a book one day. It's pretty astounding, and I don't know what else to say about it except that it would have never been possible without these people:

My big, bighearted family. My parents especially, who gave so much of themselves to me and my brother. I didn't know many of their sacrifices and struggles until the writing of this book. Mom, thank you for answering my questions without turning away from the truth, even when the truth was painful. And thank you, Dad. I hope I'm half the storyteller you were.

Gail Webb, Larry Hypes, Robert McGraw, Katie Hurley, and the many, many others who believed in me, who saw something in me before I saw it myself.

Professor John Stilgoe, whose wisdom and encouragement came at a vital time. Thank you, Professor, for having a heart for students like me.

It was a great stroke of fortune when Michael Pollan let me into his writing workshop in the fall of 2018. I'm so grateful for his expert instruction and guidance, and his genuine interest in my story and my telling it. I'm grateful he connected me with Binky Urban, my fearless agent, who's spoken to me as an old friend since our very first call. Binky, thank you for always looking out for me. Thank you for sticking with me through all the iterations of this book and the years it took to write it.

Ann Godoff and Casey Denis, my awesome editors, who broadened and shaped my thinking about this book in invaluable ways. Ann sadly passed away before this book was published, but the first time I spoke to her, she looked at me and said, "You are a *writer.*" This touched me deeply, and I've replayed those words in my head a thousand times since. They've powered me through many tough paragraphs and days.

Victoria Laboz, Michael Brown, Jessie Stratton Zhou, Juliana Kiyan, Alicia Crawford, and James McLaughlin for their above-and-beyondness in bringing this book to the world.

My Tuna, a force of wonder and creativity. Thank you for all the suggestions, ideas, critique, praise, and brainstorming sessions, and for lighting a fire under me every time I needed it. Your goodness spills all over everything. Love you, love you, love you.